THE
Queen's
Throat

OPERA, HOMOSEXUALITY, AND THE MYSTERY OF DESIRE

Wayne Koestenbaum

POSEIDON PRESS

NEW YORK   LONDON   TORONTO
SYDNEY   TOKYO   SINGAPORE

POSEIDON PRESS
Simon & Schuster Building
Rockefeller Center
1230 Avenue of the Americas
New York, New York 10020

10   9   8   7   6   5   4   3

Library of Congress Cataloging-in-Publication Data

Koestenbaum, Wayne.
    The queen's throat : opera, homosexuality, and the
mystery of desire / Wayne Koestenbaum.
        p.   cm.
    Includes bibliographical references and index.
1. Koestenbaum,   Wayne.   2. Opera—Biography.
3. Gay men—Biography.   4. Sexuality in music.
5. Opera—Social aspects.   I. Title.
ML429.K74A3   1993
782.1'092—dc20
[B]   92-34911   CIP   MN
ISBN 0-671-75457-2

Portions of this work have appeared previously in dif-
ferent forms:
Chapter 4 appeared under the title "Callas and Her
Fans" in The Yale Review 79, no. 1 (Autumn
1989).
Chapter 5 appeared under the title "The Queen's
Throat: (Homo)sexuality and the Art of Singing" in
Inside/Out: Lesbian Theories, Gay Theories, ed-
ited by Diana Fuss (New York: Routledge, 1991).
Parts of Chapter 7 appeared under the title "Opera
and Homosexuality: Seven Arias" in The Yale Jour-
nal of Criticism 5, no. 1 (Fall 1991), and The Best
American Essays, 1992, edited by Susan Sontag
(New York: Ticknor & Fields, 1992).

Illustration credits appear on page 257.

• ACKNOWLEDGMENTS •

I owe special thanks to my agent, Faith Hornby Hamlin; to my editor, Elaine Pfefferblit; to Laura Demanski at Poseidon, and James Stoller, copy editor; to Bruce Hainley, Susan McClary, J. D. McClatchy, Lisa S. Rubinstein, Jeanne Schinto, Eve Kosofsky Sedgwick, Barry Weller, Jennifer Wicke, and Elizabeth Wood; to Yale's Morse Fellowship; to my parents, for giving me words *and* music; and to Steven Marchetti, who listens, and to whom this book is therefore dedicated.

Contents

3

CHAPTER ONE

Opera Queens

· *1* ·

The first opera I ever saw: *Aida*. San Francisco War Memorial Opera House, 1969. I was eleven. By the last act I was exhausted, bored. All I remember now is the color of the sky above the Nile—beyond midnight blue, a shade redolent of witchcraft and spice.

In childhood, I stored all my programs in a crate. Recently I found that first opera program: the Radames was Jon Vickers. Only now do I appreciate the name's weight and valor. A house's foundation, even if invisible, exists—has once, long ago, without witnesses, been poured. And so as I try to compose this fragmented history, I must begin with my first *Aida*, unremembered except for the high blue sky.

· *2* ·

Am I an opera queen? My proudly gay friend David—eight years my senior, and infinitely more sophisticated in matters sexual and cultural—first told me about opera queens. (We were riding a bus in Baltimore. It was 1980. I was trying to convince him I was bisexual, not gay.) The opera queen seemed the victim of a severe, pleasureless affliction. The opera queen seemed to have given up more reasonable pastimes. I, at twenty-one, could not recognize myself as an opera queen. I told David, "I still have crushes on women." And he said, "Stop kidding yourself."

Opera queens, according to David, went to the opera on Monday nights. I couldn't afford to go to the opera at all. How could I be an opera queen? I owned only four complete operas, and they were budget recordings. Didn't opera queens put on airs? I wasn't a queen. I was delicately built, and wore black pegged trousers, and listened to *Rigoletto* at night with the lights out, and no one in years had called me "femme."

· *3* ·

Even before my first *Aida,* I saw a student performance of *Hänsel und Gretel,* from which I recall only the scalloped shape of the auditorium, and the sensation of riding in a car, over mountains, toward a townlet unfamiliar and obtuse, where opera grew among grapevines and a heat more lancing than in our development.

· *4* ·

My first three opera sets, talismanic, purchased by my grandparents for my tenth birthday:

Carmen, the Richmond/London budget set, called by a contemporary guide to recorded opera "perhaps the worst *Carmen* on records";

Aida, the Toscanini version, with Herva Nelli and Richard Tucker;

Madama Butterfly, with Anna Moffo, to which I listened only once—and I stopped midway, because I couldn't find the melodies.

But I made it far enough through the first act to be struck, when Anna Moffo entered, with a sensation I've tried to describe before, and may never adequately name. Her timbre was separate from its surroundings. Her voice wasn't the canopy, the column, the architrave; gravely self-sufficient, it seemed not a copy of life, but life itself, and, like a breathing property, it entered my system with a vector so naïve, unadulterated, and elemental, so unpolluted by the names I would later impose on the experience, that my drab bedroom shifted on its axis.

And yet, after that initiation, I waited eleven years to listen again to the *Butterfly* recording. Taking up the opera at twenty-one, I knew the ability to respond was stationed in my body, waiting for reveille.

· *5* ·

The voices of Barbra Streisand, Shirley Jones, and Julie Andrews prepared me for opera and for homosexuality. Barbra, because in *Funny Girl* she sang "I'm the Greatest Star"; Shirley, because her pitch was pure, classical, her soprano not a belter's, but a virgin's; Julie, because she was a nanny in *Mary Poppins* and a governess in *The Sound of Music,* because her haircut was short and mannish, like my mother's, and because her voice, like my idea of opera, confidently checkered the air with summary, silver, emotionless bellicosity.

The voice of Marni Nixon, ghosting for Audrey Hepburn in *My Fair Lady* and for Deborah Kerr in *The King and I,* told me everything about singing in the dark, singing without a body, singing from an erased, invisible place in the universe. No one saw Marni Nixon's body; invisibility made her voice operatic, characterless. Audrey Hepburn lip-synched "I Could Have Danced All Night": like Eliza, I listened but didn't sing. I opened my mouth, in a wide, vapid O of awe and shame, while women's voices streamed from my green Magnavox record player, vibrato so quick it was nearly undetectable.

Vibrato was best when it gave the note elasticity, length, and vigor—discreetly. On the cornet I was embarrassed to use vibrato (to tremble the hand over the three valves). Vibrato was a kind of limpness, like a wrist.

· *6* ·

Predictive sign: a fondness for musical comedy. I worried, listening to records of *Darling Lili, Oklahoma!, The Music Man, Company,* and *No, No, Nanette,* that I would end up gay: I didn't know the word "gay," I knew about homosexuality only from *Time* feature stories about liberation, but I had a clear impression (picked up where?) that gays liked musical comedy. My mother told my father, "Isn't it time that we buy the boys some original-cast albums?" I cowered as I overheard this question, because I *already* loved original-cast albums, and yet my mother bizarrely thought my predilection was still a future event she had to foster, and she thought, even more irrationally, that a taste for show tunes was a necessary rite of passage for teenage boys: *all boys of a certain age must pass through the purging fire of original-cast albums.*

Adriana Caselotti, operatic-style soprano, with a timbre that, like Jeanette MacDonald's, must have seemed fashionable in the 1930s, dubbed for Snow White in the Disney film. I owned the *Snow White* soundtrack, and wanted a photograph of the invisible Adriana Caselotti. I stared at the calves of Helen Gallagher in the photo spread of the original-cast album of *No, No, Nanette,* and connected the calf muscle's swell (unnaturally developed from wearing high heels?) with her capable voice, and knew I'd have neither those calves nor that voice, and therefore my position on the bedroom carpet, admiring the liner-note photo, was not normal, would get me in trouble someday: why was I staring in solitude at Helen Gallagher's calves, and was this passion sexual?

· 7 ·

Bart, a fourth-grader, sang "People" ("People who need people are the luckiest people in the world") at the school assembly. He wanted to be a star and claimed already to be a semistar. But he was a laughingstock.

I wondered why the boy put himself through this martyrdom, and why he thought an appearance at the school assembly would advance his career.

I also felt a grudging respect for him, and seeds of an affinity. But I pretended to be dumbstruck by his conduct.

· 8 ·

How, from musical comedy, did I make the transition to opera? The idea of opera coagulated with most density in the cover photograph of my mother's Joan Sutherland album—"Operatic Arias," 1959: Joan's face blanched and huge against a sky-blue backdrop. But here is the strange and resonant part: Joan's lipstick was the result of retouching. The lipstick didn't match the lips, but hung askew. Before I listened to her coloratura, I knew Joan Sutherland and opera as errors in makeup: I enjoyed the spectacle of lipstick separate from the lips on which it was supposed to rest.

My mother kept her records in the closet. Why? Fear of dust. She rarely played them. And so this image of female vocalism remains separate from sound: Renata Tebaldi's torso, on the *Aida* highlights album, put under considerable pressure by a too-tight costume, so an ampleness makes itself known.

· 9 ·

I never heard my spinster aunt play her records; and yet because of her old Victor set of *La Forza del Destino,* I will always associate Verdi with my aunt's maiden destiny. I don't know if she was a lesbian, but I know she traveled with women in Germany, lived with women in Venezuela, and, in old age, wore a ring given her by a San Francisco lady friend. In the backseat of my parents' car, she hummed Papageno's aria and tapped its downbeats with her fingers on my leg, and told me about the choirs she'd heard in Munich before the war.

In the late 1960s, I was in my bedroom practicing Papageno's aria, transcribed for trumpet. (At the time, I thought of it as sheer exercise. I didn't know it was an operatic excerpt.) My aunt entered the room and listened to me play the aria. Some recognition passed between us, on the back of the Mozart melody: the understanding that I, like my aunt, would live apart from marriage (bachelor, spinster), and that a fondness for Papageno's tune and *La Forza del Destino* were secret signs of a destiny we never described to each other in words.

· 10 ·

My piano teacher, who had no evident sexual life, who lived, a maiden, with her aged father, couldn't carry a tune, but when she wanted to demonstrate how to shape a phrase, she would falteringly, expressively sing it, off-pitch. I, a virgin who couldn't sing, understood this peculiar paralysis of the throat, and connected it to a life apart from marriage, a life of secrets and containment.

· 11 ·

When I speak too much or too loudly, I lose my voice: and at all times I speak from my throat, not my diaphragm. Faulty speaking means I'm perennially hoarse. Too much talking on the phone puts pressure on my throat, and it starts to ache. Though my voice is relatively high-pitched, I speak huskily, like Harvey Fierstein. I don't lisp, though I used to stutter. I've always admired the voice placement of actors, even if my actor friends are embarrassed, in casual conversation, to speak as they were trained (from the diaphragm): it sounds pretentious, oratorical, and nervously earnest.

The last time I tried to sing in public was in fourth grade when I auditioned for *Oliver!*, a children's light-opera production. All auditioning boys stood in a line and sang "Consider Yourself" together; then, one by one, we stepped out of line and sang a phrase, and continued to sing until told to stop. "Consider yourself at home, consider yourself one of the family. . . ." Doubtless I flubbed: I remember that sensation of vulnerability in the throat, of exposure, of sacrifice.

When Walt Whitman wrote so extensively and rhapsodically about the throat *("O throat! O trembling throat!")* he was urging us to liberate our throats, to imitate the wide-mouthed opera singer: "A tenor large and fresh as the creation fills me, / The orbic flex of his mouth is pouring and filling me full." We drink sound through our throats: our throats are activated, brought to life, by what we hear. Listening is a reciprocation: grateful for what the ear receives, the throat responds by opening.

· *12* ·

Cultural folklore convinces us that we can tell someone is gay by voice alone. Decadent novelist J.-K. Huysmans wrote in a letter to Marc-André Raffalovich that "sodomy changes the voice, which becomes almost identical in all of them. After several days' study in that world, from nothing but the sound of the voice of people I did not know, I could infallibly predict their tastes. Do you not think there would be research to be done on the influence of one organ on another?"

And Earl Lind, the remarkable author of *Autobiography of an Androgyne* (1918), believed that "the voice is one of the chief criteria by which to determine abnormal sexuality. I fancy that I can diagnose a man sexually simply by hearing him sing." This same Earl Lind, whose drag names were "Jennie June," "Baby," and "Pussie," daydreamed of becoming a prima donna. "At the opera I would imagine myself as identified with the leading soprano—that I was she. As is usual with professional fairies, I sought to cultivate a soprano singing voice, though singing a baritone when in my every-day circle."

Calling information (411) in Manhattan, I'm pleased by the sound of a distinctly gay-voiced male operator. Finding such an operator, I try to make my request more flamboyant and femmy: I insert an extra "please," and I push against the "please," to stretch the vowel into a diphthong. Even on the phone, voice-to-voice, I want to make my affiliation clear. (Why? No chance to meet the operator. Flirting for its own sake.)

· 13 ·

Opening my mouth wide for tonsillectomy (I can't remember the operation, but, occurring before the age of school, before I learned to read, it foreshadows my commitment to the throat), I sucked ether and courted loss of consciousness.

First French kisses with women: slow ballet of tongues.

First fellatio: surprise at the mouth's flexibility and tolerance for foreign objects.

The same year I discovered gay 69, I formed an opera club with a girl I loved (we were eighteen), and we listened to *The Marriage of Figaro* together on her couch; she sang "Voi, che sapete" down an echoing dormitory stairwell.

We planned to move on to *Norma* but we discontinued the club before making that progress.

· 14 ·

In Marcia Davenport's novel *Of Lena Geyer* (1936), drab Elsie deHaven has a crush on soprano Lena Geyer. Elsie sends the diva a huge box of yellow roses after each performance, with a note disguising her gender (E. deH.). Clearly this is queer behavior: Elsie says, "Call me a freak if you like."

Why does Elsie follow Lena around Europe and eventually become her companion? Because the diva's voice, says Elsie, "meant as much to me as parents, a husband, children, or anything most women attach themselves to"; because when she first heard Lena sing, "I was too thrilled to breathe; I remember how the pulse in my throat choked me"; because the sensation of hearing Geyer was like "fresh water pouring into the throat of someone nearly dead of thirst," a physical thrill that "gripped me and made something inside me leap into my ears and throat." Throat, throat, throat! Elsie confesses: "It was exactly like the unlocking of a prison door. The voice poured into me, and from that moment it became the one thing I cared to live for. The whole identity that my parents had so carefully created melted in the force of the singing I heard that night. All the barriers built up by convention and habit seemed to shrivel, and I felt in those few moments a free and purposeful individual. I did not even know I was repressed, or inarticulate, yet once I felt freed, I knew that I had never lived before."

Elsie comes out—her parched self watered by the geyser of another woman's voice. Elsie knows she is excited and in love because she can't breathe and because the pulse in her throat chokes her. The throat, not the ears, receives the diva: the throat, organ from which "I" speak.

The grandiosity of operatic utterance is a wild compensation for the listener's silence. Our ability to speak of ourselves has been foreshortened; we turn to opera because we need to breathe, to regain a right we imagine is godgiven—the right to open.

· 15 ·

Nuns in the Middle Ages believed they were pregnant because Jesus had *thought* of them; no wonder, then, that opera queens, nuns of an unnamed order, believe that voices entering through the ear are forms of the Holy Ghost. Freud's disciple and biographer Ernest Jones, in his provocative essay "The Madonna's Conception through the Ear," speculates on the ear's erotic significances. To hear is metaphorically to be impregnated—with thought, tone, and sensation.

How loudly do you play your opera? Loud enough to hurt the ear? In the opera house, I distinguish between two kinds of sound: the baritone, mezzo, and bass, in whose presence I remain Subject, knowing the heard voice as Object; and the soprano and tenor, which, as they ascend in volume and pitch, become Subject, incapable of remaining the distant Object. Thus opera interrupts and reverses our ground. I can't remain separate from the tenor or soprano at the height of their ranges, because high notes enter my ear, assault, make a demand. In Family Circle, listening to Cheryl Studer sing Donna Anna in *Don Giovanni,* I can't remain detached and analytical, because her voice makes incursions on my sense of volition. Listen to Rosa Ponselle. Her tones are rounded, median, warm; but then they renounce plumthickness and become sabers. Moments of being pierced, being surrounded by sound, being called, are worth collecting.

· *16* ·

And so the opera queen keeps lists. Experiences are accreted, because none can be exhaustively explained. If, once, you could describe the summons a voice sends out, maybe you could stop listening, stop looking to opera for satisfaction and consummation.

Would Proust have written his *A la Recherche du Temps Perdu* if a single enigmatic phrase from a violin had not "opened and expanded his soul" and made him wish to move linearly and at length, ramification upon ramification, room after room, through one instant? And would he have felt compelled to sip recollection from the cup of one phrase if his eroticism hadn't seemed troublingly asocial and wretched, needing to be transformed into a colossus and a labyrinth? "But while I was humming softly to myself the notes of this tune and returning its kiss, the pleasure peculiar to itself which it made me feel became so dear to me that I would have left my father and mother to follow it through the singular world which it constructed in the invisible. . . ."

James McCourt's implicitly gay novel of the diva and her fan, *Mawrdew Czgowchwz* (1975), opens with "The List"—a list of characters. A diva leaves a list of fans and friends with the stage-door guard: only those on the list are admitted. In McCourt's fan-fantasy, every character is allowed backstage; McCourt (novelist as diva) opens stardom's private recesses to all gawkers.

I keep a tiny "Opera Journal" in which I list every opera performance I attend. (I rarely include recitals.) I list the opera, the house, the principal singers, the date. But there's no room for evaluation or criticism. The purpose of a list is not to refine or browbeat, but to include, and to move toward a future moment when accumulation stops and the list-keeper can cull, recollect, and rest on the prior amplitude.

Opera queens catalogue their highs; they don't categorize or explain. Memoirs of operagoing take the form of laterally spreading reminiscences, one after another, with no sequence except chronology. Richard Edgcumbe's *Musical Reminiscences of an Old Amateur for Fifty Years, from 1773 to 1823* is a mnemonic project that leads to no conclusion—just a list of what has been heard. He recalls nothing of diva Caterina Gabrielli's voice—only an image of her judicious, antinaturalistic way with costume: "I can remember seeing her once in the opera of Didone, but can say nothing of her performance, all I can recollect of it being the care with which she tucked up her great hoop as she sidled into the flames of Carthage."

List-making is a prophylaxis against loss. Lists perform sympathetic magic: we want names (of operas, theaters, divas, roles) to be corporeal. A fan writes of Elisabeth Rethberg (in a 1939 *Opera News*): "As to the number of her roles, the other day I sat down and wrote the names of twenty-six operas in which she has sung." In such a fashion I used to keep a list (abandoned in 1969) of every movie I had seen, beginning with *Mary Poppins,* traveling through *I Confess,* and ending with—I can't recall where the list ended, which movie persuaded me it was pointless to keep a list of beloved properties.

· *17* ·

Only in 1979, at the end of college, did I begin openly to listen to opera: that same year I went to the Napoleon Club in Boston's Beacon Hill and stared, youthful and muddled behind my wire-rimmed glasses, at peacock men, gays I'd never seen in such number.

A more logical narrative of my life would have had me embrace disco, for disco was the theme music of gay sexuality in the late 1970s. But I never went dancing; I preferred furtive cruising; my desires were ruminative, oblivious to beat.

Opera has always suited those who have failed at love. I entered sexuality assuming that I would fail at it and that it had failed me, that I, by virtue of my lust for men, was where sexuality broke down, where the system stopped working, where a mistake materialized.

I remember the girl who sang the lead in our high school's production of *Guys and Dolls* (a flamboyant redhead with a large bosom). Did I love her? Or did I envy her? I spent much of childhood trying to distinguish identification from desire, asking myself, "Am I in love with Julie Andrews, or do I think I *am* Julie Andrews?" I knew that to love Julie Andrews placed me, however vaguely, in heterosexuality's domain; but to identify with Julie Andrews, to want to be the star of *Star!,* placed me under suspicion.

When I left behind my original-cast albums and began to listen, again and again, in 1980, to the four operas I owned, I had by that time acquired a boyfriend, a sexuality, and a hunger (I still can't explain the urge, I can only point to it, and surround it with anecdote, reflection, and context) to have opera take over my reason, as if opera were the antithesis of reason.

· *18* ·

Accidents of birth, of affection: all senior year of college, without pocket money, I visited record stores, and planned which Verdi opera I would buy when I had saved twenty dollars. I wanted the Deutsche Grammophon red boxed set of *Rigoletto*. I didn't know why. Or I had no coherent motivation.

Six months later, at an opera sale, I bought a different *Rigoletto,* for nine dollars: the Gilda was Anna Moffo. (I didn't notice this fact when I purchased the set.) Coincidentally, Moffo was the star of my ignored *Butterfly*. I began to put my life together. That summer I listened to her "Caro nome" repeatedly after my nine-to-five typing job. Also I had sex almost every night in a bedroom whose door wouldn't properly close, so I played music to disguise the sounds of two men in process.

One of my roommates said, "All you ever do is come home, shut your door, and listen to opera." This was a criticism: I was a recluse, a shut-in who, by accident, had garnered a boyfriend. But if I wasn't careful I would relapse into a dangerous solitude. It was unclear whether opera represented the pathway out from anomie into camaraderie, or whether immersion in opera undid the listener's social ties.

· *19* ·

The opera queen must choose one diva. The other divas may be admired, enjoyed, even loved. But only one diva can reign in the opera queen's heart; only one diva can have the power to describe a listener's life, as a compass describes a circle.

To remain loyal, one must ward off the specter of defection: the possibility, at any moment, of realizing another diva's claims, of saying (as I said yesterday), "Why not devote myself to another voice, a voice more ample, with a greater range?" But devotions are not entirely chosen.

I have floating allegiances to a dozen divas, few of them still performing. First, alone, without qualification, though always touched by sadness: Anna Moffo. Second: Maria Callas. Third: Elisabeth Schwarzkopf. (This is the heart's ranking, not vulnerable to logic.) Tied for fourth place: Leontyne Price, Rosa Ponselle, Leonie Rysanek, Jessye Norman. Tied for fifth place (singers who attract me as voice or as icon, though I rarely follow them with the personal and unqualified enthusiasm I bring to the singers listed above): Victoria de los Angeles, Licia Albanese, Renata Tebaldi, Joan Sutherland, Montserrat Caballé, Marie Collier, Kiri Te Kanawa, Mirella Freni, Renata Scotto, Elisabeth Söderström, Beverly Sills, Ljuba Welitsch, Ninon Vallin. And then some honorable mentions, women whose voices I hardly know, but whose careers fascinate me mostly because they are mid-century Met stars: Risë Stevens, Roberta Peters, Dorothy Kirsten, Eleanor Steber, Zinka Milanov. And some honorary men: Beniamino Gigli, Tito Schipa, Jussi Bjoerling, Richard Tucker, Carlo Bergonzi, Giuseppe di Stefano, Tito Gobbi.

Once I chose Anna Moffo, in 1980, ignorant of the other singers, I was set for life. I had a path. I had reference points and details, which would take pages to list. November 14, 1959: the Met debut. Mimì: her Chicago debut role. Fainted on stage after performing Lucia's mad scene. First husband: Mario Lanfranchi. Second husband: Robert Sarnoff. Father's profession: shoe repairman. Birthplace: Wayne, Pennsylvania. I had discovered an altitude, a mission. I had facts to uncover, recordings to unearth, a timbre against which others would seem too full, too old, too ripe, too controlled. I had chosen a voice which sounded to me like promise and bounty, and compared to this voice, all other aspects of the universe were scrap metal.

And so the opera queen, having chosen the diva, either tries to befriend her, or renounces all claim, and realizes that the states to be savored are absence, sacrifice, and search.

· *20* ·

Choosing a diva to love is like inaugurating any erotic arrangement. You see the boy at the pool every afternoon. At first he is just another male body. But you begin to dream of his abdomen. You blush when he passes on the street, and feel motion in your groin. You loiter by the travel books because he is browsing there. You gauge your "Hello," you want it to be restrained, not effusive. You see him sitting alone at the movies and you are overjoyed to imagine that maybe he is unattached, and his pressed peach-colored shorts persuade you that maybe he is gay, and you listen, at the pool, for his Australian accent echoing above the fast lane. . . .

Nursing a crush: one begins by noticing the person's characteristics and finding them oblique to what one had known, until that day, of the world. For me, it was Moffo's delayed, dusky, under-the-note attack on the word "disvelto" in a passage from *Rigoletto,* the way she took a word not in itself meaningful or musically crucial, and marked it with individuality and pathos; I noticed that in the performances of other Gildas, the word "disvelto" passed unremarkably, unrewarded by emphasis. I knew that when she chose, Moffo had the power to warm up a note from within, and that I had the power to listen for that instant when unspeakable complexities textured a note.

What distinguishes the diva you have chosen from the divas you merely admire is that you are interested in *everything* your chosen diva has done—even the mistakes. Leonie Rysanek pushes certain notes so they almost go flat. I'm not sure this is tasteful. And yet I wait for it to happen, and I might even stop the record and put the needle back to hear that note again—the doubtful note—because the world is alive with recognitions and quickenings when I have established a relation to such accidents, when I am not the victim of what I hear, but its willing accessory.

I want to know exactly how she sang in 1965 as opposed to 1964. It matters. I need to know what Rysanek was singing in 1972. I need to know whether Moffo's *La Rondine* was recorded in 1966 or 1967, and why Daniele Barioni (and not a more stellar tenor) was cast opposite her, and how close she stood to the mike, and what restaurants she frequented after performing at the Rome Opera House, and what she sang at her 1969 New York recital, and what she said to Callas while recording *La Bohème* in 1956. The curiosity is insatiable, and the pursuit of such knowledge is a spiritual exercise, demeaning but also secretly ennobling.

I don't have a sustained love for the voice of Roberta Peters but I almost weep when I read that she will be giving a concert on Long Island because I am pleased that her career continues, and I imagine how fond she is of the Met, and I imagine her doing warm-up scales in her studio. . . . I have more than once asked myself, "Why hasn't RCA released her *Lucia* on CD? Sure, it's not one of the best, but I'd buy it." And on a drunken spree one day I might buy her *Barbiere* because her timbre's clarity will spring-clean me. One is in love with places one could never have been, ordinary places, such as a Roberta Peters performance of Susanna in—I am guessing—Cleveland, on the Met tour, in 1955.

And before I developed a pointed love for the voice of Leontyne Price (she is rising in my estimation daily, soon I may not be able to conceive of reality without the sound of her "Pace, pace") I walked around Greenwich Village and wondered, "Which of these Federal rowhouses is Leontyne's, and if I pass by at the right time will I hear the sound of practicing?"

· 21 ·

Divas are notoriously noisy, but fans go silent to their graves.

"GIRL KILLS SELF OVER MARY GARDEN" reads a 1912 New York headline. Luckily for Garden, the dead girl's mother wrote a letter to the newspaper, exculpating the star: "Miss Garden never knew my daughter. My daughter had never even met her. She had developed a mad infatuation for her from hearing her sing. She went to Philadelphia to hear Miss Garden in *Faust* and then went to her dressing room but was not permitted to speak to her. This was not the first time my daughter had become infatuated with a celebrity. She was a very high-strung girl. . . ." A revolver fell out of the girl's muff, backstage: had she planned to shoot Garden?

A crazy fan assiduously annotated my library's copy of *Mary Garden's Story;* this fan was particularly interested in Garden's death. In the margin, the fan wrote: "There is now a fine forest on the hill where Garden's ashes were strewn. What a fitting memorial to Mary! She died in a mental home shortly before NOON (midi) of a Sunday. What a coincidence: 'Je suis née midi'—Pelléas & M." Fans sift and hoard coincidences. How mournful, to inscribe an imagined synchronicity, an astrological convergence, in a library book's margin. The most illustrious and poignant fan clubs have only one member.

I have never tried to befriend a diva, though serious opera queens usually try. I have always felt that my opera queendom is paltry and postmodern because I don't pursue it literally enough; I don't knock on dressing-room doors.

Mary Watkins Cushing, Olive Fremstad's live-in fan, was first a fan of Emma Eames: "I used to study the portraits curiously and try to imagine what the glorious sounds were like which were said to issue from between those painted lips." Mary gave up conventional society —the friendship of peers—and moved deep into her queer opera-loving self: "I no longer passed the dark winter afternoons after school on the skating pond, but in the local music shop where I sat glassy-eyed and inert, drinking in the fabulous sounds of opera from each new issue of records. I became a nuisance to the clerks and a riddle to

my schoolmates, who tittered and winked and thought me queer. . . ."
She starts to keep a scrapbook. She meets her idol, Olive Fremstad.
She moves in with Olive. This was the era of the Gerry-flapper, and
though Mary is loyal to Fremstad, she is vulnerable to Geraldine Farrar's charms: standing backstage, "I . . . felt my pulses quicken and the
fatuous smile of the 'Gerry-flapper' spread across my face when, in a
drift of delicious perfume, trailing furs, plumage, and the sparkle of
jewels, she brightened my exile in the drab gray hall."

Long lonely nights, fan Gordon M. Eby lies awake (according to
the acknowledgments page of his unparalleled *From the Beauty of Embers*) thinking of divas and of days gone by. The photograph of Eby
standing beside Rosa Ponselle in Baltimore, April 1961, makes me
laugh and shudder with recognition: the plain plump man in tux
standing proud and electric by the world's greatest living though long-
retired soprano, who holds a lily in an elbow-length-white-gloved
hand, her dress floral, her bosoms separate and intense, her waist small,
Ponselle a good three inches taller than fan Gordon M. Eby, whom I
do not mean to mock, I envy his serious industry, he who had the
pluck and vision to befriend Rosa Ponselle—and the willingness to be
small and minor beside her: for isn't it humiliating to stand next to
Rosa Ponselle and know oneself a naught? Male fans, not able simply
to gush, often feign amorous interest. I recognize that forgery of eros:
I see it in Eby's face, as he escorts Ponselle, and I imagine him saying,
"Miss Ponselle is the *loveliest* woman alive, my dream of what a woman
should be." The queeny love of women: I celebrate it, and I keep my
distance from it.

Because gush is more traditionally the prerogative of girls, the
fans most willing to blush and gush have been female. Adelina Patti
tells a reporter that a "pyramid of bouquets came from a party of
young girls, whose faces were brighter than the flowers they brought."
Nellie Melba loved singing to the "matinée girls": posy-decked debu-
tantes who attended Nellie's matinees and rushed down the aisle after
the performance to toss blossoms to the diva. A poor flower girl
squandered her earnings on Melba tickets; a one-legged soldier hob-
bled three miles to hear her sing, and presented her (Melba tells us)
with "sixteen exquisite little bouquets, each tied with a different-col-
oured ribbon, and each representing one of the first nights in the
various operas which I have either created or given in the course of my
career. Dear Jim Styles! I am thinking of *you,* and I thank you." How
dear to Nellie could this fan be, wounded man she addresses straight

in the eye, man of style, man without a leg, man who knows what Melba wants, master of the exquisite, in command of Melba trivia, man of absences and devotions?

· *22* ·

The violence of fans in Baltimore (I think Baltimore is America's queeniest city because John Waters called it the Hairdo Capital of the World, because in Baltimore I began to go crazy over divas, and because Baltimore is near Rosa Ponselle's Villa Pace): in Baltimore, Jenny Lind dropped her shawl from a balcony, and fans ripped it up and pocketed the fragments.

The fan's assault may take the form of a sonnet: one Sontag-guard (fan of nineteenth-century diva Henriette Sontag) wrote sonnets on white satin and, at a Sontag farewell, fluttered them down to the stage. Or it may take the form of an orange. Crazed servant Ann Barwick, partisan of the diva Mrs. Tofts, was arrested in 1704 for throwing oranges at Tofts's rival, Margherita de l'Épine, during a performance. Mrs. Tofts published a letter in the *Daily Courant:* "I abhor such practices; and I hope you will cause her to be prosecuted, that she may be punished as she deserves."

Fragmentation: in Russia, a young male fan breaks Dame Nellie Melba's autographing pencil with his teeth into small pieces so other "chosen friends" can have a relic of Nellie.

· *23* ·

I sink into opera depravity. I lose sense of time. I forget my obligations. I don't adore Renata Tebaldi's voice but I feel the pull of Tebaldi lore. I feel on the verge of becoming, thirty years too late, a Tebaldiano. I am really a Callas fan but long after the feud is over I soar as I read this sentence: "Callas's people gloated that their lady had the opening night, while the Tebaldi faction reminded them that Callas would appear in a seedy looking production of *Norma* whereas Renata would have the Met's first new *Traviata* mise en scène in two decades built around her." Or, we hear that on Monday, September 19, 1968, when Callas goes to hear Tebaldi open the Met season as Adriana Lecouvreur, "the Tebaldiani that evening seemed to outnumber the Corelli people" (fans of gorgeous tenor Franco Corelli). What an identity! I am one of the Corelli people. I am one of the Callas people. I am one of the Tebaldiani. The Tebaldiani are hardly a revolutionary group but they are proud of their ability to snarl the city's traffic: the Tebaldiani "stopped traffic on West 40th Street on many a night!"

The Tebaldiani see into Renata's soul. As Renata smiles and greets her fans at the Met's stage entrance, Tebaldi's biographer divines that Tebaldi is moved: "Tebaldi, always glad to see her fans, was clearly touched by the greeting, and, while she smiled, waved, and greeted a number of people by name, tears were not far away." The Tebaldiani insist that Renata is vulnerable, sensitive. They know that baritone Leonard Warren's death "on the first night of Renata's American season in 1960 must have shaken her tremendously," but Warren's death figures in this account only because his death dampens Renata's cheer; the Tebaldiano stares into the crystal ball of his imagined connection to the diva and maps the world from Tebaldi's majestic, faction-clouded point of view.

One of Tebaldi's top fans was "queen of the Met regulars" Lois Kirschenbaum. Thus named, she is my alter ego. A telephone receptionist by day (devoted to the disembodied voice), by night she haunts the Met. She goes backstage to see Tebaldi and brings two bags filled with programs and photos for the diva to sign.

I'm not a Tebaldiano, but I rescued one of her records from a yard sale last month: for one dollar I bought her *Cavalleria Rusticana* (costarring Jussi Bjoerling) because it was in its original pink Victor box and I wanted to express (to the cosmos?) my reverence for this object, for the devotion that once encircled it, before the owner decided it was junk. The Tebaldi bio speaks fondly of this set, "originally mastered by RCA in 1958, but missing from record shops since 1965. . . . It is strange that this recording, highly revered by many, through some quirk in marketing never became a cornerstone of the RCA catalogue (indeed, it was prematurely withdrawn)." I meant to continue talking about other diva factions but I got stuck staring at the photograph of Renata Tebaldi in the green room of the Philadelphia Academy of Music on December 20, 1972; the photo, doubtless the work of Lois Kirschenbaum, queen of the Met regulars, also shows the author of the Tebaldi bio (Kenn Harris) beaming beneath his handlebar mustache. I got stuck imagining what it would have been like in 1972 to stand in the green room beside Tebaldi while Tebaldi-presence showers me with intimations of the unknown and unknowable.

· *24* ·

"Your devoted little friend who has never heard you," writes a "crippled" girl flat on her back for eleven years who begs Clara Butt to wave as the diva's train passes the forlorn fan's backyard.

Must fans be loyal? Are fans subjects? Are they immobile, pathetic, slavish? The image of fan-as-vassal, bedridden and dependent, corresponds to the image of the queer person as a subordinate soul, a soul stuck in the wrong body, a soul with no connection to a body.

Fans have no minds of their own. They only figure as emanations of the diva's will, as mind readers. Dorothy Kirsten has enormous confidence in her fans: she made few recordings, and she knows that her faithful fans "search out every pirated record of my voice they can find regardless of cost." The fiction surrounding fans is that they are magically in communication with the diva (or the diva's secretary, Vicki): "When the news was released that it was . . . my farewell, members of my fan clubs from all over the country showered Vicki with letters begging her to arrange for tickets. Even though it was a special performance and not a subscription night, her task was not easy because my own guest list was considerable." To fall in love with soprano Dorothy Kirsten is a specific vocation, not open to everyone. I love the pictures of Kirsten late in her career, sleeveless dress for Manon Lescaut in San Francisco, or, young, lovely for an opera star, working with Gustave Charpentier, the composer of *Louise:* Kirsten's arms folded, her blond tresses full, Charpentier conducting, the lady smiling, teeth brilliant, dress black, the photo taking place nowhere in particular, my immersion in this photo so "pathological" and inexplicable—or constitutive of time and of my history as a gay person. Imagining Dorothy Kirsten's voice *while I look at publicity photos* is basic to this dream-sexuality we call "gay"—not really a sexuality, but for me at the moment a way of falling off the globe, a way of pursuing desires that have nothing to do with genitals.

· *25* ·

"She is the sort of person who is called 'queer,' " and in addition to being queer she is persistent, for she knocks on the diva's hotel-room door and says, " 'I've come to ask you if you would please kiss me.' " Diva Clara Louise Kellogg writes, "Of course I complied."

From there the relationship developed; whenever Kellogg sang in Providence, she stayed with the crazy lady. "She studied my 'ways' and every time I came back there was some new and flattering indication of the fact." In every opera house there are crazies and exquisites studying the "ways" of the stars, dreaming up inaudible vocalisms to match what the queer ear hears, and Clara Louise Kellogg alludes to these chimerical self-fashionings when she muses, "Who knows what sympathies, what comprehensions, what exquisite friendships, were blossoming out there in the dark house like a garden, waiting to be gathered?"

I sometimes wonder why I've never written a fan letter, and why I don't try to befriend the stars. Maybe I'm not high-strung enough— not as pulsating as Adelina Patti's number one fan, opera queen Monsieur de Saxe, whose temperament, she says, was "nervous." Or maybe I'm afraid of turning into Ida and Louise Cook, Brit sisters who scrimped and saved for passage money to sail to America and hear Amelita Galli-Curci—sisters who wrote to Galli-Curci, and befriended her, and then annexed other stars (notably Rosa Ponselle), and visited Rosa at Villa Pace after World War II, which principally made them sad because, having spent the war years smuggling Jews out of Nazi territories, they missed Ponselle's performances. Says Ida, in her memoir, *We Followed Our Stars:* "Let no one think this was a minor matter." War-work "cost us Rosa's Donna Anna and Carmen and Luisa Miller and Africana. That was what mattered." Time passes, and you miss the performances you might have heard, and no new performances will arise to take their place. So after the war they wrote to Rosa, addressing the letter, simply, "Rosa Ponselle, Baltimore, U.S.A." Magically, the letter is delivered—and answered: the girls feel "private vindication of our belief in the ultimate rightness of things."

Who knows if the girls were lesbian? Galli-Curci understood they were strange: the sisters admit, "No doubt she needed no more than a few minutes in our company to realise what kind of girls we were." They wrote Elisabeth Rethberg a note on paper of a "fierce violet shade." Their primary passion was adding star "snaps" (photos) to their collection.

A strange narcissism invests the Cook girls' attachment to Rosa Ponselle. They assume Rosa cares just as much about them as they care about Rosa. To wit, when they are reunited with darling Rosa, they aver that "she was probably as moved as we were." I doubt it, girls.

So committed were they to Rosa Ponselle that every year they threw a party celebrating the anniversary of her London debut, and at these fêtes they rang Rosa up in Baltimore so she could sing "Pace, pace, mio Dio" into the phone: "we passed the receiver round from one to another so that each of us at least heard a few notes at full volume." Is it a sign of desperation or of seraphic achievement, to hear Rosa Ponselle's voice, post-retirement, over the telephone?

· *26* ·

Philothée O'Neddy, French Romantic poet and critic, thought of Paris's Théâtre-Italien as the perfect place to commit suicide. Opera queendom isn't suicidal. But it feels like throwing the self away, giving up autonomy and production, becoming pure receiver. Once you decide that your finest experiences will come from listening to opera, you have given up on reciprocity, and you've become a phantom, a haunting. In Willa Cather's story "Paul's Case," the femmy music-lover Paul finds himself through music and operagoing and decadent expenditures but his trajectory is suicidally down, straight into the cold snow, where he freezes to death: clearly Paul was sick to find himself through singers and actors, to adore Carnegie Hall's "fine people and gay colours." The theater "was Paul's fairy tale, and it had for him all the allurement of a secret love. The moment he inhaled the gassy, painty, dusty odour behind the scenes, he breathed like a prisoner set free, and felt within him the possibility of doing or saying splendid, brilliant things. The moment the cracked orchestra beat out the overture from *Martha,* or jerked at the serenade from *Rigoletto,* all stupid and ugly things slid from him, and his senses were deliciously, yet delicately fired." He loved the opera because it matched his soul: "He felt now that his surroundings explained him. Nobody questioned the purple; he had only to wear it passively. He had only to glance down at his dress coat to reassure himself that here it would be impossible for anyone to humiliate him." But because Paul can't afford this life (he embezzles to finance his whirlwind weekend in New York City), he must kill himself rather than leave the world of opera and fancy hotels and return to his hometown room whose "horrible yellow wallpaper" (the phrase recalls Charlotte Perkins Gilman's 1892 story "The Yellow Wallpaper") is symbol of the ways in which straight civilization casts him as feminized lunatic freak, much as Cather, by titling the story "Paul's Case," impersonates the voice of medical authority, masking as a "case" this portrait of her own desire for aesthetic fulfillment and sexual nonconformity. Because the world of opera and theater is Paul's entryway to a self we could call queer (or at least oblique to conventional masculinity), and because opera in "Paul's Case" is expensive, he needs money to be gay. Without an income, he can't participate in the aristocratic milieu of opera queendom, and must kill himself.

· 27 ·

Because this book is my scrapbook, because as an opera queen I stand immobile inside a crush, and because a crush is composed of useless fragments, I give you these pieces, without commentary:

"Anna Moffo, perfectly cast as Gilda, showed real virtuosity in 'Caro nome' " (a 1958 *Opera News* phrase of praise); a 1957 photo of Anna Moffo embracing her parents on the pier ("Young and beautiful, Anna Moffo returns to her native land"); a 1960 photo of Moffo and husband on vacation in Milan ("Anna Moffo scored as Elvira in *Puritani* at Parma and Rosina in *Barbiere* at Rome this winter, both in new productions staged by her husband, Mario Lanfranchi"); a 1968 photo of Moffo, legs crossed, with caption, "Anna Moffo—who this fall filmed a cameo role in Paramount's *Adventurers,* still under production—will visit Stockholm, Berlin and Budapest during January to sing *Lucia di Lammermoor* and *La Traviata*"; a 1963 *Opera News* feature story, "Shopping With Moffo"; a 1961 candid that stops me dead because her head is cocked sideways coquettishly, her dress striped, her demeanor sterling and young, her black pumps pressing into the couch's fabric ("Anna Moffo, shown above in her New York apartment, will sing Violetta in *La Traviata* at the fortieth consecutive New York Vassar Club scholarship benefit, on Saturday evening, January 6"). . . .

These clippings have a prismatic shattering power—the power to construct me as "he-who-dreams"—that I try to explain, and then I fall silent. . . .

· 28 ·

So I understand why my opera queen friend keeps all of his records in the garage: he's afraid of them: he's afraid that listening will take over his life. The opera queen interprets his desires through a vocabulary of addiction. Love of opera seems a sickness that needs to be controlled, the infectious objects isolated. My friend let me into his garage, and we browsed together through the mildewed sets—the Toscanini *Falstaff,* the Tebaldi *Adriana Lecouvreur.* I said, "Why don't you bring the records into the house? This is a terrific collection!" He said, "You don't know what would happen. You have no idea what would happen."

· **29** ·

The solitary operatic feast, the banquet for one, onanism through the ear: taking an evening out of my life to listen to *Simon Boccanegra,* I feel I am locked in the bathroom eating a quart of ice cream, that I have lost all my friends, that I am committing some violently antisocial act, like wearing lipstick to school. In junior high I was afraid to jerk off every day, afraid I'd use up the desire, afraid that desire couldn't be replenished, and afraid that a simple unobnoxious orgasm would bring my life crashing down.

· **30** ·

Opera and pornography: in Terrence McNally's *The Lisbon Traviata,* hardcore opera queen Mendy is absorbed in a Maria Callas documentary while his friend Stephen (who loves opera but less extremely and campily) flips through *Blueboy.* Both men resort to representations, and so we're meant to see them as pathetic, adrift from the Real, though Stephen is at least on the right track; his interest in *Blueboy* means he's still interested in sex, and not, like Mendy, drowned in diva idolatry. Mendy, the character most exuberantly committed to opera, is also the least attractive member of the cast.

Pornography, like eating, falls under the shady rubric of addiction. If Mendy were to join a program called Opera Queens Anonymous, his first task would be to throw away his Callas records. Pick up *Torso,* and you enter the arena of these condemnations: you are lonely, pathetic, perverted, and you should be "relating" to someone rather than resorting to crude representations. Dependence on porn will drive you to sex crimes. Once you fall under porn's power, your self-destructions will escalate, leading to suicide, or at least isolation.

An ancient (Platonic?) prejudice against representation upholds the homophobic distaste for the opera queen. The opera queen, listening to Callas, is as removed from actuality and as enamored of "mere" images as the "lonely" gay man flipping through *Mandate*. The opera queen, unproductive, doesn't participate in any sexual or marital economies. In his most extreme incarnation, as Mendy in *The Lisbon Traviata,* the opera queen is unfit for love, and the taste for opera is seen not only as compensation for lost love objects, but as the very catalyst of loss. The opera queen is lonely *because* he listens to opera: opera isolates him from the sexual marketplace.

· *31* ·

We consider the opera queen to be a pre-Stonewall throwback because we homophobically devalue opera love as addictive behavior and as displaced eroticism. The opera queen is a dated species: very 1950s. I am an anachronism. After sexual liberation, who needs opera? But this logic would also have us renounce our fetishes, would deny us lace or leather, and would deny a taste's inevitability (those intertwining roots which determine and bind the heart). I used to be afraid that if I analyzed my love for opera too closely, I would be forced to abandon it. But the drag queen does not give up his drag just because he has cracked its code.

· *32* ·

The body of the opera queen, my body, the body I fear: overweight, not attended to, spilling out of clothes; emaciated, wasting, so hungry for voice the body consumes itself, as if listening were a digestive enzyme or acid; dressed in yesterday's fashions, wedge shoes. (The opera queen wears bellbottoms to the opera in 1980 and with the drag queen's sublime indifference to public opinion thinks the bellbottoms are still "cool.")

I used to be afraid of becoming gay because I thought gay men had eyes like holograms: I couldn't tell apart the fierce controlling stare of a Moonie and the gay man's cruising gaze, each species willing to establish eye contact on the street and to convert me.

The opera queen wants to look decent, oiled, scented, combed, contained—dressed as if dining with antediluvian authorities at a second-rate restaurant supposing itself "fancy." He has a gold bracelet discreetly tucked inside the starched cuff of his custom-made shirt but the gold shows when he gesticulates. Most of all I know this of the opera queen: he looks completely different naked than clothed. Suddenly you're home in bed with the opera queen and he wants to do outrageous things to your body.

A personals ad in a gay newspaper requests, "No fats, femmes, 'opera queens,' please!" Though the large lesbian may be signifying her renunciation of normative heterosexual codes of female attractiveness, the large gay man (unless he participates in the fat ghetto—the chubby-chasers, the bears) seems to be *failing* in his gay identity.

The body of the opera queen: afflicted with a taste for the excessive, the promiscuous—addicted to numbers, to inches, to accretion —and where do these excesses end?

The body of the opera queen: my body.

The very phrase "opera queen" performs an accusation. Who dares to wear the name? You call someone an opera queen if you want to criticize his affection for opera, or if, yourself a worshipper of the operatic, you want to elevate your own affection into *affectation,* signal your membership in a subculture, and remind the world of opera that the queens are in charge. "Opera queen" is like a beauty-prize title (Miss Cucumber); it subtly mocks the girl riding on the float, the girl rewarded with the crown, but it thrills her, too, and seems a ticket to a future, and places her in a social configuration, a lineage. The phrase "opera queen" inscribes a ceremony, even if the ring is fool's gold.

· *33* ·

I know how Moffo's voice sounds in 1956, how it sounds in 1957, how it sounds in 1958, how it sounds in 1959, how it sounds in 1960, 1961, 1962, 1963, 1964: 1964 is my favorite year, that year the tone is warmest, a mezzo's lushness, resonance as if from below. She postpones the note and then arrives at it, the note more valuable because it has been delayed. Pertness or precocity is gone; I hear only felicity and agility. This is opera, but she sounds to me like modernity, "now," "today," the smash-up 1960s. Supple, she makes other singers sound labored, hefty, and old.

We can differentiate all the different Callas sounds, like models of Cadillac: 1949 Callas and 1951 Callas and 1953 Callas and 1955 Callas and 1959 Callas and 1963 Callas and 1974 Callas. . . . The chosen diva's voice is the friend whose growth we note in snapshots from a well-documented childhood.

Listening, we are the ideal mother ("mother" as idea) attending to the baby's cries, alert to its puling inscriptions, and we are the baby listening to the mother for signs of affection and attention, for reciprocity, for world. If we "prick up our ears," it may seem we can control what we hear. Paying love-struck attention to a male or female voice, we ask it a question: will you continue, will you provide? Listening is a love factory: one produces that potion, "love," from the raw material of one's own attentiveness.

"I love Callas's voice" is another way of saying "Callas's voice loves me."

· 34 ·

The Number One Fan: I've always been afraid of that fate. Because to be a diva's number one fan is to be dead, or to be considered sick, lost, lonely, vicarious.

Judy Garland is not an opera singer, but Garland fans and opera queens have much in common. Before I learned to love opera, I loved Judy Garland. I don't know why I was driven by internal pressure to purchase, as a teenager, a remaindered copy of *Judy: The Films and Career of Judy Garland:* and I was horrified and fascinated by the discussion, in an appendix, of Judy's number one fan, Wayne Martin (of course his name was Wayne), who posed with Judy and Rock Hudson (not possible in those dark ages to know that Rock *and* Wayne were gay) at the Coconut Grove in 1958 (my birth year): Wayne Martin, according to the *Los Angeles Times* (1963), "appears to lead a tranquil, vicarious life. In a strange, semi-scholarly way, he has raised the standards of fandom at the same time as he has sacrificed himself. . . . Leaving the peculiar jumble of Judyland, one first feels pity for the thoughtful, gentle man inside. On second thought, Martin has more company than many other lonely people in this world." Poor Wayne Martin, stuck on Judy, living in his Judy museum, which he calls Judyland: "Photographs and posters pock-mark the walls." The walls are pockmarked, like the self-hating queen in *The Boys in the Band*. (Follow the homophobic equation: pockmarks = the wages of sin = stigmata of aberrant sexuality = syphilis, AIDS.) Who said Wayne Martin was lonely? Who said a love for Judy Garland constituted a sacrifice?

The dogma underlying the opera queen's body: love of opera entails a sacrifice of one's own flesh. I love the diva at the expense of normal nourishment.

Only recently have we discarded the pockmarked queer stereotype. I look at the picture of Wayne Martin in 1951 and I think, "Not bad!" though I know if I had been born thirty years earlier and had slept with Wayne Martin in 1951, he'd have cared more about Judy than about me: I'd recognize the out-of-body remoteness of his love-making, the glassy, distracted gestures: and I'd know that even though he loves to curate Judy's career, the world deems him asexual and frustrated—as if Judy were having a real life and Wayne Martin were doomed to confuse reality and representation; as if Judy were not confused about reality; as if all stars were sexually satisfied, and straight.

· *35* ·

I am afraid of the expert, the opera policeman, the connoisseur: for example, Mendy in *Lisbon Traviata,* a hypercritical queen. I'm not an expert. I remember a date who criticized my Moffo *Butterfly:* I told him to fuck off. (He, perhaps rightly, preferred the Victoria de los Angeles recording. But how dare he question my tastes!) I remember the vast Callas record collection of H., one of the first gay adults I knew: who was Maria Meneghini Callas, I wondered, and why did he have so many of her recordings? Nude photographs of this expert and his lover "pocked" their bedroom wall: like Judyland, a private museum.

Stern queeny experts who work at the best classical record shops frighten and attract me. I want to discuss the various options with them: which *Fidelio* should I buy? I long to say to them, "We love the same things! Our tastes are identical! Let's be friends!" But the object of adoration—Callas, *Gioconda,* Nilsson, the past—divides the queen from other queens. I have never had a satisfying conversation with another opera queen about opera pleasures.

The expert is such an entrenched part of opera culture, gay and otherwise, no wonder the happy fixture of the Texaco Metropolitan Opera broadcasts has been Opera Quiz. Love for opera is reduced to a matter of knowledge, trivia: you prove your love by completely *knowing* the dead body of opera, its static dinosaur bulk. When will a fan mail this question to Opera Quiz: "How many gays and lesbians are listening to this broadcast?"

Fear the opera expert, he who knows everything, who puts your humble tastes to shame, who will criticize your recording of *Turandot* or even your affection for that vulgar opera, the opera queen who only likes Monteverdi, the opera queen who doesn't go to the Met any-more, the opera queen who can't stand Sutherland, the opera queen who gave me his 1953 Callas Cetra *Traviata* because he said her voice was fingernails against a chalkboard, the opera queen who disagrees with the maestro's tempi, the opera queen who hates Wagner or loves only Wagner, the opera queen who doesn't recognize himself in this description, the opera queen who thinks homosexuality has nothing to do with opera, the opera queen who never has body odor but then, suddenly, unexpectedly, stinks, the opera queen who doesn't come out to his mother because he says it will hurt her, the opera queen who loves the local production of *Barbiere* and the opera queen who makes fun of it, the opera queen who isn't gay but seems gay because he has learned from opera queens how to be a connoisseur: the opera queen whose intense, phobic knowledge is a bludgeon.

The opera queen who is a part-time nudist and runs a bed-and-breakfast and won't go to the local *Falstaff* because Moffo isn't singing Nannetta: that is the opera queen I could be, a hack, an amateur, who will never go to La Scala, who has never met a diva, but who has his own province of affection that no one can usurp.

Homophobic, to call the queen a queen, to call the opera queen a prissy librarian, a fussy knowledge-monger, a fact policeman: homo-phobic and inevitable, to equate homosexuality with detail and trivia and superficiality (as opposed to heart and depth and substance), and then to forbid the queen from enjoying his facts and his surfaces, to forbid the queen from marshaling his details like armor.

On the other side of knowledge, look at me and my stereotypical simulacra: the opera queen with a toupee, a lisp, a pinkie ring, a poodle, a leather jacket, and a boyfriend twenty years his junior who knows nothing about opera but comes along for the ride; see the shy opera queen from Nebraska who has only heard one *Bohème* and is virtually a virgin, he slept with his college roommate, who was bi. . . .

Or begin to dream of the gorgeous opera queen who is mean, the stud opera queen who snubs you, the impeccable, cultured, frigid opera queen with god's body, unless opera listening *erodes the body.* . . .

Recognize the men who work in record stores or usher or move to New York to haunt the opera or who want to be opera singers and don't know they are gay yet and maybe never will be gay but (they can't help it) imbibe the lore and the decor of the opera queen and become dead ringers for opera queens: you know these straight opera queens, like effeminate married men who seem stranded in their heterosexuality ("Why won't anyone believe me? I *am* straight!"—as if anyone were asking or disbelieving, as if everyone had to decide).

The photographer I met at the baths, who took me home: imagine my surprise when the gap-toothed man, twice my age (I'd pegged him as "sleazy but handsome"), told me he'd been to Bayreuth, and told me he'd been raised in an orphanage, and told me I was too young to choose my sexuality (I was twenty): "Don't close off any options," he said. "Keep an open mind." He implied there was a chance I might still be straight and he regretted having been prematurely forced (anal rape at the orphanage?) to choose.

· 36 ·

After a Kathleen Battle recital in New Haven, I stand outside the stage entrance, waiting to see the diva. A group of women are the main fans: they look to me like lesbians, but maybe I'm wrong. How can I read a lesbian body if I am male? One possible lesbian says: "Hey, girls, I'm going to hop in that limo with Kathleen!" Finally glamorous Kathleen Battle appears in red miniskirt (so tight it looks like hot pants), her hair in a bun, heavy makeup; she smiles when we clap. It feels queer to applaud on the street, but we do it anyway.

I heard Fiorenza Cossotto sing Carmen when the Met came to Boston, and I remember the woman wearing sun-hat and sun-dress, though it was evening, who told me that Cossotto was her favorite singer and that she owned all of Cossotto's records. I, who may not share the lesbian regard for the mezzo voice; I, who have no attachment to Fiorenza Cossotto, who hold a grudge against Cossotto for outsinging and shaming Callas during an infamous *Norma* when Callas had lost her voice: I put myself in the shoes of the woman in whose body the bell-tones of Fiorenza Cossotto made thrilling forays. The Fiorenza Cossotto fan turned to ice when I told her I hadn't heard of Fiorenza Cossotto.

· 37 ·

In a long opera, like *Parsifal,* the audience's body functions matter. I mean the bathroom: memory of the old man incontinent at a matinee of *Hänsel und Gretel* (his urine-streaked slacks a caution) prompts me to pee before any opera, even short *Salome,* begins: I don't want to be aware of my body during the opera; I don't want to divide my attention between Salome's last scene and my importunate bladder. See the line of men in Family Circle, waiting for the urinals, reading their programs, the awkwardness of so many gay men in line, some straight men too and several undecideds; and see the long lines of expensively dressed women waiting in the Grand Tier for a chance to relieve themselves, aware that the opera might start without them. (Bathroom lines are longer at the opera than at the movies.) I look at these lines, and stand in them, and wonder if we go to the opera to get rid of our bodies or to reclaim them. Eating, listening, singing, and "micturition," as Freud and the doctors call it: in a dream, a diva whom I'd just heard sing Desdemona was performing a mad scene, and she was proffering a particularly risky interpretation, and the measure of her risk was that in place of coloratura she was urinating onstage.

· *38* ·

It is silent in the bowels of the music library, the annals of history, like Aida's living grave, among moldering scores and back issues of *Opera:* I leaf again through the Metropolitan Opera annals to look up Moffo performances, my eye caught by the names of other divas, too. Entombed, waiting to be spoken or delivered, I dwell in the downstairs silence; it's impossible to look up "gay" or "lesbian" or "homosexual" or "queer" in any of these opera tomes of sole interest to opera queens, like the gay librarian through whose opened dormer window, when I passed his house late at night, I heard the romantic strains of "Suicidio!" In these trivia-troves, the litany of performances never explains why anyone would tolerate this weight of displacement, why the pressure of a certain sexuality might bring one to this banquet of years and stars and endurances.

· *39* ·

I love the opera queens I never met, never had as classmates— men who are history now, vanished femmes, men who could or couldn't pass, who let detectable enthusiasms spill into the voice: such as the man on line for a Callas Metropolitan Opera comeback: rare interview with a member of the Line. To me he seems obviously gay, but could the 1960s radio audience tell? He says with utmost seriousness, "It's a shame that she hasn't been here, and now that she has agreed to come back, I think to miss her would be really a crime. This woman is undoubtedly the greatest singer of this century." I love the way he says "greatest singer of this century": he has absorbed the canned phrasing of star biographies, and he wants to announce a trend. He is not just a gushy femme. He is an expert on opera in America today, and that's why he stands on line in winter. I recognize the identification with Callas that produces those effusive inflections in his throat; he's a teenager, maybe in the closet, certainly in more than one closet, overlapping and discontinuous closets—for who in 1965 could afford total exposure? This fan in the Callas documentary sounds sexy in an understated, thin way, with the wide, luminous eyes I know from old porn magazines. Today that fan is nearly fifty: where are his fawn eyes now, and what do they worship?

Seventy years ago that fan might have been Earl Lind, the andro-gyne, who wrote in 1918: "I have been an unusual lover and patron of grand opera, the soprano and alto solos having an overwhelming effect particularly (because that is the manner in which I would have wished to sing). I have often been raised into sublime heights of ecstasy, generally with a sensual tinge."

And two hundred years ago that fan might have been a habitué of Fop's Alley, as described by impresario Benjamin Lumley in 1864: "It was the practice of the day for all the more 'exquisite' and fashion-able of the male operatic patrons to quit their boxes or their scanty stalls during various portions of the performance, and to fill the vacant spaces in the centre and sides of the pit, where they could laugh, lounge, chatter, eye the boxes from convenient vantage points, and likewise criticise and applaud in common. The 'meetings and greet-ings' that took place in the pit of the opera were looked upon as an essential portion of the evening's entertainment."

Fop or dandy or femme or swell or aesthete or freak or queer or misfit or dreamer: the names shift. I wonder if I, a Jew, would have had a place in Fop's Alley. I feel more at home with the sleek, attrac-tive, naked boy in a now-kitschy, then-contraband 1967 physique magazine, a sensitive boy posing nude beside a gramophone, and hold-ing a *Carousel* soundtrack album. He studies the record cover; we study him. Is opera queendom or immersion in an original-cast album a dreamland from which the body never returns, a narcotic space separate from companionship and speech, or do self-exposure and self-knowledge take root inside that moment of solitary, naked listening?

· *40* ·

The dear friends of a diva: how many of them are gay? A gay man holds a dinner party in a long-retired diva's honor; the diva is over-joyed to meet a handsome gay guest who brings a record of hers to sign and who studs the conversation with memorized facts of her career.

Gays are not always nice to each other, and opera queens rarely are. Anger (among its many uses) is a form of flirtation. Opera queens hold their heads high as divas concerned about a draft's effect on the voice: tension at Tower Records because there are three opera queens in line, three of us, too many, density in the air as if before a cat-fight or mating. We have too much in common and therefore proximity is painful. I remember Curt, the femmy boy I spurned in junior high, though I knew in my rotten heart it would be fun (and forbidden) to invite him for sleepover, original-cast-album-listening parties; he could bring *Annie Get Your Gun* and I'd play my Mae West record. Too late to invite him now.

· *41* ·

At the opera, what does your body do?

Clap until your hands hurt, so the diva will hear your tribute separate from the applause of other fans. Yell "brava" and hope the squeaky "brava" as opposed to "bravo" will make it straight into the diva's consciousness—the diva hungry for your sweet "brava," no one else's; at least you hope your "brava" will contribute to the mêlée. Or applaud at the wrong time. (I interrupted Kathleen Battle's "Depuis le jour": I thought it was over. Desecration. Will I be punished?) In Maria Malibran's time, only the men were entitled to clap; the women waved handkerchiefs.

Go forward during the final applause so that by the third or fourth curtain call you are standing close to the stage, to watch joy flood Leonie Rysanek's farewell face.

I never go backstage. How would I get there? And I don't often make it to the opera. I stay home and dream of the opera.

Opera serves as erotic go-between: during the overture to *Caval-leria Rusticana*, I'm thrilled that my boyfriend is hearing this overture, that its sentimentality is kneading his body, that we are cohabiting the music, cowriting it in air, the schmaltz entering his ear and mine, as if the music spoke me and no one else, as if I had any control over what he heard. Before our first *Traviata* I tell him the entire plot with mind-numbing thoroughness, including what Violetta feels in the final moments of the opera when she disbelieves her own imminent death ("rinasce!"), and I fear that straight couples at the other tables are eavesdropping and thinking, "What a boring queer, he's so obsessed."

Opera makes me feel two-gendered, the idea of heterosexuality blooming inside my head. Violetta and Alfredo are making love in my bloodstream and thus my body isn't just *one* body; two formerly thwarting rivers meet. Opera doesn't arouse me (opera isn't an aphrodisiac), but it presents me with an illusory heterosexual feast which I greedily eat, containing, mastering, and overpowering it. A queer person may occasionally want his or her emotions to be public and statuesque as heterosexuality, that fictive, distant, civic-minded plateau. Proust describes music's power to redeem one's paltry and oblique loves: "It seemed to me that my love was no longer something unattractive, at which people might smile, but had precisely the touching beauty, the seductiveness, of this music. . . ." Listening, the source of love in myself smiles at me like a stranger, a masked guest, and I'm assaulted by the oddest sensation of division; I become heterosexuality itself, my meek gay body hums with the magnet-sensation we call "heterosexual" because it is the dance of opposites, though is it still heterosexual when one body plays both parts?

Rubbing lazy fingertips against the velvet seat, knees sore from long sitting, you fall asleep, or close your eyes to hear better, and find yourself already drifted off.

· *42* ·

Records before AIDS: my *Lohengrin* (Bayreuth recording, 1953) and my *Tannhäuser* (with Elisabeth Grümmer), formerly the property of Bill, who died of AIDS in 1985. He bought these records while in high school. The records outlived him. On each record's label, he signed his name in large, careful, mannered script (too prissy, too curved)—establishing ownership over each record, making sure nothing escaped him. Was Bill gay yet when he discovered *Lohengrin*? Imagine Bill fifteen years old at home in Philadelphia, lonely and almost at the point of knowing the new strange word "gay," listening to *Lohengrin* and feeling separate from everything he has read about human nature; *Lohengrin* arrives in his life at the same moment as boys do, and he thinks the two phenomena—a love for *Lohengrin,* a love for boys—have no connection except that they afflict or ennoble the same body, his own. Maybe he considers a love for *Lohengrin* to be the artistic fact that lifts him from his homosexuality's squalor. Or maybe *Lohengrin* means escape, dream, story, swans, women, disappearing and reappearing men, rage, marriage, perfection, purity—and the silence in his body when these emotions storm him.

I handle with reverence the old sturdy scratched high-fidelity records: they have passed through gay hands, and they precede AIDS. No mere objects, they're invested with a glow—certain gay men before AIDS, before it was easy to say "gay men," loved these records, and didn't explain why: the love did the explaining, it was enough just to listen, the point was *not* to draw the connection between homosexuality and opera, but to pass into opera as into a safe silence.

And now I own his *Turandot,* too, and I feel a responsibility—feel pressed, by what the record has seen—to speak, as if the grooves, the scratched "Signore, ascolta," were freighted with ghost messages, significances that travel between Tebaldi and the Tebaldiani, and that are lost when the Tebaldiani have died off.

This book is an elegy for the opera queen. I am an opera queen, but I am also mourning him.

As AIDS changed my sense of gay life-span, gay pleasure, and gay politics, it made me revere the objects that have given gay people pleasure, the relics that have created gay ambience, gay atmosphere—that have created, in the boy listening to *Lohengrin* in 1965, a resonance, even if the spark couldn't yet be explained or excused.

· *43* ·

Opera queen, whether or not you choose to call yourself "opera queen": opera queen, whether or not you choose to identify yourself as "gay" (the label is reductive, but do we have another?): impresario, conductor, singer, costume designer, makeup artist, lighting designer, prompter, usher, ticket-booth agent: fan, solitary, standing-room-only habitué, record collector, weeper-at-telecasts, hoarder-of-programs: come out.

A new magazine that seems tailored for opera queens, *Opera Fanatic,* takes steps toward outing: "The Met's production of *Giulio Cesare* has parts for two catamites, played by supers. One day at rehearsal someone vacantly ordered over the squawk box, 'Catamites on stage,' —and was bewildered when half the company's administration turned out."

Opera Fanatic intrigues me, but I fear the label "fanatic." It sounds like "pervert." And yet I want to "out" opera.

· *44* ·

A singer's voice sets up vibrations and resonances in the listener's body. First, there are the physiological sensations we call "hearing." Second, there are gestures of response with which the listener mimics the singer, expresses physical sympathy, appreciation, or exaltation: shudder, gasp, sigh; holding the body motionless, relaxing the shoulders, stiffening the spine. Third, the singer has presence, an expressive relation to her body—and presence is contagious. I catch it. The dance of sound waves on the tympanum, and the sigh I exhale in sympathy with the singer, persuade me that I have a body—if only by analogy, if only a second-best copy of the singer's body. I'm a lemming, imprinted by the soprano, my existence an aftereffect of her crescendo.

Straight socialization makes queer people discard their bodies; listening restores queer embodiment, if only for the duration of a phrase. Forceful displays of singing insist that the diva has a body and so do you because your heartbeat shifts in uncanny affinity with her ascent.

Listening, your heart is in your throat: *your* throat, not the diva's. You can date the moment you began to speak as a gay person, with a gay heart, from the moment you began, truly, to listen. Walt Whitman: "A new world,—a liquid world—rushes like a torrent through you. If you have the true musical feeling in you, from this night you date a new era in your development. . . ." The star is midwife to the fan's soul, as Willa Cather describes in her aptly named novel *Lucy Gayheart* (1935): "In the darkening sky she had seen the first star come out; it brought her heart into her throat." The star comes out: so does Lucy. She finds her throat. And in Cather's *The Song of the Lark* (1915), a contemplative, passive man listens to diva Thea Kronberg sing Wagner: "he was sitting quietly in a darkened house, not listening to, but dreaming upon, a river of silver sound. He felt apart from the others, drifting alone on the melody, as if he had been alone with it for a long while and had known it all before." The discarded, reviled, queer body: find it in sound.

Or is one's body belittled and humbled by the operatic immensity of sound? Is one's silent, nonsinging body dwarfed? Does opera return gay people to their silence—but with a consolation prize?

The listener's inner body is illuminated, opened up: a singer doesn't expose her own throat, she exposes the listener's interior. Her voice enters me, makes me a "me," an interior, by virtue of the fact that I have been entered. The singer, through osmosis, passes through the self's porous membrane, and discredits the fiction that bodies are separate, boundaried packages. The singer destroys the division between her body and our own, for her sound enters our system. I am sitting in the Met at Leontyne Price's recital in 1985 and Price's vibrations are *inside my body,* dressing it up with the accouterments of interiority. Am I listening to Leontyne Price or am I incorporating her, swallowing her, memorizing her? She becomes part of my brain. And I begin to believe—sheer illusion!—that she spins out *my* self, not hers, as Walt Whitman, Ancient-of-Days opera queen, implied when he apostrophized a singer in "Out of the Cradle Endlessly Rocking": "O you singer solitary, singing by yourself, projecting me, / O solitary me listening, never more shall I cease perpetuating you. . . ."

I follow a singer toward her climax, I will it to happen, and feel myself "made" when she attains her note.

· *45* ·

The diva shatters the fourth wall dividing stage and audience when she stares straight into the crowd and finds a familiar fan's face, as when Mary Garden graciously salutes "young Billy Crawford" at her Town Hall recital—Billy, "an inveterate fan of the Golden Age, whose front row jubilations were rewarded by a rose tossed across the footlights." A reverse accolade, a rose going backwards.

A more menacing exchange of magical powers between diva and listener occurs in Willa Cather's story "A Gold Slipper." The diva, riding a sleeper train with a man who'd been conspicuously unmoved by her recent recital (he'd sat onstage, where the diva could see his indifference to her artistry), leaves her gold slipper in his berth. Mystified, he keeps the slipper—talisman of his own unexamined life. Possible questions he never asks the slipper: Does the diva know I'm a drag queen at heart? Slipper, should I wear you? Are you a symbol of the diva's voice? What can I do with you, single oddball gilded shoe, holy vessel without a partner?

· *46* ·

Two quintessentially queer sites at the opera are the line, and standing room: spaces of mobility, cruising, maximum attentiveness; spaces where one broadcasts commitment, desperation, patience; spaces where one meets other fanatics; spaces of rumor, dish, cabal.

In line for standing room, Ida and Louise Cook sit on camp stools. "The friendships and enmities of the queue!" Queer/queue. Waiting patiently, I advertise my abasement: my time is cheap. Elaborate ritualized protocols determined line etiquette at the old Met.

Standing room: the president of the Standers' Club in 1945, according to *Opera News*, is a "young divinity student." The club puts out a mimeographed newsletter, *Observations from the Rail. Opera News* avers, "For a super standee orgy, try a Saturday night *Aida.*" There's an old gay joke about getting fucked while leaning against the rail. Did such things really happen at the old Met? The old Met, as memorialized in James McCourt's *Mawrdew Czgowchwz,* is a vanished world of dreams and projections and underworlds, of mystical coherences.

Standing room promises freedom to move: room, space, liberty, ease. " 'I prefer to stand in the back of the orchestra,' said Miss Finn, 'for in this way I can not only move about as I please, but also meet other opera lovers.' She admitted that in the past two years she had made lasting friendships while leaning on the rail."

· *47* ·

Opera has the power to warn you that you have wasted your life. You haven't acted on your desires. You've suffered a stunted, vicarious existence. You've silenced your passions. The volume, height, depth, lushness, and excess of operatic utterance reveal, by contrast, how small your gestures have been until now, how impoverished your physicality; you have only used a fraction of your bodily endowment, and your throat is closed. This rushing intimation of vacuity and loss ("I mourn all I haven't seen, all I haven't said!") isn't a solely gay or lesbian experience, but unsaid thoughts and unseen vistas particularly shaped gay and lesbian identities in the closeted years of the nineteenth and twentieth centuries, the dark ages, when the shadow world of the opera queen flourished.

· 48 ·

A tableau of two throats, Maria Callas's and the opera queen's, ends *The Lisbon Traviata*. While Callas, on record, spins "an elaborate web of coloratura," Stephen, the opera queen, whose lover has just abandoned him, "throws his head back with her as she reaches for a climactic high note, but no sound comes out. . . . Stephen's mouth is open, his head is back, his eyes are closed. Callas is all we can hear." By lip-synching to Callas, the opera queen is not brought closer to the magical realm of the vocal, the articulate, the expressive, or the open-hearted. In fact, the tableau convinces us that a passion for Callas has closed the queen's throat, has taken away his power to love. While no sound "comes out" of the queen's throat (the queen is reduced to the closet by his passion for opera), Callas on record is singing Violetta, the consumptive courtesan. Stephen may regret that he can't follow Callas into her hedonistic coloratura, but the subtext of *Traviata* reminds us that pleasure will kill Violetta as surely as, in homophobic scenarios of AIDS, it has killed gays.

In the era of Silence = Death, the opera queen's silence is freighted with fatality. The silent opera queen, drowned out by Callas, is an image of gay helplessness, the persistence of the closet, and a tragic inability to awaken the body politic. But the opera queen and Callas share a biography: opera was ultimately as deadly to Callas as to the opera queen. According to the Callas myth, opera disqualified her for love, and when she lost opera, she lost her life. In the brutal, intoxicating dream of opera which framed the life of Maria Callas and the lives of countless opera queens, the gate to opera is guarded by twin thugs, Death and Silence. If you want admission to the realm of bliss and expressivity that opera promises, you must leave your throat at the door.

CHAPTER TWO

The Shut-in Fan: Opera at Home

· 1 ·

Tastes are mysterious. Where do they come from? Can we determine them, change them, refuse them? I discovered, long ago, that I had a taste for records. Some time later, I discovered I had a taste for men's bodies.

Men's bodies filled in the gap left by the loneliness of records, the vacuity of records, the sorrow of records.

I knew that people had passions and preferences, and that tastes distinguished human beings from each other. I knew about taste before I knew about homosexuality. And so when homosexuality arrived in my body, I could understand it as just another taste, albeit a grimy and forbidden one—unlike records, which were clean and wafer-thin.

· 2 ·

I found romance in the spindle, the hole, the groove, the Capitol Records tower, the word "Decca" and its suggestion of "Mecca," the deep red of Red Seal labels, the flimsiness of Dynagroove, the drama of records stacked at a slanted angle, like a fedora's brim or an airplane's wing, waiting for automatic play on my parents' turntable: these were the molecules of love and loss, of sexual wonderlands beyond my grasp.

· *3* ·

Home has grim meanings for the gay kid or the kid on the verge of claiming that ambiguous identity. Home is the boot camp for gender; at home, we are supposed to learn how to be straight. Queer identities arise against normative structures of home, whether or not we later faithfully replicate the canons of domesticity.

When, in roughly 1902, with the birth of commercially marketed opera records, opera entered the home—at first only in fragments, and later in full—opera changed home's meanings. Home bent to accommodate opera. And opera's meanings altered, too; an art of excess and display, of exteriority, it became an art of introspection and interiors.

The category of "homosexuality" is only as old as recorded sound. Both inventions arose in the late nineteenth century, and concerned the home. Both are discourses of home's shattering: *what bodies do when they disobey, what bodies do when they are private.*

Records helped kill opera by limiting the repertoire to a handful of repeated and repeatable chestnuts. Of course records weren't the only murderer. But the rise of records coincided with the fall of opera as a contemporary art. Marvelously, just at the moment that opera became a museum piece and an object of domestic pleasure, it invited gay appropriation. Suddenly opera was an art of the past. And the "homosexual"—imagined as a creature ravenous for the past, as a creature whose tastes and typical life-story involved a restless probing of first scenes to discover desire's hidden cause—turned to opera.

· *4* ·

A love for opera, particularly on record, is a nostalgic emotion, and gay people are imagined to be a uniquely and tragically nostalgic population—regressive, committed to dust and souvenirs. A record, a memento, a trace of an absence, suits the quintessentially gay soul, whose tastes are *retro* and whose sexuality demands a ceaseless work of recollection: because queers do not usually have queer parents, queers must invent precedent and origin for their taste, and they are encouraged, by psychoanalytic models, to imagine homosexuality as a matter of trauma and adaptation. My attachment to records becomes just another gay fetish: I'm a gay man identifying with transience, a gay man standing in the way of generation.

The movement of the needle in the groove degenerates the record, and yet it gives the sound—a dead set of waves—a new life.

The quintessential opera-queen pleasures pass through records: for example, the cult of Callas among American gay men has been largely a love affair with her recorded voice because her records arrived before she sang here in person. And in James McCourt's *Mawrdew Czgowchwz,* the diva appears to her faithful fans first on a broadcast, and gives them an ecstasy only later verified in actual performance.

· *5* ·

I am unhappy about opera's circumscribed audience, its association with white privilege, but I do not feel that the only ethical response is to renounce my love of opera. Instead, I want to speak honestly about the gay appropriation of opera, to render opera less monolithic.

I speak about opera records as if they were the only kind of record in the world, and as if only gays and lesbians responded passionately to them, though of course the world of recorded sound is larger than the worlds of opera and of homosexuality.

My fantasies are out of date. The CD, which has so little emotional resonance for me, has superseded the record. By focusing on the record, I turn to a former culture, a former time. This is an elegy for opera records and for those who loved them.

· *6* ·

The sound originates in the diva's throat, but it emerges on the other side of the Victrola as the opera queen's.

One important ambition of the early phonograph was to separate the voice from the body, and to take away the illusion of will and autonomy surrounding an utterance. An 1878 pamphlet, celebrating the phonograph, claimed it could captivate sounds "with or without the knowledge or consent of the source of their origin." These captivated voices were often women's; but the wish to captivate was male. And it was a desire fostered collaboratively—by Thomas Alva Edison and John Kruesi originally, and then by Chichester Bell and Charles Sumner Tainter. Another team was the Pathé brothers, their trademark "Le Coq." It's no coincidence that the phonograph was invented by men in collaboration, for there are many cases of nineteenth-century writers or scientists collaborating in order to control and impersonate mysteries imagined to be feminine and reproductive. The phonograph, like psychoanalysis or the telephone or Cubism or Surrealism, was a male collaborative invention that played with the boundaries of voice and identity (often female or maternal), and made voice seem an emanation of male will.

The phonograph could reproduce; though the invention of men, it could speak as a woman. The phonograph, according to a medical journal, would "reproduce the sob of hysteria, the sigh of melancholia, the singultus of collapse, the cry of the puerperal woman in the different stages of labor." Though a tool of male reverie and self-perpetuation, it could reproduce: the original from which recorded copies were made was called a "mother."

· 7 ·

Stealing a voice: in Jean-Jacques Beineix's film *Diva,* recording a diva's voice is an act of erotic conquest, an act of questionable legality and morality.

Diva Cynthia Hawkins has never consented to be recorded; her young fan, Jules, makes a pirate tape of her concert and, backstage, even steals her dress off a hanger—a theft that makes headlines. At the film's conclusion, as a final gift to the diva (now his lover), Jules plays her the pirate tape. ("I've never heard myself sing," she solemnly admits.) Because Jules causes the tape's music to resound in the empty theater, it appears that the voice singing Catalani's aria is the fan's, not the diva's—as if Jules has truly appropriated her sound. A voice is like a dress; playing a record is sonic drag. I'm not the voice's source, but I absorb the voice through my ears, and because I play the record—an act of will—it seems I am masquerading as that voice.

· 8 ·

Perhaps because the woman's voice was locked into grooves and waves, stolen by the phonographic scientist, the phonograph itself was considered suitable for confined spaces and confined listeners. Promotional materials promised that the phonograph would be useful to teach and tranquilize in "blind asylums, hospitals, the sick chamber," and the "domestic circle"—spaces of distress and symbolically feminine incarceration.

At first one didn't merely listen to phonographs, one spoke into them: the early talking machines could record as well as play back. Recording your voice, the talking machine seemed to be *listening* to you. A confessional, it absorbed your secrets, stored them, and replayed them. According to Michel Foucault, the institution of the confessional helped define the homosexual; the homosexual was one of those varieties of lapse, of sin, of taste, which one confessed to a shrouded, immune, omniscient, divine ear. The phonograph, then, even after its listening function became merely vestigial, remained a kind of confessional, not receiving confessions so much as throwing them back, mirroring them, producing in the listener the sensation of *having confessed*.

· 9 ·

Many of the first rhapsodic claims on behalf of the phonograph concerned its ability to record the operatic voice. Even before the phonograph was invented, there existed the wish for a contraption—a magical box—to make the operatic voice a permanent possession and to transport it from public opera house into private home. Encomia to the talking machine invoked the name of Adelina Patti as a symbol of precious and fugitive vocalism. When representatives of the Victor Company traveled to Patti's castle in Scotland in 1905 to set up an improvised recording studio, and patiently waited until the diva felt the urge to sing, they were recording a voice past its prime. But the proper function of the phonograph was capturing nearly vanished voices. In particular, early phonographic records sought to capture and immortalize vanished women.

Idolizing grand women from the past and making them come back are pursuits dear to gay culture: *What Ever Happened to Baby Jane?,* a quintessential camp film, solicits and frustrates our desire to keep the stellar images of Bette Davis and Joan Crawford intact, much as Judy Garland's comeback appearances (at Carnegie Hall, in *A Star Is Born*) staged indomitability and decay, showed us our longing for the female star's permanence, and that longing's futility.

Records are tokens of disappearance and comeback; they are also portraits. I think of records as equivalents of the degenerating portrait of Dorian Gray in Oscar Wilde's 1891 novel. A record pretends to be a boundaried, attractive, flattering portrait. But its instabilities, its mysteries, its potentially horrific features, need to be quarantined. The portrait annexes the soul of its beholder and grotesquely mutates. The portrait is vampiric. It doesn't keep a secret. It blurts out vices.

A record can't limit the voice's meaning; a voice, once recorded, doesn't speak the same meanings that it originally intended. Every playing of a record is a liberation of a shut-in meaning—a movement, across the groove's boundary, from silence into sound, from code into clarity. A record carries a secret message, but no one can plan the nature of that secret, and no one can silence the secret once it has been sung.

· *10* ·

Technological practicalities determine the way records look, and opera records aren't the only variety, but because the first operatic discs—sung by such eminences as Patti, Caruso, Tamagno, and Melba—gave class pretension and dignity to an industry that felt itself akin to vaudeville and peep shows, and because the industry depended on opera to publicize records and phonographs as alluring possessions, there are metaphorical connections between the disc as object, and the entrance of opera into the home and into a gay subcultural imagination.

· *11* ·

Buying a record, you buy the singer's anatomy and the consolations that an imaginary body brings. In 1940s *Opera News* ads for Dorothy Kirsten, Richard Tucker, and Helen Traubel records, the singers are posed inside the black Columbia disc, not an inch of flesh protruding beyond the rim, and so I think, gazing at these ads, wanting to buy a Columbia record, that the singer is incarcerated in the record or that the singer *is* the record. When Dorothy Kirsten left her voice on a Columbia record, she left more than fingernail clippings or hair or feces or other magical substances: she left her vocal soul. Buy a Kirsten record and you're buying a fragment of Kirsten.

Thus the credenza of the record collector is a necromancer's cabinet filled with immobilized, stolen souls.

Exclusively on
COLUMBIA RECORDS
Dorothy Kirsten

"It is gratifying to know that the popularity of LP grows and grows, and that this ever-widening acceptance has made possible the release of thousands of selections, from every category of music, on Columbia 33⅓ Long Playing records."

"... one of the world's most richly endowed singing actresses."
—Newsweek Magazine

Dorothy Kirsten Sings Songs of Jerome Kern—(I've Told Ev'ry Little Star; All the Things You Are; Dearly Beloved; Don't Ever Leave Me; I'm Old-Fashioned; Long Ago; Yesterdays; Look for the Silver Lining) with Percy Faith and his Orchestra and Chorus. ⓖ Record ML 2175 * 45 rpm Set A-999 * 78 rpm Set MM-999.

Dorothy Kirsten Sings Songs of George Gershwin—(Lyrics by Ira Gershwin) (Arr. by Percy Faith) (Someone To Watch Over Me; Love Walked In; I've Got a Crush On You; Mine; Embraceable You; Soon; Love is Here to Stay; Do Do Do) with Percy Faith and his Orchestra and Chorus. ⓖ Record ML 2129 * 45 rpm A-929 * 78 rpm Set MM-929.

Rose Marie—(Abridged) with Nelson Eddy and the Howard Chandler Chorus with Orchestra conducted by Leon Arnaud. ⓖ Record ML 2178 * 45 rpm Set A-1005 * 78 rpm Set MM-1005.

COLUMBIA ⓁⓅ RECORDS
First, Finest, Foremost in Recorded Music

Trade Marks "Columbia," "Masterworks," ⓖ, ⓖ Reg. U. S. Pat. Off. Marcas Registradas

Buying a record, you buy the singer's anatomy and the consolations that an imaginary body brings.

· 12 ·

In the center of the disc, the label—red, purple, blue, mauve, pink. . . .

The language of color: are there certain colors associated with homosexuality? Blue: John Addington Symonds's *In the Key of Blue,* or Wilde's blue china. Green: Wilde's green carnation. Purple: purple prose. The links aren't exclusive or absolute. But even the wish to express oneself through color, to seek correlatives between one sense and another (synesthesia), to use color as code for other states, has been associated with nineteenth-century homoerotic culture.

The most expensive opera records from the Victor Company were distinguished by the Red Seal. The less expensive records were marked by a purple label. Adelina Patti's records, each called a "Patti Record," had pink labels, and Nellie Melba, when she consented to record, was honored with her own mauve label. Melba's mauve labels are faded now, eighty years after their issue, to the lavender of prized, dilapidated seaside cottages.

· 13 ·

The two central images adorning the labels of opera records have been the dog and the angel. Bestial. Celestial. When you listen to opera, are your desires doggy or divine?

The dog was the logo of the Victor Company and of the British firm His Master's Voice. The link between the dog and the operatic disc was indissoluble; the Victor dog graced an illuminated sign at 37th and Broadway, near the Met, to show New York how close the dog lived to opera's center. Because a "master" is another word for the original from which records are made, the dog looking into the horn to find his missing master's voice is an image of a mass-produced replication (a record) seeking its original. The dog is also an image of obedience and loyalty: man's best friend. (This servitude is a little sexy: imagine the dog burrowing its warm way into the master's horn.) We, listening to opera records, occupy the dog's seat. We are trying to enter a hole backwards, trying to go back in time, through the looking glass, to find a phantom. Thomas Mann, in *The Magic Mountain*, describes listening to a record as equivalent to looking "at a painting through the wrong end of an opera-glass, seeing it remote and diminutive. . . ." My hunger for opera records is backwards, inverted. Listening, I try to reverse chronology, and the dog-label tells me my desire is devolutionary.

The other image, a nude and androgynous cherub, was the logo of the Gramophone Company in the early 1900s, and Angel Records assumed it in the 1950s. The cherub, writing with a quill on the record, represents the singer's voice, magically inscribing itself on the grooves; the cherub embodies the mystery of phonographic technology. However, it's also possible that the listener is the cherub; the quill resembles a needle, and I "write" the record by placing the needle in the otherwise mute grooves. The cherub is an image of the body before it's defined by gender or sexuality—an innocence itself homo-erotically charged, like the cherubs on baroque ceilings.

· *14* ·

When I as gay person *go backward* to find or write the story of my sexuality, I am making it up, because sexuality has no absolute origin or motivation, though because sexuality is structured like a narrative, with crux, climax, and denouement, we are always hoping to unknot its beginning. Playing a record, I move backward in time to the imag-ined scene of recording, to the real day when Amelita Galli-Curci stood in a studio and sang "Je veux vivre." Holding the Galli-Curci 78, I'm grasping a silence and asking it to speak. The groove-circle moving round and round and finding its center near the label's edge and turning into the label and never stopping, like the lines on a barber pole, or the oscillations of the hypnotist's wheel, charms and stupefies me; these never-ending spirals signify the curiosity of Oedipus who wanted to know the secret of his birth, the curiosity of the "homosex-ual" who wants to know the origin of his preference. Playing a record is like playing the Ouija, speaking to the dead, asking questions of an immensity that only throws back the echo of one's futile question, a repeated "myself, myself. . . ."

The backside of early 78s, left blank, was a shiny opaque black surface without function and without voice, a mirror that gave forth no sound, even if plied with a needle. In ads, the disc often resembles a mirror. Ads for many products—Lincoln Continentals, dishwashers —feature women; consumer goods have often been targeted for the pleasure of woman-as-shopper. But the women in record ads tell me something about the cultural meanings of listening. The Brunswick record logo shows a woman staring rapturously into a gramophone, and the Pathé trademark was "Le Miroir de la Voix," with a picture of a woman holding a disc and looking into it as if it were a mirror. (Consider today's compact disc: a lady's compact mirror, minus the puff and powder.) The Pathé disc is a mirror of the singer's voice and it is a mirror of the listener, womanish, effeminate, inactive, devoted only to pleasure and hunger, who turns to the record to verify and find a secret self, and to extend the home's borders to encompass the stars.

"Heavens, it's *me*," Nellie Melba said, upon hearing her voice for the first time on records; and Adelina Patti was even more jubilant. She kissed the phonograph's speaking-trumpet and exclaimed, "Ah, *mon Dieu!* Now I understand why I am Patti. Oh yes. What a voice! What an artist! I fully understand it all." You feel, listening to a Melba record, "That's me!" The Victor Company promises, "A mirror may reflect your face and what is written there; but the Victrola will reflect and reveal your soul to you—and what is hidden deep within it."

The quintessential opera aria is itself a mirror scene, in which the singer asks the audience whether her voice is beautiful. Massenet's Thaïs: "Dis-moi que je suis belle. . . ." Playing a record, the listener is Thaïs, asking "Am I beautiful? Tell me that I am beautiful!"

To describe the record's power of mirroring the listener's secret self, the Victor Company used the vocabulary of fin-de-siècle aestheticism—the language of exquisite, unspeakable, and implicitly homoerotic sensations. The first opera aria discs captured evanescent moments, and would have satisfied Walter Pater and his hard-burning gemlike followers, who sought to isolate the instant when "some tone on the hills or the sea is choicer than the rest. . . ." One 1918 ad uses a phrase from bisexual poet Paul Verlaine—"l'heure exquise"—to describe a disc's allure: "Into every life comes the divine moment— *l'heure exquise*—though perhaps we do not realize it till we see the event paralleled in opera." The voice we love and of which we never tire, promises the Victor Company, is the voice that expresses our own temperament and plays back our own secrets.

· 15 ·

My first record player, a kiddie monaural affair, made by Decca, was a box with a handle and a catch that snapped shut like the lid of my sister's Barbie doll case, so I could, theoretically, carry the device anywhere.

The spindle, though, was just a stub, like the eraser-end of a pencil. I admired my parents' Garrard turntable—too fancy for daily use, it moldered in the shut credenza—and particularly worshipped the automatic spindle, bent in the middle so that records could be stacked. Wanting to convert my manual record player to an automatic (I thought the difference was merely a matter of spindle size), I Scotch-taped a pencil to my spindle, eased a record onto it, and pretended that the record had moved of its own will, independent of my hand, down the canary-yellow rod.

· *16* ·

I've always been fascinated by the spindle hole. Everything on the record's face conspires to highlight it: the price circles it; the label and the round window in the protective paper envelope echo its shape. Remove a vintage Melba record from its sleeve and you see, printed on the inside of the envelope, a photograph of the diva, as if the round center of the envelope were a window onto a retreating, hermetic world.

The hole makes no single anatomical allusion. It makes many. It isn't reductively equal, even in the listener's unconscious, to any part of the human body. But it has always spoken to me of the emptiness at the center of a recorded voice and the emptiness at the center of a listener's life and the ambiguities in any sexual body, including a homosexual body, concerning the proper and improper function of orifices.

· *17* ·

Early 78 aria records sometimes had explanatory labels affixed to their blank backsides. The label translated the aria's words and briefly described the plot. Because the label lay in the record's center, the spindle hole interrupted the text and functioned like a line-break in poetry, disturbing and magnifying the sense, and reminding me of fissures in the listening experience:

The Shadow Song, a favorite concert number, is sung in Act II, in the scene where *Dinorah*, thinking her lover, *Hoel*, has proved faithless, becomes insane and dances to her own shadow—the dance being accompanied by a waltz, which is full of the most brilliant vocal effects. In the last part is introduced a florid cadenza for voice and flute, as in Lucia.

· *18* ·

The two columns of text in opera libretti, Italian and English, French and English, German and English: monolingual, I am titillated and enervated by the twin streams of text, I divide my attention between them and court fantasies of androgyny and bisexuality, left brain right brain. . . . Or I am merely confused, and long for the easy days of 1912, when *The Victor Book of the Opera* gave just the English for an aria like "Celeste Aida," and the translation fits the tune, the right number of syllables, so when Caruso sings the aria we can sing along, foolish home-confined dreamers, pretending to be Caruso, pretending to be public and whole and sure, crooning, to an invisible audience, to the chest of drawers and the shut window,

> Heavenly Aida, beauty resplendent,
>   Radiant flower, blooming and bright;
> Queenly thou reignest o'er me transcendent,
>   Bathing my spirit in beauty's light.

No latecomers saying "Excuse me" will mar our enjoyment. We are alone with our pleasure, and the pleasure is doubled, not diminished. Or it simply becomes a different pleasure: a mirror scene. We call such pleasures masturbatory and condemn them, as if masturbation ever harmed a soul.

· *19* ·

The grooves of a record suggest conformity, enclosure, entrapment: the groove pattern dooms a record to say nothing new, to replay and replay, a parrot. Grooves keep the sound coded; touch the grooves and you get no closer to the mystery. A record is like a dream; you require a needle to unravel its meanings. The groove is symbol of condensation: a sign of potential rather than actual power, a reminder that opera must be contorted and compressed to enter the home and to enter fantasy. The Victor Company boasted of these compressions when it claimed, in a 1917 catalogue, that "if you could stretch out the groove on an ordinary twelve-inch record into one long, straight line, it would reach more than seven hundred feet." But a groove will never be straightened out. It will always curve and equivocate.

Sound is locked in the grooves, waiting to be released by Mr. Right. If the rules are obeyed, the Victor Company promises liberation of imprisoned sound and sensation: "It would seem superfluous to mention the absolute necessity of using RCA Victor phonographs if you would extract from your Victor records all that is imprisoned within their shining grooves." Shining grooves, shining knight: the romance of needles promises that a spellbound urge will be awakened. Playing a record is like opening a closet: "If you desire all the brilliance and beauty that *goes into* Victor Records, choose an instrument designed to *bring them out*."

If you use the wrong needle, the intercourse won't work, and no reproduction, or poor reproduction, will take place. A blunt needle is like LSD to unborn sound: it ruins the chromosomes, and destroys vibrations that might have been. "Beware the Blunted Needle," warns RCA Victor on a 1956 Caruso reissue—as if the blunted needle were a syphilitic sex-maniac plaguing the town.

· 20 ·

I'm a neat, fussy homosexual: you know the type. I don't look for the source of my conduct (why am I neat? why am I fussy?), but I simply acknowledge the discourses looming like gargoyles at the helm of my life, the discourse of hygiene intersecting with the discourse of homosexuality, and I, trapped, shut into these languages, shaped by them—though I also find them obliquely inspiring, and a source of wonder.

· 21 ·

Record hygiene has dominated my listening life, for into a Cold War world of record care I was born, afraid of ruining my records, conscious of their vulnerability and fragility, as if the discs were an extension of my body, and the nation's last defense. I felt that to ruin a needle or to scratch a record or to touch its surface with my sweaty hands was a sin against reproduction and the doctrine of the groove.

I'm afraid to borrow records from my opera queen friends: my hygiene standards have fallen since my glory days of sanitary record practices, and I might unintentionally ruin their discs.

Here is how to wipe a record, according to the Victor Company in 1938: "The recommended method of cleaning records is to wipe them off with a soft cloth, *slightly* moistened. The records should then be dried immediately with another soft cloth." If gritty dust is left on the record, it will cause "faulty reproduction." At issue is correct reproduction—keeping the record's reproductive organs on track. As sexual liberation hit the country, new record-care devices emerged, each innovation more efficient and modern than the last. I tried to master them; I've purchased record cleaners, dust cloths, needle brushes, but have always found records intrinsically dusty and mortal. I prefer the

casual worry-free approach of 1965, the era of wash-and-wear cloth-
ing, when *Opera News* tells us that "if a record has become really grimy
during prolonged neglect, wash it with cold tap water, detergent and
a cellulose sponge, and then let it drip-dry."

· *22* ·

Does my attachment to the body of the record brand me as fetishist? And does the label "fetishist" come from a homophobic notion of
the "homosexual" as a person who has displaced a drive, who has taken
the wrong psychic turn, who is stuck in an unproductive backroad,
divorced from society, health, wholeness, and truth?

I suppose any body we love is a fetish, male or female; we can
only conceptualize homosexuality or heterosexuality if we fetishize the
gender characteristics of men or of women, and turn to those fetishes
ineluctably and mechanically.

Yes, I fetishize records; and yes, I fetishize men's bodies, make a
fetish out of groove and label and hole, spindle and turntable and
speaker, credenza and box, and the hiss that precedes the moment of

Yes, I fetishize records.

music, the unintended "click" that tells me the needle has found the first groove, and the song is about to start.

· 23 ·

I loved the idea of opera before I loved opera: and what I loved, in this idea of opera, was the boxed set. I saw the gold and silver letters of mysterious words *(I Masnadieri, Götterdämmerung)* engraved on the black spines of albums so thick they seemed books, shelved in the arcane, unfrequented corner of Discount Records: I longed to navigate that quarter of the shop, and despaired of ever doing so. I wanted to own the boxes before I knew that opera was what the boxes contained.

Records for complete operas, since the advent of the long-playing disc in 1950, have come in boxed sets. A box is the antithesis of opera—the cult of the huge, the expressive, the uncontained, the grandiose. And yet a box is quintessentially operatic, for opera involves passing air out through the voice box, and because the most privileged patrons sit in an opera box. A box is a sexually suggestive figure: vagina. A boxed-set opera in the long-playing era most frequently holds three discs, and thus has the respectable, familial stability of the traditional three-volume Victorian novel.

The boxed set contains and compresses opera's immensity, and the mythically huge bodies of singers. Operatic grandiosities of feeling need to be boxed in if they are to meet the standards of home, of family, and of confined, codified gender-role. The boxed set radiates an image of a boxed, shut-in, hampered sexual condition.

Do you remember the smell of boxed sets from the 1950s and 1960s, the odor of wax and heat and antiquity and patience, of vinyl and plastic and cardboard and years of inactivity? I felt that boxed sets were waiting for me to discover them, waiting for me to adore them. I loved boxed sets just as I loved books about the bachelorette life, like *Sex and the Single Girl,* handbooks that explained how to find an apartment and how to find a job and how to entertain your friends and how to fend off men's advances. . . . Do you remember the charm of the "bachelorette" life? I wanted such a life. I didn't know how to long for a gay life, so I longed for life-in-a-box.

· 24 ·

Record speed was not standardized until 1927. Woe betide the intrepid listener who succumbed to a variable speed: "More good music is spoiled by tampering with the Victrola speed regulator than by anything we know. Better set yours at 78 revolutions to the minute, and keep it there." Turn Caruso into a woman by speeding him up; turn Galli-Curci into a man by slowing her down. Who hasn't tried this trick? A recorded voice is genderless sound waves. Thus a disc's revolutions teach something truly revolutionary: that the pitch of a voice, which we take to be an indicator of gender, can be changed once sound passes into the home listener's magic cabinet.

· 25 ·

My parents' stereo, locked in a narrow-legged wood cabinet: I opened the cabinet and slid the turntable out, like a broiler shelf, and was transfixed by a smell I can hardly describe—a smell that seemed not horizontal but vertical, for the smell had depth and moved down, not sideways. Like the smell of encyclopedias and garage sales. Metallic, like silver polish. Rubbery and dry-cleaned, like a rented car's upholstery. The stereo console's interior emitted the fragrance of discovery—for wasn't stereo a radical new technological feat, a sign of advancement and sophistication, as mysterious and galvanic as puberty?

· 26 ·

I was born in the age of stereo, but my first records were monaural. Content with mono, I reminisced about the romantic, bygone era of High Fidelity.

The phrase "high fidelity" achieved currency in the early 1930s, and served, for two decades, to signify the ultimate in sound reproduction and fantasy fulfillment. It was a concept that meant nothing in particular and so could accommodate private yearning. "Like the concept Love, there are almost as many definitions of High Fidelity as there are writers on the subject," says a columnist in a 1956 *Opera News,* who also suggests that hi-fi equipment can be streamlined into interior design, fit into bookcases, even "hidden in a closet," so the source of sound remains unseen.

Stereo arose in the late 1950s: the distinction between stereophonic and monaural sound is real, but it also has symbolic resonances. At one time I wanted to be sexually stereo. Now I'm happy with my mono life. In the early 1960s, with stereo's arrival into the home, one might have dreamed that the bi- or polysexuality that Freud long ago promised was, with the Age of Aquarius, finally about to dawn. Remember quadraphonic? Remember orgies?

The difference between stereo and mono doesn't just refer to what happens in the speakers or in the recording studio: stereo and mono are two different states of mind. A diagram in a 1958 *Opera News* shows a man listening to mono and then to stereo. In the mono picture, undifferentiated left and right sounds bombard each ear: in the stereo picture, left sounds enter the left ear, right sounds enter the right. Stereo reverences the difference between left and right; mono jumbles them together, or isn't sophisticated enough to separate them. The possibility of confusing left and right reminds me of other games, skills, differentiations, failures: men and women; straight and gay; a world, regrettable, in which the difference between hetero and homo deeply matters and one must always vigilantly tell the two apart.

· 27 ·

An old stereotype: the collector, who, like the libertine, has no family, no social ties, no loyalties, no interior. It's not clear whether Oscar Wilde's Dorian Gray obsessively collects exotic musical instruments, jewels, perfumes, embroideries, and ecclesiastical vestments because he's gay, or whether Wilde tells us about collections because he can't mention homosexuality. Collecting is a code for homosexual activity and identity. The amoral collector is like the experimenter or the mad scientist: he takes apart the living, has no respect for the integrity of a body or soul; he stays up late; he hoards. Hoarding, Freud speculated, was a character trait affiliated with anality; we don't have to equate homosexuality with anal sex to understand the persistence of this homophobic equation: to hoard = to be anal = to be gay.

The collector hides from romance through his records; the records are a curtain, dividing the collector from human contact. In 1958 and 1960 ads in *Opera News* for Shure stereo cartridges, the connoisseur is an aloof, lonely-seeming man with a cat on his lap, or lost in contemplation, staring out at us through a spider's web of record grooves.

To collect is to go backward in time: you don't amass objects unless you believe, on some level, that you'll never die, or unless you want to defy death. The collector is a treasure hunter, and the loot is the buried, inadmissible self. According to the Victor Company in 1918, one hardly needed to listen to the Victor discs—merely choosing a record was so supremely gratifying. We're encouraged to open the Victor Catalogue at random and find the one record that will inflame us, speak to us of our dead, mirror our secrets. "Searching for that one record in the Victor Catalogue is the most absorbing of pursuits. . . . There is always the chance that the *next* will awaken echoes—echoes as precious as Spanish doubloons."

Choosing a record is a complex symbolic performance. And the Victor Catalogue is like a Tarot deck; it guides "curious voyagers," has a monstrous ability to expand and burgeon, and it is, claimed the Victor Company, a "living organism that never ceases to grow."

· *28* ·

We don't have much choice about our sexual feelings. Nor can we choose our race. Nor, in most cases, our class. But for the collector, the drama of choice is supreme. And the collector's private house-bound rituals of taste spiralled in complexity as competing versions of the same repertoire proliferated, and it grew harder for the collector to make the "correct" choice.

The collector dismisses poor taste, even considers it diseased. A Franco Corelli disc receives dismissal in a 1961 *Opera News,* and the language used to criticize this handsome tenor's record reflects a homophobic distaste for the desires that might have led gay fans to purchase it: "Since recording standard works over and over again is a chronic disease of the record industry, Angel's new *Pagliacci* with the current matinee-idol tenor was to be expected. . . . Franco Corelli's fans will rush to acquire this version. Others may feel some reservations about the tenor's impure vowel sounds, lisping consonants and irrelevantly trumpeting interpretation. . . ." The recording industry suffers from a chronic disease; Corelli lisps and performs impurely. Only a Corelli fan would be foolish enough to want this version. Only a gay person would be foolish enough to be a Corelli fan. The collector must enforce these standards and uphold them with imagery of contamination; the collector must believe that the beloved object is pure and that the "wrong" choice is contaminated. One would think that opera were a sterile solution infected by the desires of gay fans.

· *29* ·

Gay novelist Manuel Puig, in *Betrayed by Rita Hayworth,* describes a young sissy's pastime: "instead of learning how to ride on the new bicycle that's too big for him he cuts out actresses from the newspaper and colors them in with crayons." Jean Genet's imprisoned narrator in *Our Lady of the Flowers* cuts pictures of sexy criminals from the newspaper to adorn his cell walls. The shut-in opera fan cuts up *The Victor Book of the Opera* or *Opera News* and pastes the pictures on blank record sleeves or in scrapbooks.

In an archive, I found a generic Pathé envelope that some long-ago listener transformed into a collage. I don't know if that listener was gay or lesbian, but I handle that sleeve as if it were a queer relic—that sleeve on which, beside the trademark, "Le Miroir de la Voix," a nameless hand has glued pieces of a catalogue, fragments which identify the singer as Albert Huberty and the aria as "Quand la flamme" from Bizet's *La Jolie Fille de Perth.* In my used copy of the 1912 *Victor Book of the Opera,* the previous owner, who signs herself "Janet," has cut out the illustrations accompanying the descriptions of *Faust* arias available on Victor, and she has colored in the gowns (Massenet's Manon with pink crayon, and Offenbach's Olympia with orange), and she has written "This is the last!" beside several finales. *Opera News* encouraged its readers to take up the crayon: "Color the illustrations in *Opera News* depicting the artists in costume, using the tints described in the Costume section, or the remarks of Mr. Cross."

The sissy and the fan, symbolically imprisoned, respond to a policed, curtailed sexual condition by cutting out pictures. Constructing a collage, I cut out images that turn me on, awaken my past, speak my secrets; I repeat what homophobic society has already done—reached into memory's body and scissored it up.

Collage is a technique that gay artists have found useful: Joseph Cornell's homages to ballerinas, Robert Mapplethorpe's pasteups based on 1950s soft-core male physique magazines, Robert Rauschenberg's assemblages, incorporating autobiography and history. Andy Warhol reproduced images of Elizabeth Taylor and tinted them ("Blue

Liz as Cleopatra"); the shut-in fan takes pictures of Tebaldi or Galli-Curci, del Monaco or Gigli, and colors them in with pink crayon.

· *30* ·

The Metropolitan Opera House curtain, replaced several times in the company's history, has traditionally been cut up to supply fans with a memento of the golden fabric they may only know from Milton Cross's words on the Saturday broadcast, or from pictures in *Opera News*. We are forbidden to cut up the American flag, but the Met curtain's ideal, final condition was fragmentation—pieces to satisfy the collector's reliquary passion: "No sooner was the historic fabric dismantled than it was cleaned and cut into convenient fragments by The Metropolitan Opera Guild." These pieces were used to make piano covers, bookmarks, blotters, trays, and eyeglass cases.

The Met's curtain, noiseless, redolent with the thematics of privacy and the closet, of sudden graceful revelation, and rippling reinstatement of invisibility, obsessed one fan so deeply that she incorporated the curtain into her private world of myth: she loved "the smooth and graceful way in which the gold curtain was raised and lowered," and could not understand "how one man was able to raise such a big and heavy curtain with such evenness of speed and without jerking it." She practiced pulling the curtain in the dark school auditorium, and prided herself on her ability to raise the curtain flaps slowly "and then all of a sudden pull them so fast that they would 'swoosh' together like the magnificent gold curtain at the Metropolitan."

The curtain is the membrane that separates in from out, diva from fan, gramophone-horn from ear, sound-in-the-box from inkling-in-the-heart.

· *31* ·

When, in the 1960s, reproductions of record covers appeared in the center of *TV Guide* in ads for Record-of-the-Month Club, I used to cut out the small squares to build a miniature, dollhouse-size, phantom library of discs I couldn't afford and would never really want to buy: Dean Martin, Perry Como.

· *32* ·

Cutting was necessary in the 78 era: even to fit an aria on a single disc, tempos were hastened, episodes trimmed, repeats omitted. But apart from necessity, condensation had its own logic. Cut, disguised, opera can pass into the home, as a genie passes into other realms by compressing his circumference into a bottle.

Record companies applied to whole operas the same scissors that the listener-at-home used to fragment *The Victor Book of the Opera*. Of a *Carmen* medley, the Victor Company boasted in 1911, "An amazing number of the most popular bits of Bizet's masterpiece have been crowded into this attractively arranged potpourri. . . . Only such an organization as that of the Victor, which stands absolutely alone among record-making bodies, could successfully cope with the difficulties of Bizet's score." The difficulties of Bizet's score include violence and irregular sexuality. *Carmen* is not an opera that neatly celebrates the virtues of the hearth. Victor, a record-making body, digests the opera, turns it into bits, and passes *Carmen*'s sexual meanings incognito into the home.

· *33* ·

Can opera fit into the home? Does opera disrupt home values? What happens when Adelina Patti's voice emerges from the furniture?

Illogically, opera was considered a family pleasure. The first opera set produced by Columbia Records in cooperation with the Met was Humperdinck's *Hänsel und Gretel* (kids who flee home, Hansel a drag part for a soprano). But from the beginning of phonograph history, the talking machine was considered a spy in the family house, a surreptitious means of controlling child's play. A 1907 Victor Catalogue described the phonograph as a tool that could educate and control the children while adults were absent. An expert advises the parents to go over their record collections and eliminate "trashy" songs, keeping in mind the "refining influence" of the voices of great opera singers.

Opera in the theater as well as in the home can interrupt lessons in gender conduct, particularly lessons in how to be masculine. One fan writes to *Opera News* in 1944 about nearly swooning at a performance of *Tristan* he attended with his father. "The music of the second act reacted on my emotion so strongly that I almost fainted and I had to feel my way out to the stairway, not to lose control of my body. After feeling better I returned and my father said to me: 'What's the matter with you, boy?' 'The music,' was all I could answer." A 1942 *Opera News* reports the aberrant and unfathomable physical sensations that assailed a little boy named Jimmy at the opera, when, as he listened rapt to "Tu che a Dio spiegasti l'ali," he looked down at his arm and "ruefully started rubbing it." "What is the matter with your arm?" asked the teacher, and Jimmy replied, "It never looked like that before. I really don't know what *is* the matter with it." Jimmy has "gooseflesh." Jimmy is turned on by the tenor aria. Jimmy's gooseflesh is a sign of complex and unspeakable arousal.

In both of these anecdotes, a parent or pedagogue asks the little boy at the opera, "What is the matter with you?"

· *34* ·

At home, listening to opera on record or radio, the fan, girl or boy, imagines the costumes of the stars. Lush hints excite the home-stifled imagination: "In the final temple scene, Miss Stevens is a gorgeous vision in cloth of gold with a narrow gold band across her forehead." Or: "Miss Traubel's costumes, designed and executed by Adrian of Hollywood, express the 'ageless and timeless' period of the drama. . . . The lyric quality of the second act is suggested by a draped gown of pale bois de rose jersey with graceful dolman sleeves and a sweeping cape." Did young boys enjoy such prose? Did gay men write such prose? Opera-at-home involved more than simply musical pleasure; it was an imaginary fashion show, and it assumed that operatic consummations and presences could best be experienced at a distance.

In preparation for the broadcast, the listener is advised to "study the pictures of the settings in *Opera News,* shut your eyes and try to visualize them." To be passionate, must I deprive myself of sight?

· *35* ·

Photos of singers on record jackets and elsewhere are rarely explicitly seductive: they are tame. But their very cleanliness and sanctity make them fit for imaginative projection: cheap thrills. Stare at the photo of Charles Kullman as Cavaradossi in a 1944 *Opera News.* He doesn't intend to touch the listener's sexual imagination, and therefore knocks me dead with desire. (Are listeners even supposed to have

Left: Who dares to have a crush on Carlo Bergonzi?

Right: Who wouldn't feel sleazy cutting out a photograph of Charles Kullman as Cavaradossi solely for its eroticism?

sexual imaginations?) Not quite handsome enough to be a movie star, he is a good-looking tenor. One is not supposed to read sex into such pictures. And who dares to have a crush on Carlo Bergonzi, even though in an ad for *Aida* he is young and dark-eyebrowed, a masculine goody-goody with a vein visible on his broad-palmed hand? These bodies demonstrate what Roland Barthes has called the "third meaning"—not the first or second meanings, the meanings that matter, but the third, ambiguous, unassimilable meaning, like the third sex: details in photographs that represent or symbolize nothing in particular, that bear the weight of no allegory or intention, have an irreducibility that punctures the viewer's imagination.

I am drawn to a photo of Giuseppe di Stefano and Bidu Sayão, the centerfold of a 1949 *Opera News*. I find solace in the fleshiness of Sayão's arm, the specificity of di Stefano's sideburns; the garish lighting makes me edgily curious about what can't be verified. (On the same page, the quaint phoneticization of words we already know how to pronounce: Ahl-fray'-do, Vee-oh-let'-tah.) These photos may provoke neurasthenic sexual reverie, accompanied by a sense of desecra-

The garish lighting makes me edgily curious about what can't be verified.

tion. Who wouldn't feel sleazy cutting out a photograph of Charles Kullman as Cavaradossi solely for its eroticism—a photograph in which Kullman is entirely clothed?

It is futile to desire an anonymous man on the cover of *Opera News*.

· 36 ·

Opera News tempts me with its palely homoerotic images. In a 1944 *Opera News* cover photo of servicemen entertained by ladies of the Metropolitan Opera Guild, one handsome sailor confronts the viewer. The bold insolence of his gaze (a bit of undershirt showing over the collar) plunges through me, and I wonder where this event is taking place, who this sexy sailor is, with cuff rolled above the wrist, and I desire him, even though it is futile to desire an anonymous man on the cover of *Opera News,* a man who looks like John Travolta: all I know about this sailor is that he attended an opera reception long ago.

The images in *Opera News* that came closest to beefcake were photographs of dancers and supernumeraries. Neither dancers nor supers can pass onto radio or record: dance and spectacle are aspects of live performance to which the at-home fan, until video, remained blind. The dance scenes in grand opera are frequently homoerotic; supers in such operas as *Turandot, Aida,* and *Samson et Dalila* are often half-dressed. The super is like the fan: a backstage spy, an onlooker,

"Cheap thrills" beefcake in *Opera News.*

not a participant in the vocal festivities. Supers have good dish on divas.

"Their Feet Are Young and Gay," says a 1951 article about the Metropolitan Ballet corps. At least in his 1942 *Opera News* photograph, handsome Lee Foley of the Metropolitan Ballet is a dead ringer for Ramon Novarro or Rudolph Valentino: the photo is such a closeup I can see eye makeup and sweat. In photos, the young male supers playing cards in intermission or dressed in fish-scale costumes look lithe and available. Other reliable sources of subtle "cheap thrills" beefcake in *Opera News* are photos of the *Aida* ballets—one revealing 1948 photograph (captioned "High Jinks on the Road") of male dancers on tour, spreading body makeup on each other's backs.

· *37* ·

It is difficult to explain or justify the desire I feel for a photograph of Callas as Turandot in an *Opera News* ad. If this desire is not sexual, is it mystical? And is it a desire to buy and hear that recording, is it a desire to know or to have known Maria Callas, or is it just a desire to have been there in 1965 to see this image as a present-day excitement and possibility, and not, in 1991, as a fragment from an archive?

The original boxed set of Callas singing Cherubini's *Medea,* with Renata Scotto as Glauce, a "Mercury Living Presence" monaural set from 1958 (who knew that Callas recorded for Mercury?), tempts me mostly because of the photo on the libretto's cover: Callas looking like a ghost with dark painted lips and with hair braided in a pile above her head, a photograph so abstract (black background, white face) that I dare not call my emotion *sexual:* nor is it a musical attachment, because while I stare at this picture I am not listening to *Medea* (though my love for her face depends on already loving her voice). Tawdrily, I adore her, and I believe, irrationally, that she, dead Maria Callas, departed diva, is grateful for this devotion, that she intangibly depends on it; and I feel irrationally sustained by the medium of the phonograph record for including this photograph of Callas, for understanding, in advance, my desire for such an image. This image marks me, just as I'd be marked by receiving a copy of *One* in the mail, in 1955, if *One* slipped out of its plain brown wrapper.

It is difficult to explain why I respond so strongly to the mere

MERCURY LIVING PRESENCE

Tawdrily, I adore her.

perfume of the "Callas Portrays Puccini Heroines" Angel recording, in its original sleeve, from 1954.

· 38 ·

Despite these visual (and olfactory) supplements, the shut-in fan, the at-home listener, is supposed to be a mere ear: sheer auditor, disconnected from presence.

In record ads, the ear is cut off from the rest of the body, as if opera listening were dismembering, and as if the listener were exiled from continuity, wholeness, pleasure. These floating, mournful, haunted ears seem emblems of the shut-in fan's condition: just an ear, solitary and horrific as the severed ear at the beginning of David Lynch's *Blue Velvet*.

The most prominent ear in record history is the one that London Records (Decca) has used as its logo—combined with the trademark "ffrr" (full frequency range recording), its synonym for "hi fi." But the London ear is not attached to a head, a hearing canal, or a nervous system. It is disjunct. In a London ad for tenor Mario del Monaco's records, his head dominates the page, but he has no ear. The picture is cut off there.

· 39 ·

Because sound emerges from the singer's mouth, and because singers' bodies are mythically unsightly, it makes sales-sense, and it saves space, to shield the body and present only the singer's head in opera record ads. But another meaning emerges: decapitation. Do we interpret this decapitation as castration, and connect it to the imagery and reality of castration that is opera's heritage, and that is one source of opera's folkloric association with emasculation?

When Calaf, in Puccini's *Turandot,* wants to play the riddle game and win the ice princess's heart, he strikes a gong. If he can't answer her riddles, he'll lose his head: severed heads of the men who failed to answer Turandot's riddles festoon the stage. The gong is a disc; I imagine that Calaf is the listener, banging on the gong, moving the sound box or tone arm onto the disc, playing the aria record, summoning Turandot the ice diva, making her sing.

Turandot was one of the last operas to enter the standard repertory: it premiered in 1926. And the opera is itself incomplete: Puccini died before it was finished, and the scene of Calaf and Turandot's erotic union, their ecstatic duet, was composed by Franco Alfano: the ending is unsatisfying, and only reminds the listener that opera virtually died with Puccini, that *Turandot* isn't a whole body, that Calaf never finally arrived at Turandot, and that the gong, the disc, through which we first entered Turandot's vocal universe, was just a mirror.

The aria record, the 78, which emerged at the moment of opera's death, is symbolically opera's head: opera is dead, and all we possess are these discs, fetishes, remnants that remind us of the dead body and that prevent our own destruction and dismemberment by warding it off, apotropaically: we frighten off death by flashing the record, a mirror.

"Incomparable," boasts the London ad for the records of Birgit Nilsson—and yet she is not unique: the ad, in the style of Andy

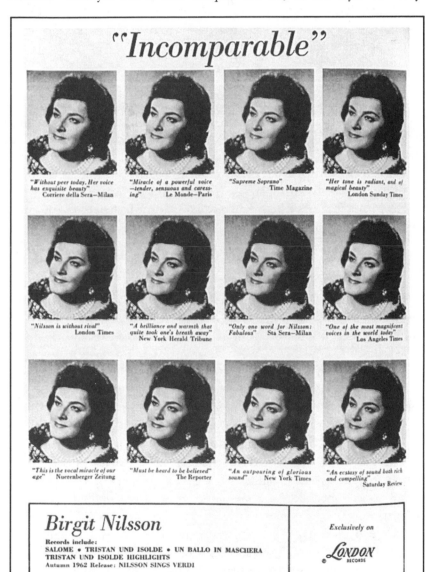

Repeat, repeat, repeat, to fill in something missing.

Warhol, shows twelve identical photos of her head. This shotgun por-
traiture emphasizes the repetition compulsion basic to the phonographic experience (repeat, repeat, repeat, to fill in something
missing), the mass-producibility of the Nilsson voice on record, and
the ability of the fan, listener, collector, or scrapbook keeper to repeat
what he or she loves, and to control the objects of desire. The fan, a
Bluebeard, has records, like the heads of singers, stacked up—substi-
tution for other, missing pleasures; booty; gravestones; proof of conquest; proof of loss.

· 40 ·

The summer before college I came down with what seemed
mononucleosis: false diagnosis. Perhaps it was sleeping sickness, or
depression. I spent two weeks immobile and languid in my bedroom,
listening to records. I'd fall asleep in the middle of a side, and wake up
to find it finished; I'd replay the record, and fall asleep again in the
middle. I don't know whether I considered records the key to my cure,
or the symbol of my sickness.

· 41 ·

Opera News, from the 1930s until the 1960s, was obsessed with
the crippled, the infirm, the shut-in, and the pathetically lonely. The
implied or ideal listener of the Metropolitan Opera Saturday afternoon
broadcasts was a girl, boy, woman, or man fated to extreme sensory
and social deprivation. There were certainly handicapped or house-
bound people who loved the Met broadcasts; but *Opera News* was also
speaking to listeners who were symbolically shut in.

The phrase "shut-in" has three meanings:

1. the fan is *shut in* because closeted;

2. the fan is *shut in* because enclosed by a sexual identity which
society imagines to be an affliction or a confinement;

3. queer meanings are *shut into* opera, *shut into* code and dis-
simulation.

Caruso records make singer Louise Homer weep; she says,
"We're all 'shut ins' in a way, and it's really *wonderful* to be able to hear
other singers and learn from them." Louise Homer is shut in by her
profession: celebrated diva, she doesn't have time to get out. Listeners
confessed more literal and exacting confinements: *Opera News* consis-

tently printed letters from self-identified "cripples." One 1942 article, entitled "Opera in the Sick Room," describes a listener's eight-year-long immobility; the voices of Lily Pons, Gladys Swarthout, and Lawrence Tibbett helped the author to forget his body. Maimed fans: a boy who was "blind and with no hands or legs"; a seventeen-year-old paralytic who was "an earnest listener to the Metropolitan Auditions of the Air"; an "ardent opera lover" who "regained consciousness just an hour before the final Metropolitan Opera broadcast of Gounod's *Faust*," and died right after the "final celestial vision of Marguerite." One fan ("I am lame and on crutches") writes to say that she dresses up for the Saturday afternoon broadcasts as if she were really attending the opera. Against odds, one teenage girl made it to the opera—to be photographed, on crutches, beside her idol Risë Stevens. The gratified girl holds a Columbia album of Risë Stevens singing *Carmen*, a gift from the diva.

The singer Marjorie Lawrence was an inspirational image for shut-in fans: in a photo, the gutsy diva (elected "Chin-Up Girl") sits in her wheelchair beside soldiers with bandaged eyes.

· 42 ·

Blind fans appear in *Opera News* to prove that you don't need your eyes to enjoy the Met broadcasts (Milton Cross will describe the costumes and sets), and to prove that opera fans are blind to something. Are they blind to the possibly queer ramifications of their taste? Or is queerness just another form of sightlessness?

The grande dame of modern blindness, Helen Keller, posed backstage beside diva Astrid Varnay for *Opera News*: "When Helen Keller, the renowned blind deaf mute, attended a recent performance of *Simon Boccanegra* she listened backstage to Astrid Varnay's rendering of one of Verdi's arias. Placing her fingers on the soprano's lips, she said the tone sounded 'sweet, like a thrush.' " No matter how few senses you have left, opera will stimulate them. We read in *Opera News* of a temporarily blinded twenty-three-year-old bombardier taken from the hospital to hear Eleanor Steber sing Violetta, and "led backstage by his mother to fulfill a life-long ambition." Because our culture blames mothers for causing homosexuality, it's significant that the mother, in this anecdote, helps her blind son achieve his gay-sounding ambition, which is to meet Eleanor Steber, who, in the 1970s, sang a concert at the Continental Baths, black towels on a peach gown.

· *43* ·

There's a dire connection between disease and listening—an act requiring passivity, and therefore suitable for the paralyzed. Since gays were considered sick until quite recently, it's not too big a leap to imagine that when *Opera News* presented a sick person as the Met broadcast's ideal audience, that sick community included gays and lesbians.

Letters to *Opera News* in the 1940s from "sick privates" connect sick soldiers and sick desires. One private writes, "In Atlanta if I spoke about opera or symphony to the local yokels they steered clear of me as though I was suffering from a foreign disease." A bedridden ten-year-old boy falls in love with opera when his mother turns on an *Aida* broadcast: "I was so entranced by the music, that I felt as if I were in a dream." Another young martyr, Betty, died of leukemia in high school: in Betty's memory, her classmates purchase a memorial membership in the Metropolitan Opera Guild. Betty's love for the Met was part of her prematurely sickened state; this innocent's passion for opera was precocious and fatal. A 1953 photograph of Giulio Gari singing for patients at a veterans' hospital shows a handsome young man, IV tubes lacing his bed; there seems a connection between incurable wounds and opera fandom, between untimely immobility and an opera star's consoling presence.

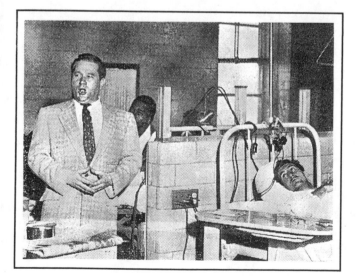

There seems a connection between incurable wounds and opera fandom, between untimely immobility and an opera star's consoling presence.

Though a taste for opera is sometimes a symbol for diseased passions, listening to opera records can be healing. The patients at the sanitorium in Mann's *The Magic Mountain* are given a gramophone. Diva Lucrezia Bori surmounted vocal breakdown by listening to her own records, and the Victor Company suggests that the public, too, might find her records curative: "Every day she listened to her own crystal clear notes on her Victrola records and awaited the time when complete rest had accomplished its purpose. . . . You will want to hear some of the records that charmed Lucrezia's voice back again." Odder is the case of Mac, who cracked up in his junior year of college (he had "gorged his sensitive nervous system"), and was treated to a long, slow cure through records of simple opera arias. Music therapy, according to the *Victor Record Review*'s expert in 1939, was successful because musical vibrations "make contact with the entire body," and give a "body massage."

· *44* ·

Images of outcasts—tomboys, sissies, nerds—fill the pages of *Opera News*. I don't know if these fans "turned out" gay or lesbian. But I do know that the misfit, the boy or girl who grows up conscious of a reigning difference, is a vital myth in modern queer culture— voiced in Judy Garland's "I'm just an in-between."

The clean-cut members of Student Opera Council, the men in ties, smiling, addressed by Miss Lucrezia Bori, look like future lighting designers who are still trying to pass. These boys wear suits; they behave; they channel difference into good works; they don't stay home, clad in pajamas, crayoning cutouts of Mignon's dress.

One parent writes to *Opera News* to describe an eleven-year-old boy's peculiarly intense devotion to opera. This kid has an autograph book: "Bampton, Moscona, Novotna, Tibbett, Kullman, Sayão, and Resnik are some of the names in his book. He always gets them himself, and is very much at home talking with the stars." For Halloween, he dressed as an astrologer, and "made little predictions" for all the guests, "and here too, he was very much at ease." What little predictions can we make about a boy at ease with opera stars and celestial bodies?

I'm intrigued by Mary Anne, eighteen-year-old hysterical opera fan, whose peculiarities her mother confesses to *Opera News*. I could have been Mary Anne. I know what it is to go "starry-eyed over the mere mention of a certain tenor," to sob "with Lakmé and Lucia over their sad loves" and "gaily" share "Juliet's joy over her party," to know all the names of the stars "from Pons and Pinza to the two-line-a-performance players," to fill my conversation with obscurities, names of operas no one will ever sing again, to eat Saturday's lunch on top of the radio. But Mary Anne's mother isn't worried about her daughter. She enjoys her daughter's raptures. She's glad that her daughter has found an outlet.

But an eighteen-year-old boy who knows the names of all the stars inspires suspicion. A 1951 article in *Opera News,* "Anyone Can Be an Opera Lover," describes a handsome young football player who loves opera and has a "beautiful natural bass voice." His participation in the choir raised "opera morale" among the student body, who distrusted the world of classical singing. Yet even this football player knew opera's effeminate reputation: it was "with a blush" that he admitted he loved to sing opera. Mary Anne enthuses; the football player blushes; the femme boy keeps silent.

Or else he solicits a pen pal. A typical golden-age issue of *Opera News* contained a plea for a like-minded correspondent. Often there are no names. *Opera News,* in the 1940s, erased gender by giving only its correspondents' initials. Perhaps *Opera News* didn't want to reveal that these hysterical fans were men. (Even when there are names and addresses, they sound fabricated: Bruce Stevens from Queen Street in Canada writes in 1943 that he would like to hear from other fans who collect and trade opera star photographs.) "A Loving Opera Fan" wants a pen pal who will be willing "to consider a friendship founded on our mutual love of opera." Such requests—clawless and poignant —imply a terrible isolation. One young buff asks *Opera News* for a fourteen-year-old pen pal, and confesses, "I am the only person around our neighborhood of my age who is interested in opera." Another lonely aficionado admits, "I am an opera-lover and a faithful reader of *Opera News,* but I have a problem"—none of his friends care about opera. A nineteen-year-old opera lover says that he is very lonely because he has not "found anyone." The young readers who write to *Opera News* looking for "others of like taste" have no communities; as one opera lover puts it, "I actually do not know a single person who is interested in opera."

· *45* ·

As a young outcast I considered opera embarrassing; I still do; when I'm stuck in a traffic jam, I'm afraid that the man in the next lane will hear my cassette of Montserrat Caballé singing "Tu che le vanità" or Maria Callas singing "Convien partir," and that he will laugh at me or sideswipe my car. Paranoia? I understand he will think it strange, excessive, and effeminate that I am listening to opera. When I play Madonna, I leave the car windows open. When I play Callas, I close them. I fear the consequences of announcing my tastes.

When the Met broadcast comes on, Saturday afternoon, I find any frail excuse to take a long aimless drive. I consider the gas pedal an extension of the diva's throat: when she crescendos, or ascends in pitch, I speed up, in sympathy, in emulation.

· *46* ·

Backstage, long ago, in children's theater productions, I saw late adolescents undress—the Scarecrow in *The Wizard of Oz* in his underwear, Marian in *The Music Man* changing quickly between scenes. I, a curious extra, a voyeur, walked by and saw her underclothes in theory if not in fact: I saw the possibility of exposure and attainment, and learned to associate that distant, mournful boon with backstage.

Opera records bring us backstage; bring us closer to the singer's mouth than we would ordinarily be allowed to stand; bring us to the microphone—our proxy, our spy, feeding us information.

Backstage musicals of the 1920s and 1930s (*Footlight Parade, Dames, 42nd Street*) depict "backstage" as a capitalist's gold mine, a space of chance encounter, lucky break—a school of hard knocks. Backstage is the place where show-biz dirt is stored and spilled. Because we can't see backstage, or know what goes on there, it permits projection and fantasy. My projection: backstage, like anything rear-end, is symbolically anal. And the Freudian connection between anality and gold helps me decode the allure of the Met's gold curtain.

Backstage knowledge: a knowledge of origins. Sexuality is inscrutable and we are made to feel the burden of unknowability: to feel responsible for finding, proving, remembering the source of this affliction, this benediction; for tracing it back to a scene or a fancy, to say, "*Here* my desire began."

· 47 ·

Opera News in the 1940s and 1950s devoted much space to fans who built miniature opera stages at home. Miniature opera is an oblique variety of drag: the fan takes on the desired attributes not only of the diva but of the entire operatic mise-en-scène.

One industrious miniaturist constructs her diva dolls out of chicken wishbones, using cotton for the heads, and embroidery floss for the hairdos; this wishbone artist is "much more thrilled over wearing pink lace to the opera, than to a Junior high school dance."

Playing with dolls is taboo for boys, and so staging miniature operas is a willfully effeminate pursuit. And yet these performances take place in the family room, near the domestic bibelots. Billy stages little operas for his family, and he's not afraid to make the costumes from fragments of his sister's cast-off clothes. Through miniature opera, he cuts and restitches gender to suit his fancy. His "red velvet, sequin-trimmed curtain came from a discarded formal dress belonging to his sister," and he has fashioned a second curtain, "salvaged from his sister's old dancing costume, before which the 'stars' take their bows." He receives *Opera News* on Monday, and by Saturday, his cardboard performance is ready. He plays flute and piano, and sings in the choir, but he confesses that "back-stage knowledge is his final goal."

· 48 ·

While I was researching this chapter in an archive of recorded sound, the curator approached me with a tantalizing offer: "Would you like to see Adelina Patti's shoe?" He opened a huge drawer. Beside rolls of microfilm in boxes, there rested a tiny white high-heeled satin slipper, signed, in willowy cursive, "Adelina Patti." He removed the shoe from the drawer and handed it to me. Here was a diva's shoe! One shoe only. Too small for me to try on. And yet it was real. It was rare. It was a relic. What should I do?

I felt like the man in Willa Cather's "A Gold Slipper"—the clumsy philistine who finds a diva's shoe and locks it in a vault and studies it, like a mirror, in private. I was being offered a chance. I didn't understand the nature of the invitation. Silently, I held the shoe, turned it over, peered within. Then, mystified, I put the shoe back in the drawer, beside the microfilm.

I've spent my whole time in this archive looking at records as objects, and no time listening. But I asked the curator for one favor: could I hear an original pink-labeled "Patti Record"? The obliging curator played me Patti's rendering of "The Last Rose of Summer," recorded nearly ninety years ago.

Or, to tell the story properly, I should say that he played me *two* versions. In the first, her sound is muffled, as if she were standing behind a heavy curtain. She sounds beautiful but very far away.

The second record was not released at the time, because Patti stood too close to the machine; her voice, reproduced on home equipment, would have been deafeningly loud. But modern technology can reduce her volume. So with the curator I listened to this alternative, secret performance of "The Last Rose of Summer." The curator said, "It sounds as if the curtain, separating Patti from the listener, has been lifted."

I wish I could say I heard the curtain rise to reveal Patti's voice in its original splendor. But I still heard the intervening ninety years, the curtain, the turntable, the hiss of reproduction. It sounded as if Adelina Patti were whispering something I could not understand, or as if the medium of reproduction itself were whispering instructions, codes, opacities.

CHAPTER THREE

The Codes
of Diva Conduct

· Diva Prose ·

I crave backstage knowledge about divas. I have burrowed into the lives of Frances Alda, Marian Anderson, Clara Butt, Emma Eames, Geraldine Farrar, Olive Fremstad, Amelita Galli-Curci, Mary Garden, Clara Louise Kellogg, Dorothy Kirsten, Jenny Lind, Maria Malibran, Blanche Marchesi, Nellie Melba, Grace Moore, Adelina Patti, Adelaide Phillipps, Rosa Ponselle, and Leontyne Price. All but the last of these divas are relics of opera's golden ages. They are not contemporary artists. I relish bygone divas because the heyday of gay opera culture predates Stonewall and depends on the institution of the closet. In a culture without closets, would I have adored divas? Coming of age in a civilization of the closet, I have wanted to know how divas debut and bomb and blitz and survive and fail and dream and die, and I've cut these stories out and assembled them here in a scrapbook. I quote generously from the prose of diva auto/biographies because I adore the trashy cadences and idioms of *diva prose* (whether penned by the diva, an admirer, or both at once); I'm affirmed and "divined"—made porous, open, awake, glistening—by a diva's sentences of self-defense and self-creation.

I don't claim to prove any historical facts; instead, I want to trace connections between the iconography of "diva" as it emerges in certain publicized lives, and a collective gay subcultural imagination—a source of hope, joke, and dish. Gossip, hardly trivial, is as central to gay culture as to female cultures. From skeins of hearsay, I weave an inner life; I build queerness from banal and uplifting stories of the conduct of famous fiery women.

By the twentieth century, homosexuality already meant more than just sex acts or desires shared by bodies of the same gender. It implied a milieu and a personality—flamboyant, narcissistic, self-divided, grandiose, excessive, devoted to decor. These stereotypes have shaped behavior, and have been reinforced by gay people when they have made the transition from enduring their preference, to choosing it.

There is nothing prosaic about a diva. But diva prose is often banal: an ordinariness touched by sublimity. The diva writes to amplify herself, to state the obvious—floridly. (When a nondiva writes diva prose, she writes to admire or to impersonate.) Diva prose is amusing and pathetic because the divas who write about themselves so grandly are often dead, no longer household words. Because a diva is rarely a dictator, we can afford to be charmed and transported by the tragicomedy of diva prose, and not insist on greater circumspection.

Diva prose never offers a new or surprising fact. Its cadence is imperial yet practical: for example, Nellie Melba's declaration, "At any rate, I went. I sang. I got my fee." Household and empire converge in the diva's mouth.

Diva prose is an acquired dialect—attractive, and utterly imitable. Unlike genius or voice, inborn qualities that confer on the diva her near-divine status, diva prose has nothing to do with actual merit; I could approximate diva prose but never diva voice. I write diva prose if I am weak but want to pretend to be strong, if I want to cut off opposition, if I want to feign beauty while knowing I'm plain, if I want to bully but seem polite, if I want to praise myself lest no one else praise me. Diva prose is the style of the outsider who has arrived inside, but still fears the sentries.

These meditations are pro-butch, pro-femme, pro-drag. I want to use the particulars of diva conduct to chart a method of moving the body through the world, a style that gay people, particularly queens, have found essential. It is a camp style of resistance and self-protection, a way of identifying with other queer people across invisibility and disgrace. I am not sure whether we must prove queenly conduct useful and efficient in order to justify our idolatrous love of its decor. The milieu of divas and queens is a cultural monument worth our respectful, nostalgic revisitation. It is possible that the era of the queen is past, though the homophobia that made such conduct necessary is still blistering and present.

· *Me, Myself* ·

The magisterial diva doesn't fear solitude; for her, no act of self-authorization is small or fragmenting. Narcissism doesn't seem silly when a diva practices it.

The diva hasn't yet arrived at herself; she is in a continual, gratifying state of becoming. Frances Alda proclaims, "I became, in the very essence of my being, Frances Alda." A diva is not afraid to risk tautology: "I am myself. I am turning into myself." Long ago in the diva's life, she was not herself; she tries to forget that alienated prehistory.

Mary Garden writes: " 'My,' I would say to myself, 'I played a different mood of Thaïs tonight.' " Or: "I, Mary Garden, wouldn't allow any but my own mentality to go into Salome." Or: "I always had my audience, from the beginning to the very last day, in my hand —just as I have it now, speaking. Then it was Salome, Thaïs, Mélisande; now it is *me, myself.*"

In junior high I made a list of twenty women whom I considered mine—my women, emanations of me, women who assisted me in my metamorphosis, women I wanted to become. I've forgotten their names.

· *Closets* ·

A diva's tones go *out* of her mouth and into the theater. So Nellie Melba's high C seemed to Mary Garden: "it left Melba's throat, it left Melba's body, it left everything, and came over like a star and passed us in our box, and went out into the infinite. . . . It wasn't attached to anything at all—it was *out* of everything."

To project a role, the diva must throw it *out* of her body and bestow it on the audience. Garden writes, "All my creations went into me and out. They were there inside of me, and I threw them out to the public." And: "I have a horror of being shut in." Before, I was shut in, but now that I am a diva I am out.

A diva is said to *come out* from behind the curtain for her bows: after a successful performance, Clara Louise Kellogg "had to come out again and again." When we see a diva she is, by definition, out. We know she is there only because she has projected a self for us to hear. Once she is a diva she may have the liberty to articulate a self loudly; but when she is in apprenticeship, or when she is a young girl, far from the city where her career will one day bring her, she must keep her vocation secret. For Willa Cather's heroine Thea, in *The Song of the Lark* (a novel inspired by soprano Olive Fremstad), diva vocation is an unspeakable secret she can share only with the town doctor. Only with the sympathetic doctor can she lift the lid of her box and look at the "open secret" of her desire to sing.

It is a nightmare to have camouflage imposed, like a religious order, patriotism, or heterosexuality. Marian Anderson felt apprehensive whenever she sang in her studio: she feared she was disturbing the neighbors. Anderson had more reason than Mary Garden to dread what the neighbors would think, and yet every diva opens her mouth and makes loud sounds, and even if she says "I am for camouflage," she must long ago have given up masks and meekness, and decided to disturb the neighbors.

· *Trauma at the Origin of the Diva's Voice* ·

A singing identity, like any identity, is an artificial system, part choice, part circumstance. Identities coalesce around catastrophes, later forgotten; the process of forgetting builds the new self's groundwork. The diva can't separate self from vocation: her body is her art. When she discovers her diva-incipience, she's discovering the nature of her body, and she coins that body, that inseparability of election and damnation, in a scene of trauma or embarrassment.

Emma Eames's mother scours the girl's mouth with ash because she tells a lie; Mrs. Price whips Leontyne for refusing to play "Blessed Assurance"; Marian Anderson, in her room, sings to her floral wallpaper; a classmate sees Nellie Melba's underwear when at six years old she stands on a stool and sings "Shells of the Ocean."

Not every origin of diva vocation is traumatic. But the conviction "I will sing!" begins with a primary alienation and unhappiness. I am locked up; *voice* is the key to the prison door, but it is also part of the prison, the body I am shut inside.

· *Divas and Their Dolls* ·

According to mythologies of operatic singing, the voice comes out from a fathomless vacancy. Does the diva know where her sound comes from? Or is she a doll, an unconscious commodity?

Divas are my dolls; I play with the stories of their lives, and I learn from these fables how to transcend affliction, as a little girl is supposed to learn proper femininity from her dolls.

The diva, in childhood, may be strongly attached to a doll: Clara Butt's first performance was singing the ballad "Tommy make room for your uncle" to an audience of her battered dolls. Emma Eames, child of a missionary in Shanghai, stood on stage with traveling circus dwarves and embraced them, inviting them home with her to be her "dollies." Adelina Patti, at an early age, stood on a table to sing "Una voce poco fa" and referred to herself in retrospect as a "little bit of a doll": she was billed as "The Wonderful Child Prima Donna." The soprano Olympia, in Offenbach's *Les Contes d'Hoffmann,* is one operatic image of the soprano as inanimate doll.

Looking at a photograph of diva Bessie Abott from the early years of this century, I remember the immobility of queer youth. She appears dazed, as if she's just been released from a locked trunk. Her weak, plump hands hide her breasts. Is she anticipating a trauma, or has the trauma already occurred? She lists to her left, like a column in a temple not structurally sound. I identify with the diva's inability to

I remember the immobility of queer youth.

She is already a diva and no one can harm her.

choose her life, though her willfulness and indomitability make us think that she has sculpted her fate.

Girls, not boys, play with dolls, but I am playing with the image of Bessie Abott, as if I were once again seven years old, trying to extract perfume by pressing rose petals against a rock.

Looking at a photograph of Adelina Patti at the age of nine (at an early performance she gave her doll a seat and said to it, audibly, "Here, little one, listen to your mamma sing you a pretty song"), I recall what it felt like to stand on the verge of puberty and wait for sexuality, fierce and unexplained, to rescue me. Of course sexuality performs no rescue; it complicates rather than simplifies. Patti has already discovered her voice, and so in this picture she looks old and humorless. A book is open before her but she has no intention of reading it. She is already a diva and no one can harm her.

· *Puberty and Fatality* ·

Amelita Galli-Curci "first sensed the psychic world at the age of sixteen." Sometime later, she bought herself a fifteen-carat diamond.

Her biographer speculates, "Was there a hidden charm in this talisman? Who knows what influence those pure white rays had upon the imprisoned vocal cords?" But to conceive of the diva's vocal cords as "imprisoned" implies a philosophy of puberty as well as of history: an assumption that the entire grown adult body, complete with secondary sexual characteristics and drives, lies dormant in the child's body—that destiny sleeps in the genes, already plotted, waiting to be catalyzed by an expensive gem. Neither puberty nor history is that simple.

· *Tomboy* ·

Roberta Peters exclaims, "Of course I was a tomboy." Clara Butt began as a tomboy. One of Ernestine Schumann-Heink's first teachers was a woman who "dressed like a man" and smoked cigars. This butch pedagogue seems lodged in an indelible, fatal lifestyle—lesbian. But a tomboy is just a phase on the way to becoming a butterfly; tomboy is not a vocation—only a temporary, endearing, transcendable affliction. It is excusable to say "I was a tomboy" but less permissible to say "I remain a tomboy, I choose to be, in middle age, a tomboy."

· *The Will to Power* ·

Her confidence that she will be a diva lifts her from an obscure, immobile, difficult childhood; the vocation of diva permits her to read her life backward and see clear meanings, hints of tremendousness, where there was once shame.

"There is Nature . . . there is Art . . . and there is Clara Butt!" exclaimed Sir Herbert Tree; "MARY GARDEN, SUPERWOMAN," proclaimed the headlines after her New York debut as Thaïs. And Galli-Curci, according to her biographer, sang "even at the risk of antagonizing everyone."

How can a doll be a force of nature? Only if her plastic, paralyzed head conceals a masterplot.

A woman who ends up queer will later read this certainty into early fantasies and pastimes, and imagine that there was something queer in her deportment from the very beginning; that her queerness was like Lotte Lenya's in *From Russia with Love*—a sign that she's a spy, affiliated with shady organizations, longing to conquer the world.

For the diva-to-be, difference is power; she seeks profit in her deviance. For the nondiva, difference only leads to ridicule.

The diva's will to power culminates in a scene of vindication. What a thrill: the most monumental and unrealistic vision of herself turns out to be accurate! Nellie Melba said about her first New York *Traviata:* "In thirty seconds—I must say it, though it may sound boastful—I knew that I had won. The rest of the performance was one long triumph, and when it was over, I walked through the corridors full of massed bouquets." Lucky Melba, whose confidence and self-love are so absolute and so deserved. Imagine your own version of Melba's corridors decked with flowers, corridors of "I told you so," corridors of "And you called me queer. . . ."

Here is a conversation between Amelita Galli-Curci and her grandmother. Amelita says, "I shall be one of the few and more—I shall be the greatest of Milanese singers," and her grandmother quips, "Don't forget Grisi," and Amelita returns, "But I must surpass even Grisi." The diva-in-training thinks like a bellicose nation. But a diva is a solitary woman, not a country; all she wants is sovereignty over herself.

· *The Art of Personality* ·

Legend has it that Frank O'Hara called Mae West the inventor of "small-town faggot psychology." Mae West was not an opera singer, but she thought like one. She pontificated: "Personality is the most important thing to an actress's success. You can sing like Flagstad or dance like Pavlova or act like Bernhardt, but if you haven't personality you will never be a real star. Personality is the glitter that sends your little gleam across the footlights and the orchestra pit into that big black space where the audience is."

Do you have a nice personality? At the drugstore, test your personality by depositing a quarter in a machine that senses body heat. Change your personality if it is neurotic or unpleasant. What was it like, however, in the days before personality was invented? Before personality, if you wanted to be loved and couldn't resort to witchcraft, how could you gain access to erotic electromagnetic fields? Opera is the art of personality; by the nineteenth century, opera began to sell its patrons the elixir and ideology of personality—convincing its consumers that certain human natures were more vocal and magnetic than others, and that the listener should surrender to the tidal wave of a strong stage presence.

The word "personality" has faded and turned neutral: we now think of it as etiquette, not energy. But when Willa Cather wrote that a "voice is personality" and that "it can be as big as a circus and as common as dirt," she meant that the divas who sold us the doctrine of magnetism were dirty and dangerous, and that, like circuses, they had the power to seduce us with their freaks and marvels.

· *Mimicry and Flaunting* ·

A diva often begins by imitating her mother, even if the mother's voice hurts. On hearing her mother sing, Emma Eames cried, "Oh, Mamma, Mamma, don't, don't! You have such a lonesome voice." Eating and speaking, opening and closing—the simplest movements and emotions arise in imitation. So do the fine points of diva conduct. Dorothy Kirsten describes the utility of living with Grace Moore: "Living with her those two weeks in Cincinnati, I learned a great many of her habits, some of which I eventually adopted as my own." Two weeks is not a long apprenticeship, but a diva has to learn quickly. Who invented the gestures we associate with the diva? Who taught Renata Tebaldi how to bow, how to extend her arms and open and shut her hands, "which in her native area means 'I will come back!' "? I know the drag queen's pleasure in imitating histrionic gestures. I want my natural affections to have the minutely calibrated artificiality of Tebaldi's bow.

Gay men have counteracted the regime of the closet by enjoying sex in public places; we want to flaunt our sexuality, after years of camouflage, even if we are flaunting a conduct that we are in the midst of inventing.

· *Debuts and Discoveries* ·

The diva, debuting, invents herself, imposes herself on an audience unaware of her magnitude until she opens her mouth. Impossible, to be queer before the moment of announcing that predisposition, though in retrospect it seems that queerness existed before it made a formal debut, before it discovered or inherited its name.

More suggestive than the debut is the moment *before*. Before Maria Malibran's La Scala debut, she said (hearing that her great predecessor Giuditta Pasta, creator of Norma, was in the audience): "I am not afraid of Pasta. I will live or die as Norma." Inimitable Mary Garden, before her debut, told herself (she repeats the story many times): "Mary Garden, this is your moment. Tomorrow Paris will be at your feet!"

It is impossible to narrate a life—a queer life, at any rate—without imagining such a moment: the instant before arrival, when a spirit guide, the one who foreknows and assists, takes charge. On hearing Melba sing for the first time, the great teacher Mathilde Marchesi yelled to her husband, *"Salvatore, j'ai enfin une étoile!"* (The moment when the star is born helps us all to see.) Then Marchesi told the surprised Nellie, *"Alors,* if you are serious, and if you can study with me for one year, I will make something *extraordinary* of you." Marchesi is the good fairy telling the little "nelly" that she is not unnatural, she is supernatural: she is not odd, she is extraordinary. She has been granted a divine dispensation. If she is very serious and does her exercises she will finally earn the privilege of floating a voice apart from her body disguised in a Gilda costume, a voice that will force everyone in the world who was not present on that forgotten night to look elsewhere for their one impossible founding scene.

Then the debut moment becomes hypothetical, an evening that exists only by deduction, by inference. (She must have sung then, because history, legend, or rumor says so; if the sounds she made are gone, how can I participate in the glow of this career's commencement?) A reviewer of Melba's first concert in Australia described the tendency of origins to disappear and to make us, in retrospect, hunger for their phantasmal clarity: "everybody who heard her will desire to hear her again and everybody who did not hear her is at this moment consumed with regrets at not having been present." Did the debut really happen, or did I invent it because my life is predicated on it?

Grace Moore has the right to proclaim, the morning after her Met debut as Mimì, "My bed was covered with telegrams from all over the world—and I suddenly realized I was an opera star!" Did Grace Moore feel like an oddball? Is that why she must suddenly pronounce herself a diva, extraordinary and elect, the center of attention, the shrine, the source, the dimestore-novel heroine, the Empress, the Absolute and Only?

Mary Garden in retirement, flourishing her pearls.

· *Divas and Protégées: The Mystery of Succession* ·

It is a mystery, how power is passed between women, how divas discover each other, how girls apprentice themselves to divas. I want to be present when a diva and her protégée meet—when the diva decides to pass on her fairy dust.

Mary Garden raised Helen Jepson to the "opera throne" by bestowing on her the privilege of impersonating Thaïs. The *Toledo Blade* reported in 1936: "The crown that was Mary Garden's rested today on the brow of her protégée, blond Helen Jepson, and the hand which placed it there was that of her abdicating predecessor as queen of the opera." The protégée kissed the queen's hand, and the queen commanded, "Go, go sing." The love between an aging diva and a diva entering her prime is erotic, but we are not supposed to imagine their bodies as they observe each other with mingled reverence and jealousy.

Once, Mary Garden was herself the young protégée, crowned by a more seasoned star; Sybil Sanderson taught Mary the role of Thaïs, and told her, "Mary, Thaïs must have pearls." The diva acquires divinity when her predecessor passes on privilege, stature, beauty secrets, fashion tips, and vocal tricks. Garden's crowning of Jepson is full of pathos in retrospect because the diva rules over no particular territory and has no crown to give. Despite the invisible nature of diva sovereignty, it would sustain me to become a Mary Garden and to hear from Sybil's lips, "Mary, Thaïs must have pearls," and to know thenceforth that finding my gender is just a matter of developing a knack for the right accessories.

It is particularly contraband and delightful for me as a man to contemplate the bond between two elegant divas, because I am absent from the scene, and I can't feasibly participate in it except by identifying against my gender with the experience of being crowned.

Mary Garden in retirement, flourishing her pearls, was full of advice for younger divas. She told Dorothy Kirsten, "Dorothy, that first impression is very important. Exude confidence and let your bosoms lead you." And when Grace Moore sang *Louise,* Garden's great role, the crowd clapped for the retired diva as well as for the debutante, and so Garden stood in her box, bowed, unpinned a bouquet from her chinchilla wrap, and threw it to Grace on the stage. And then Grace Moore, trained in the mysteries of succession, passed on the crown to Dorothy Kirsten, who wrote, "The evening was over and I

Callas and Sutherland assume identical expressions, as if they graduated from the same school of diva conduct: jaw raised for glory, smile wide, teeth even, spray-stiffened hair an unnatural halo.

was Grace Moore's protégée. The following day a press conference was arranged and our picture together hit every paper. . . . I was launched."

I love photographs of divas embracing each other—such as a dressing-room candid of Joan Sutherland with Maria Callas, the younger diva placidly beaming, the elder diva worn down by trauma and tremendousness. Callas and Sutherland assume identical expressions, as if they graduated from the same school of diva conduct: jaw raised for glory, smile wide, teeth even, spray-stiffened hair an unnatural halo. In few public forums dare I say that this photograph of diva succession—though it's not a "snap" of me—confirms my place in the universe. Both women are absolutely sure of themselves, and I, who treasure the picture, who try to learn from it this mysterious business of *how to live a queer life,* want to ask these women how they succeed in being so public, creamy, and colossal.

· *Divas and Their Mothers* ·

Joan Sutherland copied her mother's scales and exercises; Clara Butt said, "I believe that I owe my voice to the fact that my mother had a beautiful voice but did not sing"; Ernestine Schumann-Heink said, "I sang what my mother sang." But if the diva sings by imitating her mother, eventually the voice itself becomes a demanding child, and the diva must, as Galli-Curci phrases it, "mother the insistent flow" of the voice.

Does the diva mother her voice? Or does the diva give voice to her mother? Geraldine Farrar felt like a member of her mother's body, and considered her own career an avenue for the two women's joint expression. She even wrote half of her autobiography, *Such Sweet Compulsion,* in her dead mother's voice. Impersonating her mother allows Farrar to describe her own body with unrestrained erotic admiration: Farrar, in her mother's voice, calls herself a "seductive vision" with gleaming décolletage.

The diva's grandest moments may exist for the mother's contemplation and regard. Clara Louise Kellogg's mother admiringly describes her daughter's performance as Donizetti's Linda di Chamounix: "Thursday 9th. Saw Linda. Magnificent. Best thing. Called out three times. Bouquet—dress—yellow. *Moiré* blue satin apron—pink roses—gay!"

Little has been said seriously about gay men and their mothers, or lesbians and their mothers. Much has been said carelessly or to instill prejudice. The figure of the diva captures some of the electricities and erasures of being a gay man looking across gender at the mother, or (here I speak from imagination) a lesbian looking within her own gender at the mother. The gay man has left his mother behind (and what we leave behind we must refract and reiterate); the lesbian has resumed her mother, chosen her.

· Gay, Queer, and Flaming ·

Like her mother, Clara Louise Kellogg valued gay art: she wrote in her autobiography, "I often think that the art, or the ability,—on the stage or off it—which makes people truly and innocently gay, is very high in the scale of human importance." By gay art, Kellogg means cheerful art. But I as gay person do not feel "gay"; I distrust the word and dislike its everyday straight significance as "cheerful." I am not a cheerful person. I am not gay. When I say the word "gay" the vowel "A" sticks in my throat; "gay" is one of those difficult words, almost as hard as "homosexual"—impossible to handle the second O, the hoMO, without opening one's mouth too wide, embarrassingly wide, like a singer finessing a pianissimo.

What does Kellogg mean by "queer" when she says that "tenors are queer creatures"? Or when she says, "I must have been a rather queer child. . . . Even as a little thing I liked clothes. When only nine years old I conceived a wild desire for a pair of kid gloves"? Probably the same thing as when Clara Butt senses a "queer silence in the room" after she finishes singing, or when Grace Moore calls her idol Mary Garden "so lovely, so flaming, so much a woman," or when the novelty of Maria Jeritza's "Vissi d'arte" (for the first time sung while the diva lay prone on the stage) appears the next day "in flaming headlines."

I who am "gay" and "queer" and "flaming" am interested in the origin of these words, and their telling occurrence in nineteenth- and twentieth-century diva prose.

The diva's gaiety is qualified, shadowed. She has reached merriment by passing through shame and despair. She felt gay aboard the *Titanic,* but then it started to sink. She's gay but also horrified. The bouquets and telegrams distract her from terror; she calls this state of distraction "gay."

A singer is queer because she presents the ear with unexpected bounty, and because she's distinguished by a gift that makes her not ordinary. She begins as a "rather queer child." Mathilde Marchesi, doyenne of voice instructors, taught solely women—except for the boy who came to her studio disguised as a girl. When he reached puberty, Mme. Marchesi grew aware of a quality in his voice that was "very queer, extraordinarily queer. . . . The queerness that appeared suddenly in the voice was the change from boyhood to manhood." The moment when it grows impossible to judge the gender of a singing voice is the moment she names "queer."

Divas are not always gay; they are often cheerless. As Emma Eames said, "During my entire career I never knew a day without pain, and my private life was not a happy one. Yet I believe I can congratulate myself on having impressed all who knew me as always being perfectly well and perfectly happy."

For divas and for gays, cheerfulness or gaiety is part of the profession. But during my entire career ("my career as a fairy," as Earl Lind says in *Autobiography of an Androgyne*), I never knew a day without pain.

· *The Lesbian Diva* ·

Male composer, librettist, conductor, and impresario surround the diva, and yet her career evolves because of crushes on other women. The following stories have convinced me that the diva's desire for women is not incidental to her power and her allure, or to the emotions that motivated actual women to be divas.

Frances Alda chooses to become a diva because she has a crush on the American actress Cora Brown-Potter. Most of Alda's allowance goes to buy photographs of her idol; when the fan and the star meet, Brown-Potter kisses Alda on the mouth.

Emma Eames, in early life, thrives on feverishly affectionate girl audiences: "Such pretty girls in such feminine clothes as formed my audience and gave an ovation to another young girl!"

Fan Gordon M. Eby knows: "Men (as such) were not much to Miss Bori."

Grace Moore had a crush on a teacher who wore "various shades

of lavender" and spoke in "subdued throbbing faraway tones." Then
Moore began to worship Mary Garden. Meeting Garden, Moore passionately knelt, kissed the queen's hand, and exclaimed, "You are my
goddess."

Olive Fremstad had a female companion, Mary Watkins Cushing
—a so-called "buffer." "To be a buffer to Olive Fremstad," writes
Cushing, was "all that any girl could desire." The diva and her buffer
slept in separate rooms, but a string led from the diva's bedpost to the
companion's toe. If Fremstad needed attentions in the middle of the
night, she woke the compliant girl by pulling the string ("This she
tweaked at need"). Of her vaguely erotic servitude, Cushing remembers, "One not only survives such things but finds them exciting."
Another of Fremstad's techniques for copping a feel: because the diva
insisted on payment before a performance, the buffer would obtain
the check, stuff it in her blouse, and present herself to Fremstad, who
would inquiringly tap the girl's "flat and heaving bosom with an anx-
ious finger." One day backstage Lilli Lehmann told Fremstad, "Put
your hand down my back under my wig and cloak." Fremstad com-
pliantly ran "a respectful finger" down Lilli's "erect and handsome
spine" to discover that the great Lehmann, unaffected by nerves, was
perfectly dry though she had just performed.

Mary Garden had a crush on her first teacher, who was "handsome, tremendously charming, and oh! so French in manner. . . . She
was *so* everything that I had dreamed of, and never seen in my life.
After I sang for her, she came up to me, seized my hands in hers, and
said warmly, 'Oh, but I must keep you as my pupil!' " Later, Garden
had the chance to see Debussy's wife near-naked: "The surgeon went
to Lily's side and opened her nightdress, and in my life I have never
seen anything so beautiful as Lily Debussy from the waist up. It was
just like a glorious marble statue, too divine for words!" She admits
that sleeping alone gives her "a shiver of freedom," and muses, "Sometimes I wonder why I've never been crazy about men like so many
other women."

These are only stories. They are not theory or history. Stories are
the only pieces of a diva, other than records, that I can hold and repeat.
And so I take stories seriously: I take them as ritual and as belief, and
as reflections of larger systems. These anecdotes tell me that divas
required other women as models, mentors, and admirers. Without the
example of other forthright, independent women, how could a diva
imagine and pursue this vocation in which subservience to men

Mary Garden: "Sometimes I wonder why I've never been crazy about men like so many other women."

seemed to play no part? Eroticism could be openly acknowledged, because many of these divas flourished before female bonds were classified and condemned as "lesbian."

At least in the nineteenth century, the diva is usually not from a wealthy family, and so she earns an income by singing; if successful, she can avoid marriage, or can choose to marry only after her career ends. Maria Malibran insisted that "I never feel the slightest desire [for men]. . . . I feel such disgust!" And asking her husband for a separation, she writes, "I think a theatrical life demands a great deal of calm and the life of a virgin which is what suits me perfectly *I am very happy as I am now.*"

The diva exposes her capacity for independent pleasure: her joy comes from the body, the throat, the cavities no one in the audience can see. She presents the uncomfortable and antipatriarchal spectacle of a woman taking her body seriously—channeling, enjoying, and nourishing it.

· *Fat* ·

Singers are supposedly fat. The body must be huge. The body must spill over, embarrass itself, declare immensity. There are cultural and emotional affinities between large women and gay men; both are entrusted with understanding the body as shame and as difference, the body all mouth, unable to stop making statements, signifying too extremely—the body a clue that a mistake has been made.

We care about the bodies of singers, and not only about the sounds those bodies produce. The Met made Zinka Milanov lose weight and Grace Moore gain weight. Contemporary music journalists refer obliquely to a singer's size through such phrases as "majestic appearance," "colossal stage presence," "too robust to make a convincing Mimì." And there are theories, however tenuous, that larger bodies make a more powerful sound.

Some dishes named after divas: Pêche Melba, Turkey Tetrazzini, Coupe Fremstad, Chicken Ponselle, L'Aile de Bresse Sutherland, Beignets Soufflés with Sauce Callas. Sometimes singers fashion their own dishes: I've made Galli-Curci's "Prima Donna Cocktail"—a tablespoon of strong coffee mixed with milk, sugar, and ice—so I can imagine I'm connected to Galli-Curci or that I'm ingesting her. Eat Melba toast and you ritually consume a piece of Melba's body in a diva Communion. But Melba toast won't satisfy our hunger for Nellie Melba. As a dish, it is a tease.

We want to consume the singer; we go to the opera to eat voice, to eat trills and cavatinas and the failed or successful "Ho-jo-to-ho." Astrid Varnay compared the Metropolitan to a stewpot, with Rudolf Bing as lid, the singers as meat, the chorus as vegetable, the conductor as fire. And Farrar spoke of the public's cannibalistic urge to see a singer served to it already overcooked by hard work, a talent "fried brown and curled at the edges."

Singers, too, are hungry creatures—hungry for fame, money, glamour, artistic satisfaction. Maria Malibran, in a love letter to her great predecessor Giuditta Pasta, confessed, "If I were near you, you would have neither face nor body, because I would eat all of you." Balancing the legendary stories of postperformance feasts are such ascetic tableaux as Geraldine Farrar's mother spooning bouillon to the diva between the acts of *Butterfly,* or the story of Mark Twain's daughter, Olive Clemens, an aspiring singer who starved herself to death. The process of singing, a sublimation, figuratively wastes the singer's body, turns her to wraith.

Eating is a reigning metaphor for operagoing and opera singing because both singing and listening have vestigial and unconscious connections to sacrifice. We consider the diva fat because *we* are the hungry ones; we want to ingest the diva through our voracious, vulnerable ears. And so we project onto the diva's body an image of our own cannibalistic orality, an image of how grotesque we consider our desires to be.

"Fat," in diva iconography, means "presence." I love the voice but I am not supposed to pay attention to the body behind it, a body with questionable, shifting boundaries, a body able to absorb mine through vocal osmosis, a body with an open mouth emitting spit, a mouth that might swallow me as the whale swallowed Jonah (Rossini described his pupil, the diva Marietta Alboni, as an "elephant that swallowed a nightingale"); the diva's mouth openly speaks its wish, its demand, and so it's an infantile mouth, the mouth I wish were mine, as I listen, close-lipped, suppressing a cough.

· *Divas and Disease* ·

Divas, like gay people, fall under the sign of the sick, the maimed, the deranged. The diva is associated with disease and with injuries that prevent adequate voice production; in crisis she undergoes operations. Paradoxically, the successfully produced voice is perceived to be a sort of sickness—because it is secret, gnomic, and because it is an exception to natural law, even as it upholds a doctrine of Nature as divinely infused. The diva supports cosmologies, and she shatters them.

Diva self-mutilation helps the show go on: before a performance, Maria Malibran took a pair of scissors and cut away the blisters around her mouth; Geraldine Farrar told Carl Van Vechten that "at every performance she cut herself open with a knife and gave herself to the audience."

There's a bizarre affinity between divas and dismembered anatomies: diva Brigitta Banti died in 1806 and left her larynx, preserved in alcohol, to the city of Bologna; Olive Fremstad's piano was graced by a pickled human head sliced in half so she could show students the vocal and breathing apparatus.

Nondivas also undergo operations, but in the diva's case, the very process of probing the body and of opening its mysterious inner recesses has a bearing on her art: a diva, when she sings, operates on herself, reveals her body, exposes an indwelling secret. And we will either call that secret a sign of health, and applaud the diva as a specimen of humanity's finest; or we will consider her vocalism, her exposed element, to be an abnormality on which we nonetheless depend.

Galli-Curci lost her voice and regained it (however imperfectly) through surgery. During the operation, she sang a fragment of *Barber of Seville* to test her voice. When a diva sings, an operation is implicitly taking place: a body is being opened.

Judy Garland, in her last film, *I Could Go On Singing,* is jealous of the attention that opera singers receive from doctors. When she can't go on singing, her ex-lover, played by gay-seeming Dirk Bogarde, is reluctant to treat her. Garland assumes that he would be happy to heal an opera star; she mentions Tebaldi and Callas as examples of superior, classy eminences. Symbolically, doctors and gay men share curiosity and compassion about occurrences in the diva's throat: doctors can help divas (even as their laryngoscopes and other implements seem to violate the diva's oral privacy), while gay fans can only listen, applaud, and sustain the singer in her addiction to performance.

Diva iconography casts the successful, prominent woman (the woman who makes a large fee and a large sound) as a diseased anomaly: or it portrays her *failure* to make sound as a disease, a bloody lapse. "The cords of my throat were bleeding profusely," says Nellie Melba of her voice in crisis. Diva voice production is a scene of sickness, an occasion for the body to appear nonconforming, internal, festering, underground, and interrupted. Singing, the diva interrupts our ideas of health, because what she produces is unnatural but also eerily beautiful. The diva, when she sings, exposes *interiority,* the inside of a body and the inside of a self; we may feel that the world of the interior that the diva exposes is a diseased place, but we learn from the diva's beautiful voice to treasure and solicit those operatic moments when suddenly interiority upstages exteriority, when an inner and oblique vision supplants external verity. The diva's voice may come shadowed by sickness, but I learn from it to revere my own derangement and to value those moments when hysteria interrupts the story, when territories like homosexuality, which dominant culture casts as sick, seem more compelling than health.

· *Divas and Difference* ·

The diva is demonized: she is associated with difference itself, with a satanic separation from the whole, the clean, the contained, and the attractive. Mythically, she is perverse, monstrous, abnormal, and ugly. Though divas have been firmly associated with queens and with the perpetuation of empire, they have been considered deviant figures capable of ruining an empire with a roulade or a retort. Mozart's librettist Lorenzo da Ponte condemns diva Brigitta Banti as "an asp, a fury, a demon of Hell, capable of upsetting an Empire, let alone a theater."

The diva overturns the world's gendered ground by making femaleness seem at once powerful and artificial; and so the diva has often been associated with ruptures in the earth. When Mrs. Elizabeth Billington debuted in Naples, Vesuvius erupted; Neapolitans blamed the natural catastrophe on the diva. And the San Francisco earthquake, in myth, has been linked to opera singers. Olive Fremstad sang Carmen in San Francisco the night before the earthquake; she gave her roses to the wounded. In the Jeanette MacDonald movie *San Francisco* (1936), our modern Sodom crumbles because of loose morals and because of MacDonald's increasingly operatic voice. She defects from dance hall to opera house, exposing fault lines in the city's class system, and fault lines—difficulties in saying what we feel, difficulties in coming out—in the audience's collective body.

The beauty and magnitude of a diva's voice resides, so the iconography suggests, in her deformity. Her voice is beautiful because she herself is not—and her ugliness is interpreted as a sign of moral and social deviance. Reading biographies of divas, I can't ignore the repeated references to physical flaws—for example, Benedetta Pisaroni's "features horribly disfigured by small-pox," prompting spectators to shut their eyes "so as to hear without being condemned to see." Audiences speculated that Maria Malibran was not anatomically a woman, but an androgyne or hermaphrodite—an aberrant physique to match her voice's magic power.

The diva can assist gay self-authorization because she is a deviant figure who has an "ugly habit of pressing her hands against her bosom when executing difficult passages" (Mrs. Billington); who has a "slight squint perceptible in the right eye" (Caterina Gabrielli); who is willing to say "I adore the unusual" (Jessye Norman); who has a sympathy for abnormalities (Marian Anderson "wanted to be a surgeon, to do something grand like correcting deformities"); who is worshipped and revered but began as a "small, ugly, broad-nosed, shy, gauche, under-grown girl" (Jenny Lind). . . .

The diva may object to her role as demonized difference, as a creature labeled "perverse, unreasonable, and turbulent," "ungovernable and malevolent"—as Regina Mingotti was called by an angry impresario in 1756. She retaliated in a pamphlet, accusing him of using "female Arts of Intreaty and Lamentation, which I have no need to practice." Mingotti may have protested, but most divas don't, probably because their artistic and financial success vindicates them, and turns their deviance into proof of supremacy. The ungovernability of a diva's performance contributes to its power.

Do I want to be an earthquake—an eruptive force, rather than a closed vault? Before ACT UP, gay people didn't explode—unless we consider a stereotypical style of gay male self-presentation (for example, Anthony the swishy stutterer in *Brideshead Revisited*) to be a slow-motion Vesuvius, power partitioned into oblique, thwarted, resistant gestures.

When I enter a space (waiting room, restaurant, theater, street) that seems predominantly straight and where my abstention from heterosexuality seems suddenly conspicuous, visible, risible, I feel my muscles involuntarily, defensively contract. I want to make sure my body doesn't express itself, doesn't accidentally (through swish, buoyancy, curve, elasticity) speak this mythic, impermissible "homosexuality." And at such moments, in the midst of rigidity and self-cancellation, I long to be a diva, to have the privilege of impersonating a quaking, fault-lined earth.

· Divas and Darkness ·

Many great divas of the last thirty to forty years have been African Americans: Grace Bumbry, Martina Arroyo, Shirley Verrett, Leona Mitchell, Betty Allen, Mattiwilda Dobbs, Kathleen Battle, Leontyne

Price, Jessye Norman. And yet, until recently, opera was a white enterprise. Most opera houses forbade women or men of color from singing or attending. Few blacks attended the Metropolitan Opera, even in the absence of strict segregation policies, and no blacks sang leading roles there until Marian Anderson made her postprime debut in 1955 as Ulrica the gypsy witch in *Un Ballo in Maschera.* Rosalyn M. Story's recent study, *And So I Sing: African-American Divas of Opera and Concert,* details a long history of African-American women achieving fame either through recital work or through operatic performances in all-black companies.

In Jean-Jacques Beineix's film *Diva,* the diva, Wilhelmenia Wiggins Fernandez, an American woman of color, subverts the traditional image of the white diva and reminds us that divas, though usually white, have been linked to racial otherness, darkness, exoticism, and "blood." Long before the recent flourishing of the African-American diva, opera culture used images of darkness to demonize the diva. Color is one of the primary metaphors for the qualities of vocal tone. Singers are taught to avoid the "white" sound and to cover the tones, to make them darker. Roles like Carmen rely on the notion of the diva's "Latin blood." When divas have been made up to appear Asian or African for such roles as Aida, Selika, Cio-Cio-San, and Iris, they were expressing opera culture's insistence on the dark nature of the diva, as well as underscoring, in a problematic masquerade, the white diva's separation from the women of color she portrays.

The voice of the black operatic or concert diva was imagined to emanate directly from her ethnicity: commentators referred to Marian Anderson's "Negroid sound." And listeners have used metaphors of darkness and of racial essence to describe the appeal of certain female operatic voices even when the singer was white. Maria Malibran and Pauline Viardot were frequently described as having non-European features; one friend of Malibran speculated on the diva's "negro blood." A journalist, describing Adelina Patti as a child, notices her "little brown throat," her "dark arms" clinging to her girl playmates' "white little necks"; because of her darkness, she is a "born exponent of the Spanish type." Italian origin was itself considered a sign of darkness: Margherita de l'Épine was called the "tawny Tuscan."

The diva brings her vocal treasure abroad, on tour to the colonies; and she finds there, among the colonized, a reflection of her abjected organ. Galli-Curci's biographer, narrating the diva's tour of Asia and Africa, alternates descriptions of her "native" audiences with accounts of her larynx's increasing vulnerability to medical specialists and to disease, as if the diva's voice, sent to tame and tranquilize the colonized, were itself the empire's possession, doomed to mysterious maladies and uncontrollable passions. Galli-Curci was like a missionary bent on conquering darkness; but her voice, because it was female, hidden, and inscrutable, was already aligned, in the imagery of empire, with the colonized.

· *Queens* ·

I crowned myself; no one crowned me. In my most elevated, mournful, and diva-identified moments—the instants when I understand it would be grand to sweep across a stage with a long dress trailing behind me—it is possible that the word "queen" washes over me as a consolation ("I am a queen!") and a caution ("Don't act like a queen, don't think like a queen").

Only one mark, one letter, separates queen and queer: n/r, the "r" an incomplete "n."

Some divas who have been named queens: Patti was "Queen of Song"; a letter addressed "Madam Galli-Curci, Queen of Song, London," actually reached the diva; Marian Anderson sang her historic concert at the Lincoln Memorial in Washington with the "dignity of a dusky queen," according to the *New York Post;* Kate Douglas Wiggin wrote a poem to Geraldine Farrar which exclaims, "She's a rosebud, still in its sheath of green, / In the singing garden of girls, the Queen!" "Queen" implies supremacy within a girl community—like a Brownie troop leader or a prom queen.

Though fêted by crowned heads, the nineteenth-century diva, like other musicians, was not considered part of polite society. A silken cord at private gatherings separated her from the wealthy partygoers she was paid to entertain. Nor did she have full civil rights: governments classed her as a prostitute. Many performers in Europe, whether musical or dramatic, were similarly disenfranchised. France gave theatrical players their religious rights (Communion, marriage, burial) only as late as 1849.

And yet the diva masquerades as regal. Queens and divas understand each other. The diva believes—and this may be not grandiose delusion but truth—that she and the queen are secret sharers, conversing in winks and nods.

The diva loves queens because pretending to be a queen is an occasion to divorce the body from the soul, to assume lofty and hieratic alienation; pretending to be a queen also helps the diva imitate figures in her past who might have ignored or abused her. Imitation is a form of mourning-through-identification: you imitate what you wish you could explain. The diva's mother once floated by with serene, oceanic detachment. And so the diva herself assumes that posture— just as Christina Crawford, in *Mommie Dearest,* pretends before a vanity mirror to be cruel Joan Crawford practicing her Oscar acceptance speech. The daughter of diva Giulia Grisi wrote, "My mother was almost haughty in her movements, and had a stately way of walking which suited her queenly head": here one sees the diva's manner through the daughter's eyes, and recognizes that the diva acts like a queen so she can impress this imaginary, abject witness. Fremstad's "buffer," Mary, watches the diva walk onstage: she "marched to her ordeal with the exalted, other-world look of a queen led to her crowning. Olive Fremstad had now cut herself off from reality with a completeness which was terrifying." The diva's queenliness resembles a madwoman's or Richard II's: it signals comatose, gelid indifference to fact. The diva pretends to be royal, and at any moment her illusion might be shattered. She is a carnival queen, queen-for-a-day, an ordinary woman indulging in detailed drag of queenliness.

Is the royal manner revolutionary when assumed by divas and by queers? Or is the gay queen a royalist? "Queen" is a term of reproach and defamation because it means a willed or hapless effeminacy, and male effeminacy is one of the least accepted behaviors in Western culture. But the word "queen" also subtly puts down the queer because it implies that he wants to be a woman and he wants to be a queen and, pathetic soul, he never will attain either incarnation.

Queenliness has long functioned in gay culture as a shield against insult and disgrace: the queen pretends to be above scorn because he is so often scorned. A diva, too, may act like a star long before she becomes a star and long after she ceases to be a star. It insulates one from harm to pretend to be royal. In prison for some imbroglio with operatic management, diva Madeleine Guimard said to her maid, "Never mind, I have written to the Queen to tell her that I have discovered a new style of coiffure. We shall be free before the evening." Only a diva could purchase freedom so easily. The assumption that fashion tips have the power to reverse prison sentences may be thoroughly Wildean, but Oscar Wilde himself had no such recourse during his own imprisonment. It is subversive—but sometimes futile—to treat arts of dress, manner, style, language, and gesture as if they were monumental.

· *Impersonation* ·

In turn-of-the-century diva prose, the roles are termed impersonations and are sometimes italicized. Maria Labia "sang *Mimi, Nedda, Santuzza,* and *Marguerite,*" and she studied "the parts of *Tosca, Carmen,* and *Marta* in 'Tiefland,' which latter rôle she created and sang eighty times." The impersonations pile up, conquests on a dance card: Kirsten Flagstad's 182 performances as Isolde, her 7 performances as Serpolette in Planquette's *Les Cloches de Corneville,* her 2 performances as Rezia in Weber's *Oberon,* her 47 performances as Micaëla in Bizet's *Carmen.* The diva, like the shut-in fan, is a collector: she collects roles, cities, accolades.

Two photographs of Adelina Patti, one as Norina in *Don Pasquale,* another as Lucia di Lammermoor, are identical: the same

NORINA, 1863   LUCIA, 1863

Patti imperiously refuses to alter her gestures from role to role, and her indifference to realism thrills us.

expression, angle of head, position of body within the picture's frame. Only the costumes are different. Patti imperiously refuses to alter her gestures from role to role; and her indifference to realism thrills us. She doesn't fall short of her role; she surpasses it. Our pleasure derives from her acting's insufficiency, its laxness, its willed remoteness from truth; realism is beneath Patti, for no diva needs to be realistic in order to achieve her ambitions.

It's camp, and it's vindication, to receive applause for maintaining a haughty distance from the role you're supposed to inhabit; to be rewarded for not relenting, for not altering your hungers, for saying "Get off my property," for barking "I am who I am, do not disturb the regime of my desires!"

· *Names and Gush* ·

Any diva, when she lists her roles, sounds off a salvo of sonorous foreign names that function as opera culture's primary decor. These lists give the pleasure of a collage—pieces of the world robbed of authenticity. But the erased histories beneath the names inspire fear. Rita Fornia "made her début in 'La Juive' as *Eudoxia* at Hamburg." Rita Fornia, La Juive, Eudoxia, Hamburg: these four names summon and silence stories. Don't ask questions of the names in opera; only admire their majesty, the sparkle of an impersonation associated with a city, a year—my 1913 Paris Azucena, my 1975 Buenos Aires Leila.

Divas lose their names and become their titles: La Stupenda, Miss Sold-Out, Queen of Staccato. Sometimes it is sufficient merely to precede the diva's name with the definite article: call Lina Cavalieri "The Cavalieri."

Gush: a young man tells Clara Butt, "Madame Butt, you are a poem!" Hyperbole conceals diminishment: is Madame Butt really so grand, or is the young man calling attention to his own insignificance? Does this comment—"you are a poem"—describe Clara Butt's aura, or the Paterian, love-struck, diva-ruled world of the young man?

The young man's gushy statement is affected; he willingly surrenders to enthusiasm. To emote, to exaggerate, to express whim: this deportment is countenanced in women and vilified in men.

· *Fevers and Police* ·

Whole cities succumb to the infection of the diva. San Francisco falls prey to the Adelina Patti epidemic. Broadsides in London proclaim "THE JENNY LIND MANIA." London falls sick with Galli-Curci Fever. In Sweden, during Marian Anderson's tour, Marian Fever is catching.

Where there is fever, the need for police arises. Police manage crowds at the stage doors of Covent Garden when Patti sings. (A crowd that gathers to buy tickets for a Jenny Lind night is called a "Jenny Lind crush.") Do crowds that pay homage to a female star have a political agenda, however tangential and concealed? Certainly the assembly that rioted at the Stonewall—just after throngs gathered to mourn Judy Garland at Campbell's Funeral Home—suggests that fans might assemble for purposes other than shiftless curiosity. Enthusiasms and affections, particularly for absent figures, are potentially violent, though rarely revolutionary: no clear political program motivates the crowd that follows Henriette Sontag home to her hotel and serenades her.

Marian Anderson's mother told her, "Remember, wherever you are and whatever you do, someone always sees you." This advice had sharp meaning for the African-American child, who needed to beware of watchful, threatening, armed presences. But the warning also applies to the performer, who builds an identity from the experience of being watched, and who must learn to police herself.

Powerful social institutions roost in our bodies; the normative category—man, woman, straight—rakes one's body, inspects it for error. We want to conform to our categories, and rarely do. The boy in *Tea and Sympathy* wants to walk like a straight man; he tries to learn; he tries to shed his swish. But he can't help himself. The fevers that hurt and sustain can't be policed away.

Diva is a specific female role (a woman opera singer of great fame and brilliance), but it is also a pliant social institution, a framework for emotion, a kind of conduct, expectation, or desire, that can move through a body that has nothing to do with opera, that can flush the cheeks of a nonsinging, nonperforming body, a body called "private" because it does not depend on being seen or heard.

· *Flowers, Sonnets, Curtain Calls* ·

Divas receive flowers, though Louise Homer claimed that "the smell of flowers is bad for soprano throats." Flowers form a language, its articulation choreographed with military precision: "la bataille des fleurs" is what Fremstad's companion called the bestowal rites. Adelina Patti's floral tribute, at Albert Hall, was an eight-foot-high constellation of yellow chrysanthemums. "Like most prima donnas," according to Leontyne Price's devoted chronicler, she has a "deep love for red roses." Giving flowers, the audience caters to the diva's pleasure. Or does the fan toss flowers selfishly—to make a mark on the evening?

Apparently, it was customary in the nineteenth century to throw admiring sonnets onto the stage. Adelaide Phillipps, traveling in Italy, was deluged with sonnets after a performance. One was published the next day in the newspaper: "Adelaide, tu canti!"

The diva counts her roses and her curtain calls. Several divas report having to come back onstage over fifty times. The diva may come out with feigned or genuine traces of the role's emotion marking her face, to prove that impersonation took its toll, that she served the public well, that she suffered in reality and not merely in masquerade. I love the aplomb, the antinaturalism, of the diva's resurrection— Gilda, Lucia, Carmen, Butterfly, dead women revived for the curtain call, the diva so deserving of kudos that she can rise from the grave to receive them.

Flower-throwing, like placing flowers on a grave, can't overcome the obstructions that stand in the path of presence. The gift of flowers will never be reciprocated. Like a fan letter, it is a tribute to the void: a gesture of faith and despair. To throw a flower is to say: I am imprisoned. (Remember Jean Genet's *Our Lady of the Flowers*.) Violence and brutality are buried in flowers: sometimes a bouquet's projectile force can wound, particularly if the flowers conceal jewels. The fan who throws flowers at the diva is shut into the language of flowers —shut into falsehoods of petal and scent.

Love for deep red roses can't sustain the diva. No one wins "la bataille des fleurs," because the romance falls short of speech and knowledge. In payment for the diva's ritual sacrifice, flowers pile up like carnage at her feet, and confetti from torn programs—snowflakes —fall on her, but these fragments, these clipped buds, these shredded pages, don't satisfy, because the context for this adulation—the love that queer fans send across the footlights—remains unspeakable and internal.

I have never bought roses for a diva, and maybe that means I'm a selfish fan. Or maybe these fragments are my roses: flowers for an imaginary diva, for the identity of diva, toward which, against reason, against gender, I aspire.

· *The Art of Anger* ·

It is possible that divas feud because they are powerless to battle the patriarchal system that rewards them with token acclaim and independence. But this hypothesis doesn't attribute enough intelligence or volition to divas, and doesn't account for what is inspiring in their rivalries. Battling divas offer lessons in the art of anger: how to fight an oppressive order by inventing a resilient self.

Lesson one. Nellie Melba says within earshot of Mary Garden, after their joint recital: "What a dreadful concert this would have been if I hadn't come!"

Lesson two. Geraldine Farrar, in her autobiography, offers Mary Garden this faint praise: "I am sure it will make no difference to Mary Garden when I say I did not care for her Carmen, but she had her own ways and a devoted public, and it was probably a pleasant change for her from the pale Mélisande and the touching little Jongleur. . . ."

Lesson three. Olive Fremstad turns on Geraldine Farrar, who has her own dressing room—a "bijou"—at the Met, while Fremstad shares a room with the rest of the prima donnas: "these artists sing trifles like Manon or Nedda or Marguerite—but for Fremstad and Isolde anything is good enough!"

Our social selves—the selves that believe in order and humility and staying in one's proper sphere—are shattered by the liberating spectacle of a diva standing up for herself against propriety. Reading about divas, I capitulate to the pushy diva's forceful example; I open myself to a gesture or a coup d'état that I didn't expect, that I didn't dare hope for. When I behold the scene of two divas fighting, cattiness strikes my body with a lightning bolt; the scene singes my soul, as if I, inadvertent witness, were a celebrant in a secret cultic ceremony.

Bitchiness is reputed to be a gay mode. Repartee, cat-fights, and one-liners are staples of works embodying one kind of gay taste: Oscar Wilde's plays, Ivy Compton-Burnett's novels, George Cukor's *The*

Women. These cadences aren't limited to "high" art; they show up in drag shows, in John Waters films, in bar argot. Quips, backtalk, and sneers are weapons that conquer severely limited terrains; the fruits of the queen's victory are trifles like a dressing room without a cracked mirror, or a pair of cha-cha heels.

The *sublime* is a thrilling infusion of paranoia and grandiosity into the gay fan's patient, watchful, unobtrusive soul. Suddenly the subject-object axis is reversed. Suddenly your private world is public, your internal monologue audible. Diva rivalry reverses the queer soul's isolation, and makes the world of private gestures and grudges seem shared, gregarious, legitimate. Everyone knows what you are thinking, everyone is watching your motions, everyone is judging your mood. Everyone is taking cues from you. A minute ago you were nobody, but now you are the diva, the victim of a conspiracy. So when Gloria Swanson says, at the end of *Sunset Boulevard,* "All right, Mr. De Mille, I'm ready for my closeup," she is speaking from the heart of diva rivalry: narcissism, a delusional godhead, makes her feel universally visible.

The opposite of rivalry is posed, treacly bonding, when divas are so established in their supremacy that they can be nice to each other. Bonding divas assume that everyone cares about their mutual fan club. Leontyne Price says: "Giulietta Simionato . . . is one of my pet loves. Callas is fabulous, and so are Tebaldi and Farrell. From these girls you can get a wealth of anything you want as a singer." The phrase "pet loves" doesn't cheapen Price; it gilds the reader, and kindles a reversal, the words of divas suddenly becoming an accessible, familiar currency.

Whether bonding or feuding, a diva is never alone; her solitude is peopled with reflections of herself. In Cecil Beaton's photograph of Marguerite D'Alvarez, he's trebled her face: he gives us three images of Marguerite staring beyond the picture's frame. The act of self-contemplation has divided her; she is looking for her self and never finding it. Or she's split into parts because Cecil Beaton, the gay photographer, loves her so intensely. Admiration engenders repetition. Gay adoration brings on the diva's split-personality syndrome (the three faces of Marguerite), and turns a happy lady into a schizoid dreamer. Or does it take three heads to convey her monumentality and self-absorption? The photograph attempts to be transcendent by imitating a saint's portrait or a cameo, and by sheathing her body—the problematic body of a diva—in a black that hides the figure; but the

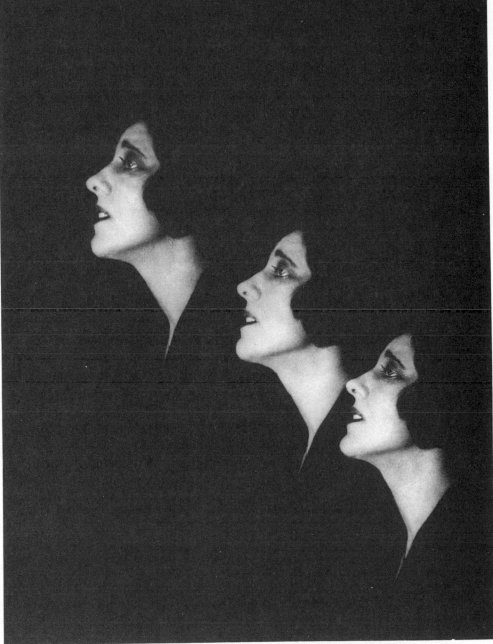

A diva is never alone; her solitude is peopled with reflections of herself.

picture more closely represents the divisions, ascensions, and arousals that shake a queer soul worshipping a diva.

In another photograph of Marguerite D'Alvarez looking heavenward, she is visibly aged, and a beatific upward gaze helps her avoid reality. She worships a cross, and she is surrounded by flowers that represent her own fragrant evanescence and the enamored photographer's tribute. The diva looks upward because she's immersed in images of herself and because she's past her prime; it strengthens one's chin to hold it aloft, which is why divas so frequently raise their jaws when they sing or when, bowing, they strain to greet all quadrants of the opera house in one sweeping glance. Marguerite D'Alvarez stares upward because she needs a miracle. "Give my career a lift!" she might as well be praying. For bisexual Carl Van Vechten, who took the picture, this image is a religious fix. He worships the diva's vulnerability to time; she can tamper with time but she is also time's victim. Like Dorian Gray, the diva has a peculiarly poignant relation to the fiction of eternal youth, which we all may want, but women and gay men are imagined to want most intensely.

"Give my career a lift!"

· Camp ·

Susan Sontag defined "camp" as the anarchic jolt we experience in the face of artistic artifacts that try to be serious and fail. But it is not the object's or the artist's failure that makes the artifact campy: the camp sensation is produced by our own joy in having discovered the object, in having been *chosen*, solicited, by it. Experiencing the camp glow is a way of reversing one's abjection, and, by witnessing the depletion of cultural monuments, experiencing one's own power to fill degraded artifacts to the brim with meanings.

When we experience the camp rush, the delight, the savor, we are making a private airlift of lost cultural matter, fragments held hostage by everyone else's indifference. No one else lived for this gesture, this pattern, this figure, before: only I know that it is sublime. Words-worth, in *The Prelude,* describes the experience of crossing the Alps and not knowing it, only realizing afterward, in retrospect, that he has had an experience of magnitude. When I watch divas, when I read about a gesture of Dorothy Kirsten's or Leontyne Price's, I feel that I've crossed the Alps, that I've witnessed something tremendous and boundary-shattering, but that no one else around me realizes its signif-icance and luminousness. I'm grateful, however, for the world's si-lence, for the privacy in which I study the image of Nellie Melba telegraphing *"Either Alda or myself"* to the conductor Cleofonte Cam-panini. It's more sublime and more camp to keep quiet about joy and then rescue the story later, once everyone else has abandoned it. The pleasure I take in diva lore ("This moment, this aside, this tableau is useless and therefore I claim it as mine!") is like the pleasure I take in a forbidden sexual sight. I sequester the erotic image in my inner museum: time never enters this gallery, whose pinups no one can alter or destroy.

· Divas and Their Dogs ·

A photograph of Rosa Ponselle with her pet dogs catapults me to camp heaven. I wonder why she poses with them. To thrill me? To prove she's down-to-earth? Or because the dogs are her cherished companions, and she wants to give her fans an accurate image of her life?

Rosa Ponselle with her pet dogs.

Divas cherish dogs because divas are aristocratic, interested in breeding; and dogs embody the unspeakable, panting, wet delight we take in the diva's voice. Mary Cushing describes listening to her beloved Olive Fremstad sing: "I would sit there in the dark auditorium with Mimi panting on my lap, dreamily wallowing in the delicious strangeness and excitement of this new world." That sentence's baffling syntax obscures exactly who (Mary or the dog?) is "dreamily wallowing."

The dog seems the diva's familiar, haunting her, providing her with forbidden, howling, magic vocal powers. Like Dracula in disguise, a dog mysteriously recurs in Mary Garden's life. Reminiscing about the horrid dogbite of her childhood, Garden symbolically alludes to other unspeakable violations—rape, incest: "my white silk dress was one mass of blood. . . . When I think what might have happened if that vicious brute had taken me just a bit lower down—at the throat. . . . He was jealous, you see, because he thought I was coming into my aunt's bed. I still carry the marks of his teeth." Years later, while Garden the grown-up diva is cutting a book's pages with a nail file, a dog jumps up and drives the sharp implement into her ear: "A small trickle of blood appeared, and I suddenly found myself deaf." This is the second time a dog has nearly ruined Garden's musical life.

Even when Galli-Curci initiates "her pet cat 'Dinorah' into the secrets of song life," the relationship of soprano to animal seems less a comment on the diva's pampered predilection for pets, than a way to make her seem demonic and hybrid (like the Catwoman), and to downgrade the fan's pleasure—to portray listening as animalistic. The diva is a stubborn species, fated to survive: the Darwinian logic that drives most diva prose associates diva pleasures with the "lower orders"—with darkness, undergrounds, persistence. The diva, dogged, may appear aristocratic, but she slobbers and howls. Blanche Marchesi describes a dramatic soprano voice in its early, undeveloped stage as "like a new-born Newfoundland dog, clumsy, heavy, shapeless; you can hardly believe that it will become manageable, beautiful and balanced, reaching easily the top notes and behaving like other voices." Blanche Marchesi may compare a dramatic soprano to a dog, but she disapproves of subjecting her pupils to the "dog's breath" exercise—making the young soprano pant as a dog does after running. The diva masks her heavy animality and learns to behave decently; when the diva develops her voice, she rises above her animal inheritance, as if a woman's career could recapitulate the evolution of the species.

Consider two stereotypes: gay men and poodles or other "effeminate" dogs (J. R. Ackerley's *My Dog Tulip* is the definitive story of gay men and dogs, though Tulip is a German shepherd); young girls and horses *(National Velvet),* an interest that precedes the love of boys. Are lesbians supposedly fond of dogs? What is the lesbian pet of choice? In *The Autobiography of Alice B. Toklas,* Gertrude Stein describes her own comic affinity with animals: "Gertrude Stein had always liked little pigs and she always said that in her old age she expected to wander up and down the hills of Assisi with a little black pig. She now wanders about the hills of the Ain with a large white dog and a small black one. . . ." The image of the dog persuades us that queer passions, the perversities of women who love women and men who love men, are bred into the blood, and are mute, domestic, and subhuman.

· Diva Gowns ·

I've never worn women's clothes—or just once, trick-or-treating as the Wicked Witch, at an embarrassingly late age. I made a convincing witch, but I didn't enjoy the plain serge skirt, the hat, the tacky blouse. Once, at a Christmas party, an acquaintance came as Elisabeth Schwarzkopf's Marschallin—an impeccable impersonation, except for the hairy chest. I admired his wig, his beauty spot, his gown.

Diva prose is more devoted to gowns than to timbre. A good gown gives the diva's possibly bestial voice an appropriate sheath, and masks the less acceptable meanings of the female voice—its ability to open us, expose us, renovate us; its inexorable independence and gall. Diva gowns don't assist heterosexual seduction; the gown's folds and follies speak to women and to gay men—or to men interested in women's clothes, if that is a population separate from gay men.

A good gown vindicates the diva by making her glamorous, and it inspires the queer fan by showing gender's dependence on costume. A woman is a woman and a man is a man but not entirely so; clothes give gender its social meanings.

When I heard Kathleen Battle sing a recital, she wore a stark strapless gown with a Grecian aspect (it looked like a Corinthian column) whose train took up half the stage, and the care required to maneuver that train was lush and unannounced, like an encore.

A gown confirms status, corroborates secret fantasies of self-worth. "At last I was dressed as befitted my talents!" comments Frances Alda on the experience of wearing her first gown. But for divas less privileged than Alda, the gown serves as camouflage and helps the diva pass as an aristocrat. Before an important Town Hall engagement, Marian Anderson broke her foot, and she had to wear a cast onstage. A reporter noted that the "flowing folds of her gleaming

Clara Butt in her "grape dress": a law unto herself.

white gown hid her cast-encased foot." Her foot was *caste*-encased; the gleaming gown whitened and elevated her caste.

The dress permits a spectacular display of pride and nerve: witness Jessye Norman's unembarrassed and opulent gowns. Gowns proved Clara Butt "a law unto herself." Butt gave one favorite dress a farewell party to commemorate the two hundredth time she wore it, and she was famous for her grape dress—embroidered with clusters of artificial grapes. Clara Butt of the grape dress was six feet two inches tall.

My fantasy: circumstances change, I become a diva and I must acquire a gown. I don't know how to walk like a diva or dress like a diva but because I'm already famous the salespeople bustle when I enter a shop in clouds of scent (I'm wearing Gardenia—the perfume named for Mary Garden) and say, "I have a big concert to give, please fit me for a gown"; I require endless adjustments, and I emerge with a huge ribbon-tied box, like Jean Harlow in *Red-Headed Woman*.

Diva gowns tell stories. Narratives arise from the seams and the turbans and the fine threads of many colors. Each part of the gown or the coiffure carries with it a period reference, a vanished code ("In the second part of the program appeared Galli-Curci, dressed in a spangled white gown, with hair a little curled, which gave an aspect of the Directoire epoch"). And gowns inspire doubt—a skepticism which fan Gordon M. Eby represses: "Surely no one who saw Miss Bori in the gorgeous red velvet and gold lace creation of her first act 'Traviata' or the striking white tulle garden dress with its voluminous skirt, garlands of flowers and ruffles and her large picture hat of the 1935 'Don Pasquale' revival will doubt her fastidious taste." The secret that the diva gown conceals is a lack of taste, or too much taste, taste grown grotesquely independent of its context.

One is not supposed to pay attention to what a diva wears. One is supposed to listen to the music. But divas themselves have adored the art of masquerade, even if it means upstaging the loftier pleasures of music and drama. Lucrezia Bori's favorite roles were Violetta and Manon because of their "costume possibilities." Frances Alda's moment of glory came when some queen told her: "I have never forgotten how beautifully you sang, and what a lovely dress you wore. . . . I remember I asked you who made it and you said Doucet. I will tell you now. I went round to Doucet next day and ordered one just like it." The queen imitates her subject: towards this kind of reversal, all queenliness of the drag or diva variety tends.

All I remember from a Janet Baker recital was her electric blue gown. All I remember of Hildegard Behrens's Tosca was her gown's noise: while she moved across the stage, her many skirts rustled, announcing the gown's autonomy as an object of desire, showing how to be graceful in the midst of possible shame.

The diva's fashion needs are the same for home and for stage. At home, Rosa Ponselle washes dishes in her *Traviata* costume ("altered for personal use"), her sleeves pinned back and "soap suds to her elbow." It makes a fan's pulse race, to imagine Ponselle doing dishes in her Violetta party gown: the image is silly (it shows Ponselle to be grandiose while pretending to be humble), and the image is uplifting. I wash dishes in blue jeans or in khaki shorts, but if the diva can alter opera for personal use, if she can bring opera into the home, maybe I can use diva mannerisms to help me endure the perplexities of private life.

· Divas at Home ·

Diva iconography erases the distinction between stage and home. In three publicity photographs of Joan Hammond—as Aida, as Tosca, and at home—she looks most at home as Tosca; in the "at home" shot, she is serious and unsmiling before a studio backdrop. What is homey about erasure?

The diva's home, a stage, is a shrine to herself; it teaches the fan that home should be grand as opera, that home is *not* a place in which one should tolerate diminishment. At home, as rendered in diva myths, the great lady expands, unwinds, and creates memorials to her own magnitude. The diva's home is not necessarily the location of repressive domesticity, or the bastion of traditional femininity and masculinity.

Rosa Ponselle, unmarried for most of her long retirement, had the privilege of luxuriously redefining "home" as a monument to her triumphs, her tastes, and her roles. In Villa Pace, she enjoyed a life "compatible with the grandeur of her fame and her personality." Her doorbell was inscribed with a phrase from her signature aria, "Pace, pace, mio Dio." Oddly, Rosa Ponselle captioned a photograph of herself standing stiffly at the head of a staircase at Villa Pace, "Informal portrait taken on my seventieth birthday." Hardly informal, she descends a stair as Katharine Hepburn in *Suddenly, Last Summer* comes down speaking in an elevator. Montgomery Clift (gay or bi?) waits downstairs for Hepburn's entrance, as, in this picture, the photogra-

Above: Joan Hammond as Aida
Top right: Joan Hammond at home
Right: Joan Hammond as Tosca

She looks most at home as Tosca.

pher waits downstairs for Miss Ponselle. The trip to the first floor is a stylized *condescension,* a descent from the upstairs of flux and private ruin, to the downstairs of command performance, display, and queenly composure.

Adelina Patti, whose husband called her "Ma Divine," abolished the distinction between home and stage by building a small theater at her Welsh castle so that she could perform for guests. She attempted a home *Traviata* with the butler as Alfredo. When indisposed, she silently crossed the stage in a flower-decked gondola while guests applauded. Here is a sample of dinner-table conversation chez Patti:

Guest One: "Is she not divine to-night?"

The trip to the first floor is a stylized *condescension,* a descent from the upstairs of flux and private ruin, to the downstairs of command performance, display, and queenly composure.

Guest Two: "Be quiet, there are no words to express her beauty."

Patti was not the only diva who transformed her home into a place of ritual and simulated royalty. Mlle. Desmâtins liked playing queens so much that in her own household she set up a throne.

In her retirement, Giuditta Pasta wore a dress that was "an extremely original medley of oddities." With her collage-dress, her assumption of motley, of gypsy eccentricity, her adoption of "fragment" as costume and vocation, she endured her silence.

· *Vocal Crisis* ·

The tendency of a diva's voice to break down makes queer people feel at home. Collapsing, the diva says, "I am discontinuous. I am vulnerable. I cannot bear the marytrdom of performance and exposure." In crisis the vocal organ calls attention to its schisms, narrates its own history, and reveals to the queer subject that voice or identity is always torn in half, broken, dispossessed. You own your voice only when you lose it. You find out who you are only when singing's ground has been taken away, and you are exposed to danger and decay. For he or she who is ruptured by the impossibilities and paradoxes of speaking as a queer person, vocal crisis offers one solacing outward sign that the condition has spread, has gone public.

Vocal crisis can be sudden, even instantaneous, like crib death. Of Leontyne Price we hear, "Suddenly the bejeweled voice had absented itself completely from the throat of the soprano who stood at the pinnacle of the operatic world."

Vocal crisis arises like an inward, physiological Fury, voice *contra* voice, the larynx punishing itself for its hubristic excess, its commitment to vertigo. According to Blanche Marchesi, fame caused the hysterical decline of Etelka Gerster: "Gerster cakes, Gerster hats, Gerster umbrellas were the fashion, and her success was so overwhelming that it began to tell on her highly strung nervous system." Marchesi is confident that a strained nervous system produces vocal disorder. For singers' breakdowns, she blames morning baths, poor training, or excesses of conduct: "if a person is of a violent temperament, or too gay, or allowed to shout since her childhood, or howl a song in a rumbling train in a tunnel," the voice will surely become diseased, and the symptoms will resemble the hysteric's aphasias and absences.

The diva is allowed to sing but not for too long; she is granted the power to soar in a phrase, but only under certain conditions; and when the voice breaks down, she shows us how beggared and partial the terms of her triumph have been. Vocal crisis is a form of communication. It tells us that opera is an art of interruption, rupture, and bodily danger. The singer in vocal crisis has been punished for sublimity. But vocal crisis is also the moment when the queer meanings of opera begin to speak—because at the moment of vulnerability and breakdown, the diva proves that seamless singing had been masquerade, and now her cracked, decayed, raucous, and undisguised self is coming out.

It is tempting to treat the diva's vocal crisis as a cautionary tale: "I should remain silent; after all, look what happened to Christine Nilsson." Or this discontinuity in a diva's vocal self makes rupture seem pleasant. Even if I want to sing, I may also wish to be silent. Even if I want to move melodiously through a phrase, I may also want to shriek it, tear it, ruin it. Diva vocal crisis is anarchic: it threatens the foundations of opera. And yet opera tantalizes us with the ever-present possibility of diva breakdown.

Certain post-*bel canto* operas are famed for ruining voices. It's plausible that voice-wrecking parts show the character to be in psychosexual crisis, and unsettle the distinction between the diva and her role; singing the part of a martyred, hysterical woman destroys, in turn, the diva's voice. Blanche Marchesi reports a voice doctor angrily telling Richard Strauss, "I have advised . . . all my lady singer clients, to stop singing your music until it shall be written for the human voice." The audience is excited by the danger that hysterical or extreme parts pose to the voice: opera requires the preservation of a singing instrument, and yet opera also explodes the boundaried, obedient self, moving listeners and performers away from respectability and toward rage, even if the throat is silenced by the travail of speaking out.

A broken voice has brought the self's private woe, the body's history and flaw, into the Olympian art of singing. A broken voice *exposes,* and what it exposes is a sadness (not gaiety) which may be the listener's.

Imagine the collapse of an operatic voice as a movement downward and the development of a voice as a movement upward. Imagine that there are only two directions in which a life may proceed—up and down—and imagine that desire may be only expressed or repressed. But this up/down axis tyrannizes sexuality: either straight or gay, either male or female, either passive or active, either virgin or initiated, either a masturbator or not, either frigid or hot. What if, instead, desire moved laterally through the body, and a voice or a career never went *down* or *up* but floated and meandered? Lillian Nordica confessed to Schumann-Heink, "I didn't sing well last night. I know it. . . . My great days are over, Ernestine, all over! I am going down, down, down —and you are going up and up and up." Nordica dies of pneumonia after being shipwrecked in Java, and her friend muses: "Poor Nordica, her time had come. And it was perhaps for her the best. She never could have endured the disappointment not to be still the great star."

Vocal crisis is a physiological emergency, a bodily catastrophe. A movie star's popularity may fade because of fashion changes, but divas fail for organic reasons, or because of seizures, accidents. After a horse-back fall whose effects would prove fatal, Maria Malibran put makeup over her bruises and sang four nights in a row. In a carriage crash, Anna Maria Crouch's dressing case, containing all her theatrical prop-erties, fell on her throat and nearly choked her. Thenceforth she had to transpose downward, and later she suffered "internal derangement." The iconography of vocal crisis connects internal derangement to vocal derangement; the diva who can't go on singing is insane. Mrs. Cath-erine Tofts, an early eighteenth-century diva, went mad and thought herself a queen. In "a remote part of her house" she wandered "in her fancied royalty," wearing her opera costume, singing "I was born of royal race, / Yet must wander in disgrace."

Eighteenth-century diva Francesca Cuzzoni lost her voice and ended up making buttons in Bologna. There are worse fates than button-making: but the spectacle of Cuzzoni's economic fall, her class descent, is meant to inspire pity and terror. The worst fates that Blanche Marchesi can imagine—and they will befall the girl with the misused voice—are singing light opera and serving as a lady's compan-ion.

Though the most elaborate myths of crisis involve the female voice, there is a famous tale of male vocal crisis: Jean de Reszke, so obsessed with his condition that he carried around a laryngoscope, regained his voice—lost for twenty years—on his deathbed. *"Enfin j'ai retrouvé ma voix!"* he cried, and spent his life's last three days in bed singing his old roles.

"Vocal crisis" means *a crisis in the voice,* but it also means *articulate crisis, crisis given voice.* Hardly an interruption of diva art, vocal crisis is the diva's self-lacerating announcement that interruption has been, all along, her subject and method. And in her interruption, I hear the imagined nature of homosexuality as a rip in meaning, in coherence, in cultural systems, in vocal consistency. Homosexuality isn't intrinsically an interruption; but society has characterized it as a break and a schism, and gay people, who are molded in the image of crisis and emergency, who are associated with "crisis" (Gay Men's Health Crisis), may begin to identify with crisis and to hear the interrupted voice as our echo.

· *Farewells and Comebacks* ·

At their farewell performances, divas sometimes speak. What they say is bland. But the sound of a diva speaking her own words breaks the operatic contract, and lets something unforeseen, queer, and embarrassing enter the ritualistic opera house. Emma Eames, after a *Tosca*, tells the Met audience, "I wish to tell you that this is the last time I shall sing for you." Saying farewell to Berlin, Jenny Lind says, "I thank you—never, in my whole life, shall I forget this!" Nellie Melba's adieu to her Covent Garden audience: "Goodbye is of all words the saddest, the most difficult to say." Olive Fremstad, at her farewell, told a sobbing audience, "I have never made a speech in all my life." When Geraldine Farrar said farewell as Zazà, the Met "dissolved in tears. You could hear the weeping rise in great waves and flood onto the stage." The Gerry-flappers were especially heartbroken: "With reddened eyes and swollen noses they snuffled and wept openly and unashamedly because the one they loved was no longer to lead them."

Margherita de l'Épine sang farewell concerts beginning the first year of her career (1692) and gave them for thirty-four years. Patti sang goodbye for twenty years. At a certain point her farewells gave fans the shock of *temps retrouvé,* mingled with the terror inspired by failed drag. Schumann-Heink describes the Grand Guignol of Patti in her last years: "I almost wish I hadn't seen her, because it was at the end of her career. Her singing days were then over, and when I saw her there she was at the breaking point. . . . The remnant of her greatness still clung about her. You could feel her triumphs, so to say, in her presence, which is always so with the great ones. . . . She was made up like a doll, with her hair bleached red."

To come back is to push against silence and ignominy, to move from seclusion and confinement into a wide open scornless space of total commitment, self-exposure, and risk. When Cuzzoni came back, she issued an advertisement before the performance, saying that only pressing money needs prompted her return. To come back and to come out are similar excursions. One fan imagined Henriette Sontag's comeback (alas, he couldn't obtain tickets) as the reappearance of a "prodigy of the stage, whose loud ovations had rung in my ears when a child, and who now, like a long-hidden treasure, was raised once more to the light to be seen, heard, and admired." The scenes the diva has wrapped around her, like a gown, are primal and irrecoverable. Any staging of desire involves the comeback sentiment, which Freud called "uncanny": the long-hidden treasure (a body part, a beloved) rises once more to consciousness. So when a desire first comes to mind, it is really a return: homosexuality, when it makes its first appearance, its debut in the mind and the flesh, is actually making a comeback.

When the diva returns for a special appearance she will not necessarily sing. These nonvocal comebacks are appealing because any silent person can imagine herself making such an appearance: no talent is required, only a conviction of one's singularity. Olive Fremstad is silent when she appears on the Met stage for the last time in 1933, a gala party for general director Gatti-Casazza: "Of course she did not sing, but as she swept graciously if none too firmly across the boards, which of old had known her wind-blown stride, the audience rose to her, though the greeting had a note of sadness, of infinite regret. The great days were gone beyond recall."

Rosa Ponselle made a comeback on records, seventeen years after her last operatic appearance; but she insisted that the session be held in her Villa Pace. Because she is making her comeback without leaving home, the event is paradoxical, unfathomable.

I scan the *Times* for news of comebacks. Leontyne Price is coming back! Elisabeth Söderström is singing another recital! Will Anna Moffo return? I skip the news of the up-and-coming divas—Aprile Millo, Barbara Hendricks. Instead, I haunt the comeback circuit. I want to know how the old-time divas are doing. I want to be present at their resurrections. Comebacks intangibly assist me: the familiar, long-absent diva opens her mouth, and a lost property, a lost capacity for mortification and catharsis, says, "I'm back."

· *Divaspeak* ·

Divas aren't afraid to praise themselves. Divas talk like Oscar Wilde. Or Oscar Wilde talked like a diva. The diva *turns* a phrase and reverses it—substitutes praise for blame, pride for chagrin, authority for vacillation, salesmanship for silence. I long to imitate this language, if only to inhabit, for a sentence or two, its sublime lack of respect for the truth.

Few dare conceive that the diva can't speak, though Giuseppina Grassini was called "heavy and dull in conversation."

Divaspeak is succinct, epigrammatic. How many words need I expend to vanquish you, to work my own will? Is it possible to condense my anger, make a flourish of my failure? Shirley Verrett remembers an early performance—her own—as Carmen: "It was marvelous —the body was lovely, and I had a lovely voice." Nellie Melba on Nellie Melba: "I am Melba. I shall sing when and where I like, and I shall sing in my own way." Melba's "I am Melba" is a tautology before which we must fall silent; we can offer no reply to Verrett's "the body was lovely"—her ability to handle her own body with the tongs of a definite article.

Mary Garden commands an incomparable divaspeak: "I began my career at $50 a month and ended it with $3,500 a night. I call that a lot of fun and adventure." The speaking diva achieves succinctness because the slope between beginning and end (early shame versus later fame) is so sheer.

Divaspeak, a language of vindication and self-defense, works only because we know the tale's moral. The diva is always right. And she assumes that we share her interpretation of the event. Blanche Marchesi cancels a performance, an understudy is called, but then Marchesi changes her mind and shows up anyway to find the understudy already there and expecting to sing—but Marchesi insists on singing (screw the understudy!): "Tell Mr. Simpson that I will be on the platform in due time, that there is no reason whatever why I should not sing, and that I absolutely refuse to enter even into any conversation about it, as I fail completely to understand what he means. I am engaged, I am here, and I will sing."

Divaspeak helps the diva steal the show and then, with a rhetorical question, assert that the show was her property all along. When, at a party, someone calls Donizetti's *La Favorite* "trashy," Adelaide Phillipps rushes to the piano, accompanies herself in one of the arias, and says, "Do you call that trashy?"

Divaspeak is the language of put-on (faked aristocracy, faked humility) but it utterly believes in the effectiveness of its gestures—or pretends to. Divas know many languages, and divas tour the world, so they rise above trivialities like nation or law, and blend different tongues into a comfortable, aristocratic, complacent Esperanto. "Un-be-*liev*-able!" repeatedly, slowly, and mirthlessly ejaculates Wilhelmenia Wiggins Fernandez in *Diva;* her English, against the film's French, expresses her alienation from the land and the culture in which she finds herself. The diva, like other international stars, is a stranger, a wanderer—free to assert a paternalistic fondness or disregard for entire continents. To a Russian admirer, Patti cries, "Ah, how I dote on Russia!" For Patti, countries are condensed into representative individuals, as the queen of France might once have been called simply "France." American diva Clara Louise Kellogg fumbles through foreign tongues to speak: to each role she claims to have brought "a clearer vision, a surer touch, a more flexible method, a finer (how shall I say it in English?) *attaque* is nearest what I mean." We are lucky she can only go so near her meaning, because she means attack.

Divaspeak is not limited to opera culture. It is a gay dialect. It resembles the techniques of "shade" and "reading" that Latino and African-American drag queens use (as documented in Jennie Livingston's film *Paris Is Burning*): a way of asserting power, preeminence, and invulnerability through language alone, of speaking strong though one is really weak.

Divaspeak is the ideal language for slap and sting and cut. No one can answer its assaults. Mathilde Marchesi said to her protégée Nellie Melba after her London debut, *"Ma chère* Nellie, how is it that you forgot the two notes in the Quartette?" The coy French phrase, *"ma chère,"* can't disguise the fact that Marchesi is a martinet. Use divaspeak and you can pretend to be wounded while remaining invulnerable to arrows. When a fan backstage told Olive Fremstad that after hearing her sing Sieglinde, he now understood Wagner, the diva retorted, "Isn't that nice, you are more fortunate than I who have given my whole life to the study and still know so little!" Fremstad conceals a bludgeon beneath her saintly sackcloth; she uses the fan's statement as a springboard for her own solo backstage cadenza of pique and retaliation.

Using divaspeak, Fremstad says of the role of Brunnhilde: "It is the end. Further one cannot go!" She means that is how far *she* went. She means that was *her* end.

Codes of extravagant female behavior have arisen around the diva: these mannerisms, collectively, are as famous and influential as any masterwork in the operatic repertory, and they transcend the borders of opera culture. Diva conduct, whether enacted by men or women, whether, indeed, we feel that diva conduct differentiates between men and women, has enormous power to dramatize the problematics of self-expression. One finds or invents an identity only by staging it, making fun of it, entertaining it, throwing it—as the ventriloquist throws the voice, wisecracks projected into a mannequin's mouth. Geraldine Farrar dared to tell Arturo Toscanini, "You forget, *maestro,* that *I* am the star." One need not be a star to relish Farrar's concise way of gathering a self, like rustling skirts, around her; he or she who will never become a diva, no matter how many social or vocal revolutions occur, may still wish to imitate Farrar, to say, "You forget, *maestro,* that *I* am the star." No single gesture, gown, or haughty glissando of self-promotion will change one's actual social position: one is fixed in a class, a race, a gender. But against such absolutes there arises a fervent belief in retaliatory self-invention; gay culture has perfected the art of mimicking a diva—of pretending, inside, to *be* divine—to help the stigmatized self imagine it is received, believed, and adored.

CHAPTER FOUR

The Callas Cult

Maria Callas, immortal, died on September 16, 1977. I've seen documentary footage of mourners sobbing outside her funeral: as the hearse drives away, disconsolate fans applaud the departing body and cheer "Brava Callas!"—grimly acknowledging that she will give no more performances, that she will never hear this applause, that she craved applause and died for lack of it. To mourn Maria Callas: there, cult happiness begins.

She was Callas long before she died, but she would be a little less Callas if she were still living. Untimely death assists her legend and connects her to themes that have shadowed gay culture: premature mortality, evanescence, solitude.

I never heard Callas perform in person. I am a post-Callas opera queen, looking back. I confess that during her life I knew of her only in the role of Aristotle Onassis's mistress. Even now, I don't have an exemplary collection of Callas recordings or a thorough command of Callas lore.

Listening to Callas posthumously, I feel like a necrophiliac: but haven't other gays fallen guiltily in love with departed matter? To be a dandy—a useless thing!—is to waste time and fortune; and the worshipper of Callas *is* a waste, going nowhere with his feelings.

Callas became an international star in the early 1950s, a time when gay people, though silent and secret, and seeking assimilation and acceptance rather than radical action, were developing a rich culture. Callas remains the operatic diva most closely (if only tacitly) associated with gay fandom. (Many Callas commentators are gay; virtually none consider gayness worth mentioning.) Though opera is an elite form, and though Callas's fans were usually at least middle-class, and usually white, her image circulated beyond opera culture's borders.

Worshipping Callas, am I behaving like a vulture? One critic who objects to the gay cult of Callas is Catherine Clément, who writes, in *Opera, or the Undoing of Women:* "Come on, men, shut up. You are living off her. Leave this woman alone, whose job it was to wear gracefully your repressed homosexual fantasies." Callas, an icon already circulating through culture, was not placed on the market at gay men's instigation. Worshipping her, I don't affect the woman sleeping inside the image's shell: my love can't harm dead Callas. And yet homophobic society wants me to abandon my fantasies. To demand that I renounce my veneration is to suggest the desirability of erasing what makes me gay. Gays are considered a dispensable population. Listening to Callas, we become less dispensable: we find a use, a reflection, an elevation.

Imagine that one has a soul or an interior. Imagine that one tries to name the sensations of exhaustion or elation buried there. I call my expansions "gay." (Is the word "gay" an armor, a disguise, a uniform: a trait of the moment, resonant today, useless tomorrow?) You may feel similar exaltations and not be gay, or may not choose to call yourself gay, or may not choose to connect your Callas adoration and your sexuality. But for political, ethical, combative, and ineluctable reasons, I consider my interest in Callas to be a piece of my sexual and cultural identity.

Here are a dozen attempts to explain the gay cult of Callas. But it's impossible to circumscribe love. As a commentator, one can only operate like a skylight at a premiere, advertising a location.

· *1* ·

Ask a gay man, a Callas nut, why he loves Callas, and he may say, "Because she's the best." We need to like the best. (Excuse the "we." I say "we" without knowing the group's contours. "We" are not all alike. I say "we" wishfully, hypothetically.) We have been considered the dregs, and so we have constructed hierarchies of taste in which—

sometimes against reason—we elevate certain stars to the summit. Because she recorded the soprano repertoire so exhaustively, because every historian and journalist knows she was her era's operatic divinity, and because everyone agrees she transformed the repertoire by reviving forgotten coherences of song and drama—for these reasons we're doing nothing exceptional by loving Callas. We pretend we like her for solely musical reasons. She's a safe object of adoration. She has snob appeal. She recorded for Angel. What opera lover doesn't recognize and revere Callas, despite querulous, catty reservations? And yet because of the flaws in her voice, the taste for Callas allows room for argument. To prove Callas's worth, a posthumous, dispersed claque emerges—a nation of solitudes.

It is marvelous to adore a queen so undisputed, so deserving; to contribute to a cultural phenomenon (the Callas revolution) that isn't a back room or a closet.

Luchino Visconti, in a photograph, kisses Callas's cheek, which makeup foundation has made unnaturally pale; Leonard Bernstein exclaims, "Callas? She was pure electricity." Visconti and Bernstein loved Callas not because they were gay but because she was a genius; it is easy and conventional to deny the link between a woman's artistry and a gay man's sympathetic rapture. Bernstein and Visconti would probably have rejected my reductive association of Callas fandom and gay identity. They loved Callas simply because she was sublime. But sublimity has particular currency in gay culture.

Greatness of Callas's sort requires reiteration. The comet is gone in a moment; someone needs to stand around afterward and praise it, recall it, verify it. Callas still needs promulgators. Even now, she seems to demand a jury—of gay men—to vote her Not Guilty.

· 2 ·

I worship her because she made mistakes, and because she seemed to value expressivity over loveliness. We don't believe in nature anymore, but Callas put forth the effect of nature as opposed to the appearance of order, and offered an acceptable, digestible anarchy, a set of sounds on the verge of chaos—but enjoyably so. Here lay the danger, the lure: she was a mess *and* she was a goddess.

Her voice gave evidence of long attempts to domesticate the unacceptable. Recording producer Walter Legge commented that in her muted middle range she sounded as if she were singing into a bottle.

(Sometimes in her middle range I feel I am traveling on a tour of her sinuses.) Enjoying Callas's muffled voice, one declared affinity with hidden things.

Her voice dramatically took advantage of the listener's assumption that the opera would go as planned. She ambushed. In Mexico City in 1950 she unfurled a high E-flat without warning, dominating tenor and chorus at the end of the Triumphal Scene in *Aida*. Though her mediocre costar, tenor Kurt Baum, was furious, the audience loved her unexpected domination. Classical music may seem to demand servility of its performers, but with her high E-flat, Callas stopped serving.

Callas's upper register wobbled—a "flap." With time, the flap grew less controlled. Commenting on a 1955 *Aida,* John Ardoin points out her "flapping high C through which the Egyptian army could have marched." Too much wobbling may sound indecent, schizoid, but to Callas's fans, the indecency was endurable and gratifying. Lapses made her a sympathetic figure, a vocal underdog. Some notes, pressed too hard, turned to steel; and when we heard the steel we sympathized with her plight. The steel and the wobble announced a predicament; we loved the mistakes because they seemed autobiographical, because without mediation or guile they wrote a naked heart's wound. And if her notes had a tendency to wobble, to grow harsh, then this possibility of failure gave her fans a function. The infallible performance does not require an audience.

Callas's unattractive sounds forced her audience to reevaluate the difference between the beautiful and the grotesque, and spoke to gays, who have often made use, as spectators and creators, of the gothic. From homophobic culture's point of view, a gay person's soul is a haunted house full of moldering antechambers and dead-end staircases. Can a gay interior be lovely? Or is it, at best, plush?

With peerless technique (I'd call it a form of insouciance if it weren't so intensely willed) she hid her flaws, and curbed her unconventional, through-a-glass-darkly timbre. In her Paris 1961 rendition of Thomas's "Je suis Titania," she holds an awkward high note for its full value, even though the tone is unpleasant; she outstares the ugliness, dares it to ruin her good time. In her 1957 *Manon Lescaut* or in her 1964 *Tosca,* she prepares for the ambiguous high notes with such control of phrase and rhythm and portamento and pitch and attack, that we acquiesce, and forgive, and imagine that the note's wretched aspects are a mirror, reflecting the greedy demands *we* make of the

Like her idol Audrey Hepburn, Callas embodied a Wildean stylization of manner and gesture, as if the depths were dull and lethal and it were salutary to hover on the surface.

singer, and asking us: "How would *you* manage such a note?"

During the harsh high note, we are closer to Callas. We befriend her. Through error, she seems to implore: "Art is punishment, and I am vulnerable. Have you ever been exposed, opened up in public? Find parallels in your life to this almost unacceptable note that will make the audience hiss."

· *3* ·

We love Callas because she revised her body. In three years she dropped from 210 pounds to 144, and changed from ugly duckling to glamour queen. Bodies can't always be altered, but Callas's self-revision, like a sex change, makes us believe in the power of wish.

Careers with gay followings often have moments of rupture and reinvention: moments when the star's body or persona radically shifts, and proves the former self to have been a fabrication. The gay fan, schooled in the gap between public manner and private feeling, may identify less with Callas's newfound glamour than with her former plainness; or he may identify with the rift between the two. Callas revised her image twice: when she lost weight, and when she lost her voice. Her body was a liability she had the power to revise; her voice was a virtue she lacked the power to retain. (Even when Callas had a voice, she seemed to be losing it: and so a gay interpretation of Callas's career was always, from the start, possible.)

We know and adore the difference between the queen's two bodies: plump awkward Callas in Athens before her fame; slimmed Callas with dyed blonde hair, for the Visconti production of *Vestale*; Callas in Egyptian drag—dressed as Queen Hatshepsut—at the 1957 Waldorf Astoria Imperial Ball. Callas in fancy dress was one of the marvels of the 1950s, for, like her idol Audrey Hepburn, she embodied a Wildean stylization of manner and gesture, as if the depths were dull and lethal and it were salutary to hover on the surface. The typical Hepburn plot traced her transit from pixie quirkiness to obvious beauty: in *Sabrina, Funny Face,* or *My Fair Lady,* no one knows that Hepburn is a knockout until a couturier gets hold of her. But while Hepburn seemed born to be beautiful, Callas had an effortful, wounded relationship to her glamour. What she couldn't wear when she was fat, she wore with spite when she was thin. And she did not make neat distinctions between art and costume. "I want my art to be the most perfect," she wrote to her husband; "I also want what I wear to be the nicest that exists." At her loveliest, she looks vindictive: she will make people pay for their former indifference.

Her operatic performances seemed real; her real life seemed operatic. Since Oscar Wilde, this confusion between mask and truth has been a cornerstone of gay culture. Even in private life (if we call "private" the studied scenes of Callas at the airport, at Maxim's, at dressmaker Madame Biki's), she painted her eyes in the Medea style: long kohl lines, like a latter-day Cleopatra. The excessive eyeliner proved that she was in charge of her image, that her face was a tablet on which she wrote her life, and that femininity was a lot of work. The labor's reward? Saying "I told you so" to a cruel world. Callas's radical weight loss, and her stylized approach to matters of dress and makeup, gave poignance to her life's plot: she seemed, despite her fame and wealth, a victim of the gender system.

Callas's "Audrey Hepburn" persona—the perfectly groomed society lady—was particularly camp when seen against her feud with her mother, Evangelia Callas, who wrote a scandalous exposé entitled *My Daughter Maria Callas*. (Evangelia's own excesses are exposed in *Sisters,* the confessions of Jackie Callas, Maria's sister.) Mrs. Callas publicized her work as jewelry saleswoman at the shop of Jolie Gabor (mother of Zsa Zsa and Eva) to humiliate Maria for refusing to send money. Maria wrote to her mother: "Don't come to us with your troubles. I had to work for my money, and you are young enough to work, too. If you can't make enough money to live on, you can jump out of the window or drown yourself." No ordinary gal, Callas had the effrontery to break with her mother *and* dress up.

Queen Callas emerged from the chrysalis of the dumpy diva; another fabled trajectory was rootless, nationless Maria turning into a Greek woman profoundly identified with her homeland. Her apotheosis was singing Norma at Epidaurus; some say her voice had a quintessentially Greek timbre. As a Greek, Callas was an outsider to La Scala, Covent Garden, the Paris Opéra, the Met—turfs she conquered: the outsider who enters a field and vanquishes all opposition is an appealing figure, and not only to gays. Born Maria Anna Cecilia Sophia Kalogeropoulos, Maria Callas was imagined to hide an authentic and exotic Greek nature, which explained her notorious romance with Aristotle Onassis, and which gave her the status of a goddess, just as her overweight and impoverished beginnings emphasized a "realness"—a stigma, a wound—beneath the jet-set splendor.

· *4* ·

We love Callas because she disciplined her voice. The realm of discipline is itself a part of gay culture: weight lifters, S/M—pageants of control and self-mastery. Callas cleaned up her voice with excruciating and exhilarating thoroughness, and disciplined her phrases as severely as she disciplined her servants. She gave her staff an authoritarian list of house rules: "When you are summoned by us, you will come immediately, and always perfectly dressed"; "One will never say no to what has been asked, and no more of that 'Yes, sir' 'Yes, ma'am' nonsense"; "Everyone, including the housekeeper, will wash and iron their own garments, especially intimate items." At home and on stage, Callas commanded.

Callas was a trouper, a perfectionist: on time to rehearsals, willing to sing an aria again and again to get it right. Musical exactitude justified her caprices, and proved to her detractors that she behaved strictly, without excess or indulgence. She spoke fondly of doing vocal exercises, and of various mentors. Of Tullio Serafin, she said, "I'm afraid he's the last of those kind of maestri." She loves the word "maestri" and the notion of mastery. When Callas gives every damned pitch in a difficult run from *Lucia* or *Norma* (another singer would not be so thorough and clean), or when she reminds my listening ear that there is a vast difference between eighth notes and triplets, or between half steps and whole steps, her precision makes my mouth gape, and tells me how callused her feet must be from walking without shoes this far up the hill to magnificence.

Maria Callas, like Joan Crawford's Mildred Pierce, was a model of the career woman who succeeds only because she is viciously ambitious and because she has given up her capacities to be a good daughter and a good mother. One can enjoy the self-lashing aspects of Callas's career, however, and jettison the underlying antifeminist moral, by taking Maria Callas as proof that roles can be reversed, that destinies can be chosen (whether or not it is actually possible to alter the material conditions underlying our fates). The story of Callas, a fable, makes us believe in the power of individual fantasy. Similarly, we imagine that *choosing to be gay,* even at the cost of martyrdom, is a cataclysmic act, capable of transforming private destinies and public systems.

Callas swore by these axioms: *Study the words of an opera, and you will understand how to color the note or shape the phrase. Give each note its proper value and weight, and you will reveal the score's internal mysteries.* Each musical moment stamped with Callas-the-perfectionist simultaneously thrills us by its sublimity ("Thank God I am alive to hear this phrase from the *Barbiere* sung so accurately") and by its masochism ("She sacrificed so much to achieve this perfection, and may I, by God's grace, learn to find ennobling uses for my inborn or acquired masochisms").

We love her for intruding, via magisterial discipline, such a range of mannerisms—a control of how a phrase might always, every moment, *mean* something. This control made her an avatar of speakability, of the ability to say painful and illuminating truths and to shroud those truths in a medium that leaves its messages shadowy and subliminal. Music conceals the arguments it sinuously advances. We consider music to be merely expressive. But when "expressivity" happens, something particular is usually being expressed.

Sometimes her singing sounds like weeping. The suffering seems to arise from the discipline of music-making, and the discipline of woman-making.

· 5 ·

She's irretrievable and so I want to retrieve her. She departed before the world could surround her with sufficient adulation. Evanescence and transience: modern gay literatures are obsessed with the desire to be immortal and to press against the moment's confines. Gay figurehead Blanche DuBois mooned, "Don't you just love these long rainy afternoons in New Orleans when an hour isn't just an hour— but a little piece of eternity dropped into your hands . . . ?"

Callas sang in the era of *Sunset Boulevard:* in legend, she became a Norma Desmond, unable to bear very much reality, dreaming of impossible comebacks. After the affair with Onassis began, she had a vocal crisis, retired, and then returned to the stage. She collapsed at the Paris Opéra after the third act of *Norma*; she sang one more *Tosca* in London, and then she never sang an opera again. She returned to the recording studio; the results were too ambiguous for release. She taught master classes in 1971 and 1972 at Juilliard. I love the picture of Callas at Juilliard in black pants-suit and dour reading-glasses because I love to see a divinity become practical and serve a function: I

Most of the time the room is closed off to knowledge and to memory.

love to see majesty drop to earth in no-nonsense black, majesty in need of glasses, majesty in the fashions of 1971, which were flattering to no one. She returned to the stage with di Stefano in 1973–74 for a world tour of duo recitals: a voice in ruins, say witnesses. The has-been inhabits a mythical neighborhood. I am not a has-been. I am, like most fans, a never-been. Has-beens and never-beens have much in common. And so I visited the Avenue Georges Mandel, in Paris, where Callas lived, isolated, before her death; I wanted to experience that neighborhood of silence. I wanted to verify the photograph I've stared at so long: an often reprinted shot of Callas opening or shutting the curtains of a spacious window that looks like it never lets in light, an image of a soul shut into a role and not knowing the way out. Zeffirelli's movie of *La Traviata,* an elegy, an homage to Callas, a memorial to her vanished voice, shows us Violetta's apartment, first, from the outside. We see Violetta's window; it is just like Callas's! That aloof window is the sign of a grandeur and a sickness—a consumption—forever closed. Think of the spaces shut to us. Think of the rooms—our rooms —we have never named. Voice is a room: it opens, for an instant, in a great operatic career. But most of the time the room is closed off to knowledge and to memory.

On the cover of Callas's reissued recordings are photographs of the singer after retirement, to underscore the tragedy of the woman who outlived her voice. She smiles, radiant in simple outfits and pearl earrings—but we know better. We know she is miserable. We know the record within the sleeve contains the trace of her past; Callas and her legendary voice have parted company. Gay people have compensated for silence by enjoying the ironic or tragic transformation of power into pathos. We relish falls. Sublimity turns into degradation, and our interest quickens—not because we are sadistic sickos but because we like to see reputations, or the very idea of "reputation," decompose.

· 6 ·

When we value Callas for creating a revolution in operatic performance practice, for singing neglected Bellini and Donizetti operas as if they were tragic vehicles of undiminished power, we are valuing her for opening up the opera box, the closed space of a genre that never seemed to let us in or to let our meanings out. And yet, ironically, her revitalizations of dismissed *bel canto* operas only emphasized opera's moribund nature.

Innovators like Peter Sellars highlight opera's anachronism, and turn opera's liability into an expressive strength. Anachronism was one aspect of opera that long ago opened it to gay appropriation; opera seemed campy and therefore available to gay audiences only when it had become an outdated art form, sung in foreign languages, with confused, implausible plots. Opera's apparent distance from contemporary life made it a refuge for gays, who were creations of modern sexual systems, and yet whom society could not acknowledge or accommodate. Opera is not very real. But gayness has never been admitted into the precincts of reality. And so gays may seek out art that does not respect the genuine.

Superficially, Maria Callas took away opera's campiness by making it believable and vivid. And yet by importing truth into opera, an art of the false, she gave the gay fan a dissonance to match his own. Bestowing verisimilitude on Lucia or Norma or Elvira, Callas perforated the operagoer's complacency; her voice and her presence, arsenals of *depth,* when brought to bear on music that had become *superficial,* upset the audience's sense of perspective. Though it seems sacrilegious to call Callas's musically compelling creations *camp,* she performed the same kind of reversal that camp induces: she shattered the codes that separate dead from living works of art. To crosscut rapidly between yesterday and today is an effect that, in different circumstances, we recognize as camp. Callas "camped" *Lucia* not by mocking it (*Lucia* is too easy to mock) but by taking it seriously. Resuscitating *Lucia,* Callas challenged our belief that history's movement is linear, that there is a difference between past and present, and that modern reality is real.

· 7 ·

We love her because she incarnated vocal multiplicity and heterogeneity. She had three voices: chest tones like a contralto, an inconsistent, cloudy, yet beautiful middle register, and a piercing top that was fleet in coloratura but often metallic. One colleague said that Callas had three hundred voices. Callas, a chameleon, stepped in and out of registers like quick costume changes.

But she was often criticized for the multiplicity. She couldn't cross over the bridge between voices and then make the bridge vanish. We often heard the bridge; and so her voice seemed a Cubist painting composed of angles not organized into easily interpretable wholes— an eye, a nose, a brow.

Like *The Three Faces of Eve,* Callas's vocal split-personality affliction was a timely image of what society believed to be woman's intrinsically various and Circean nature. And gay men could identify with this vision of fractured woman: Callas's divided voice seemed to mirror the queer soul's incoherences.

Callas became famous for singing *Die Walküre* and *I Puritani* three days apart at Teatro La Fenice, and for taking only a week to learn *Puritani.* In one throat, she reconciled two vocal types—the dramatic soprano and the coloratura lyric. Even her rival Renata Tebaldi admitted the pleasurable shock of hearing Callas's heavy voice in the light repertoire. Callas's assumption of *bel canto* roles, after establishing credentials as a dramatic soprano, was an affront to fixed vocal categories and to the gendered distinctions built into them. Commentators describe Callas as a reincarnation of a kind of singer that flourished in opera's golden age—a singer who could span all ranges and styles. We admire Callas for exceeding and giving the lie to modern measurements. No note she sings remains the same; she changes voice *inside* the note, as if to say: "Try to catch me, to name me, to confine me in your brutalizing classifications!"

Every body is a civil war. Callas sang the war.

Most singers of Callas's caliber hide the register break. Callas couldn't. The naked break shows her to be, though a genius, a bit of a freak—delightfully self-embarrassing, unable to control herself in this tiny matter on which *bel canto* art depends. The break between registers is the moment when the voice proves itself to be of two minds. Compare her 1953 *Lucia* and her 1959 *Lucia:* although her tone is darker in the 1959 version, her register break is tranquilized, and so she travels up and down without disgrace—a subdued Callas, a Callas about to quit.

Callas took in breath dramatically, audibly, as if she were gasping. She turned the need to breathe into an expressive opportunity. But the gasp also revealed the cost of music-making: phrases need to come from somewhere in the body—some lode, undiscovered, where power sleeps. The gasp is the price tag on the expensive garment of the aria.

Words like "gay" or "queer" are crude, and Callas would not have approved of them. But I imagine she would have approved of this task: revealing the abjection and the sadness that lie buried in listening.

· *8* ·

I adore Callas because she so frequently expresses fury—a wrath that is its own reward and its own argument, that seeks no external justification, that makes no claim beyond the pleasure of drive, of emotion, of expressing *why I have been wronged*. A tribunal, she doesn't just express what *she* feels, but expresses what the *universe* should feel about her predicament. Every great Callas phrase of jealousy and fury becomes a command: "Universe, listen! Universe, obey! Universe, assume my point of view!" And we have visual images for her voice's tendency to radiate anger: think of Callas as Medea or Tosca, holding the knife, her eyes shooting sparks, her painted mouth a line-drawing of rage—as in the "tigress" photo taken backstage in Chicago when process servers tried to hand her a summons.

But sometimes she sings like an innocent. John Ardoin calls this sound her "little girl" voice. She mutes the tone, makes it reedy and demure, holds back power. She uses this restrained voice to impersonate virgins like Amina, or to mark the difference, in a role like Butterfly or Lucia, between schoolgirl piety and murderous maturity. Pretending to be innocent, she portrays, instead, her detachment from naïve states. This coy voice sets in relief the rage she more frequently and convincingly expresses. (Sometimes the "little girl" voice doesn't convey innocence, but a spectral emptiness.)

Gay men may identify with demonstrations of female wrath and willfulness because such behavior so wholeheartedly exceeds the bounds of acceptable gender behavior; displays of masculine power are alienating and depressing (they reflect patriarchy's sway), but displays of feminine power show the universe executing an about-face. Her vengeful volleys give us courage, and inspire us as we struggle to be open and not closed, serene and not erased, human and not degenerate.

I feast on her walkouts, her cancellations, or the scandals emanating from these outbursts, which have nothing to do with music, but which seem to emerge from her vocalism, her sudden flashes of chest tone, her searing, firecracker diction—the rolled "r" and the pugnacious dental and the narrow, nasal, oblong vowel: these terrifying effects denote revenge, murder, and the realm of *wish*, pushed to pathetic yet enviable extremes.

She fought impresarios and conductors—a feud with Serafin because he recorded *Traviata* with another soprano, Antonietta Stella; battles with Rudolf Bing; the Edinburgh cancellation; the time she threatened to brain a hostile impresario with a bronze inkstand and then—her husband said she weighed over two hundred pounds—forcefully drew her knee into the offender's stomach. But the most famous disobedience was the Rome walkout. Although ill, Callas was persuaded to sing a scheduled gala performance of *Norma*; the Rome Opera had hired no cover, and Italy's president was in the audience. Callas sang the first act, but was in poor voice. When she refused to go on for the second act, management begged her at least to speak her lines. Adamant, she left the theater through an underpass, like the Phantom of the Opera: "Scandale!"

One can purchase a pirate recording of that failed first act (I've withstood the temptation): I imagine that the record circulates primarily among gay fans who love, as I do, the aura of a woman who walks out of the closet of her role, defies the president, and places her throat's health over an opera house's rules.

About the furor, Callas later said, with her inimitable, blinkered rhetoric of self-defense: "There was a lawsuit. We fought twice, and I won twice. I had deceived nobody. I never do. I am a very simple woman, and I am a very moral woman. I do not mean that I claim to be a 'good' woman, as the word is: that is for others to judge; but I am a moral woman in that I see clearly what is right and wrong for me, and I do not confuse them or evade them."

Adoring Callas, I am admiring breakdown, resistance, walkout, flight, and feud.

· *9* ·

Because of the Tebaldi-Callas feud, choosing Callas isn't a neutral or pacific experience. It means taking sides, and shutting down the faculties of sympathy and softness.

Callas called Tebaldi her "dear colleague and friend," but Renata, unable to match the breadth of Maria's repertoire, finally left "the Scala." "Rivals I have not," claimed Callas. Eventually the two women embraced backstage after a 1968 Tebaldi opening-night Met performance of *Adriana Lecouvreur* (Maria had already retired).

Even on records, Callas seems to require devotion, not toleration; to enjoy Callas, one must renounce Tebaldi's virtues, and adopt Callas as a cause-for-life. Though Callas often piously thanked God for her good fortune, as if God cared about Callas's career, her fan must forswear decency and embrace the pleasure of partisanship; the Callas claque is an underworld order, like a revolutionary cadre, the Communist Party, or the Mattachine Society.

Fetishist that I am, I focus my shame on the word "Callas." I'm embarrassed to say the name as she and her crowd said it—the huge A, CAH-LAAAS, neither syllable emphasized at the cost of the other, the two syllables distinct from any others in the world. Saying "Callas" fills my mouth with fruity sensation. "Callas," an odd, invented name, is a telling near-anagram of Pablo *Casals,* cellist who nobly refused to play in Spain after Franco came to power, and who performed at the Kennedy White House. Casals represented the interpreter as a saint; Callas, too, was a kind of saint, but a rearranged one. Turn the word "Callas" inside out: fans at La Scala cheering "Callas, Callas, Callas, Callas" found their chant turning into "sCalla sCalla sCalla sCalla," as if Callas were the container as well as the object contained.

Deciding to love Callas, you fall into a category: the Callas fan. It's a sweet, drowsy membership: I can stare all day at the photograph of Callas in offstage life wearing a veil and white gloves and pearls, her ineffably sad eyes elongated by makeup, her ears large, her mien arrogant and refined, her regal brutishness distinct from her musicianship, which was a matter of gift, work, intelligence. . . . Built into the love of Callas is a fear of not doing her justice, never doing her justice; the attempt to account for the love of Callas is a sham and a transgression.

· *10* ·

All divas, when they sing, when they emerge from apprenticeship into the spotlight, come out: but Callas came out vocally, with unique flamboyance, at a time when coming out was nearly impossible for queers. Even within operatic singing's straitjacket (Callas used the word "straitjacketing" to describe the first stage of studying a new role —that phase when she learned the notes exactly as they were written), she appeared always to be exposing a secret shame and a corresponding power. She was celebrated for tailoring phrases in an opera to suit a specific extramusical situation—for aiming a death-threat line at the box of La Scala's impresario, Antonio Ghiringhelli, or giving a rendition of Medea in Dallas with a fury that seemed directed at Rudolf Bing, who had just cancelled her Met contract.

Her uniquely emotive singing style parallels the Method acting that was fashionable in 1950s North American cinema (Brando, Dean, Clift, Monroe). Method acting is a style of the closet and of the closet's collapse: the actor brings private, undisclosable woes to bear on the part. And yet the strain and effort in Method performances— the seething and stammering and stumbling—prove the sturdiness of the walls locking in the not-yet-spoken self. The performer needs to grunt and moan and cry in order to break through the policed border between private and public. Callas makes us sick of camouflage. After hearing Callas, who could tolerate the closet? And yet the evidence of Callas's broken spirit makes us nostalgic for the closet. Maybe, for a moment, we want to step back in.

· 11 ·

It is easy to see why Callas appeals to the drag queen in me, because Callas in motion (I rely on the evidence of films) is a sinuous, studied spectacle that one could forever simulate but never match: long arms, hands gliding slowly toward the shoulders to acknowledge thunderous applause, large nose and archaic eyes, hair usually piled in a voluminous chignon but sometimes loose and sometimes flat as Hepburn's Left Bank bob in *Funny Face,* each different hairdo transforming Callas's features so it's hard to know precisely what she looks like. I don't want to steal, imitate, or distort Callas's gestures. But I notice them, and I feel noticed *by* them; her greedy manipulation of physical space draws me into fuller life, even if, on the day of her funeral, September 20, 1977, I was marking my nineteenth birthday, and had never heard Maria Callas, whose voice and image would posthumously drape tapestries over me.

Her speaking voice was odd; she always seemed to be setting the record straight, or proving herself to be oblique as a Modigliani, simulating behaviors she couldn't pass off as genuine. Her English was affected, and full of non sequiturs. In an interview, she said: "Every time a taxi driver recognizes me it astonishes me. It irritates me. You know, I don't go out very much. I don't put myself on exhibit. I live in seclusion. I am wild. Very."

Only the banality of an exceptional person, like Callas, has the power to induce in the observer that dizzy pleasurable sensation of identification which is my subject here. Rilke wanted the angels to answer him. He knew they wouldn't. Every modern sad soul wants an answer from the void; Callas is one figure to whom some gay men have recently looked for reciprocation and confirmation. Confirmation of what? Life's grimness, and the power of expressivity to alleviate the grimness, or to give the illusion of succor.

Late in her short life, she begged Tito Gobbi to take her out for an ice cream. She imagined that the world had abandoned her. The epigraph to Charles Ludlam's *Galas:* "Only my dogs will not betray me."

· *12* ·

In a photograph, Visconti wraps his arms tightly around Callas and kisses her on the cheek—it looks to be a firm, authentic kiss—and she smiles, flattered and gratified to be kissed; Zeffirelli, doughy and devoted, kisses Callas, and she smiles radiantly, knowing the limits of the kiss; Bernstein holds Callas's hands and studies her, and they seem to be playing a seesaw game, figuring out whether their bodies are equivalent; gaunt and shirtless, Pasolini directs Callas as Medea, and she is attentive, obediently holding her hands to her face. These photographs attest to a specific historic configuration: the gay man venerating the theatrical woman and the woman responding gaily, the woman imitating the gay man and the gay man imitating the woman, the gay man directing and then listening and admiring, the man and woman collaborating.

Poring over Callas, I'm like Manuel Puig's Molina, the gay window-dresser in *Kiss of the Spider Woman,* who sustains his cellmate and himself in prison by reciting the plots of movies. One of the movies he recites is Nazi propaganda. But Molina doesn't understand the film's sinister ideology. He thinks it is a wonderful romance. His love for stars blinds him to political emergencies.

Of course I feel guilty for my imaginary romance with Callas's voice. But I don't know who is harmed by the worship. Certainly not Callas. Are you harmed? I imagine that you harbor similar attachments, that you, too, send your love to a vague, aloof star in the cultural firmament, a radiance that will never reward you with a glance, though you have spent your life in patient, earnest, fruitless attendance.

Visconti said of Callas that she was "a monstrous phenomenon.

Callas
and Visconti

Pasolini and Callas

The woman imitating the gay man
and the gay man imitating the woman.

Almost a sickness—the kind of actress that has passed for all time." Is Callas, within gay culture, the embodiment of "homosexuality" as the monstrosity we are and abhor and adore? No, Callas was not a sickness. Callas was a refuge, where a forbidden sexuality, a forbidden alienation from masculinity, could spread its wings. Listening to Callas, I acquire spaciousness. If consciousness, as determined by gender and sexuality, has certain limits, a voice like Callas's has the power to turn the mind's closed room into an immensity: she bestows the illusion that the view continues endlessly on the other side of the mirror, and that wherever you expected to confront limits, instead you find continuations.

I have been speaking about gayness as if I knew what it meant. I don't. It is a mirage.

Gayness isn't my rock-bottom nature. Rather, I listen *for* and *toward* gayness: I approach it, as one approaches a vanishing point, or as one tries to match a pitch that is fading into a vast silence.

Walter Legge, who produced many of Callas's legendary recordings, once peered inside her mouth and remarked that it was shaped like a Gothic cathedral. In imagination I am staring into Callas's mouth to see her upper palate's high spires—like far Christminster to Thomas Hardy's Jude, who gazes at the horizon but will never reach the imaginary city that gleams there.

CHAPTER FIVE

The Queen's Throat: Or, How to Sing

· Embarrassment ·

I started listening to opera because the convulsive vibrato of a trained voice embarrassed me. It filled me with an uncanny discomfort that I now call pleasure. But in those dim days I didn't call it pleasure. I didn't try to imitate Carmen, Don José, or Escamillo. I didn't try to fill the room with magnificent sound. Instead, I wallowed in embarrassment; I cringed; and I silently vowed, "In shame I will find paradise."

· Imagining the Interior ·

I can't sing. If I could sing I would not be writing this. I would not envy the singer's self-possession. Nor would I need to imagine the interior of the singer's body: throat, glottis, resonators, mask. The singer's face is called a mask, as if a voice were never capable of telling the truth.

Singers, be warned: I am not accurately describing your experience. My task is more pedestrian. I am recounting myths and stories, culled from forgotten manuals. The search started at a book barn: I found a rain-warped copy of Millie Ryan's *What Every Singer Should Know,* and though the author warns that "singing is an art which cannot be taught from book or correspondence," I tried to learn it, and have failed, and am secretly glad to have failed, for if I'd succeeded in demystifying voice, I would have no god left.

In Western metaphysics, the spoken or sung word has more authority than the written word. Voice accords presence—a myth that remains compelling, even though we are supposed to know better: we believe that no one can steal a voice, that no two voices are exactly alike, that finding a voice will set a body free, and that anyone can sing. This conviction that having a voice means having an identity is a cultural myth, just as sex is human nature but also a myth.

The physiology of opera singing is a set of metaphors; when we hear an opera, we are listening not only to the libretto and to the music, but to a story about the body, and the story of a journey: the voyage of "voice," traveling out from hiddenness into the world. This fable, so ingrained we do not remark it, is also the story of sexuality. Just as breath surges out through the voice box into the ambient air, so our unmarked, unformed soul loses its imaginary innocence and becomes branded for life with a gender and a sexuality.

We are unaccustomed to thinking of voice as a discourse located in history. But voice uplifts and degrades us as forcibly as sexuality does. Voice is a system equal to sexuality—as punishing, as pleasure-giving; as elective, as ineluctable.

By operatic singing, I mean the classically trained voice. It is remote from speech; it is dexterous; it strives to be strict in pitch and to obey the letter of the law; it projects; it forbids flaw. I can't give a definition of the operatic voice that will encompass Monteverdi and Wagner, lieder and oratorio, Bach and Berg. But you recognize an operatic voice. Deanna Durbin had it. Tito Gobbi had it. Conchita Supervia had it. The sophomore down the street practicing for a glee-club audition with embarrassingly sterling vocalise wants to have it. The operatic voice pretends to be polite but is secretly stressed, huge, exorbitant: it sings its training: it exclaims, "A price has been paid." You may think the operatic voice sounds like a parrot or a locomotive or a windup toy or good taste or piety or cowardice or obedience: traits we don't appreciate. Or you may agree that the operatic voice is the furious "I"-affirming blast of a body that refuses dilution or compromise.

This blast, this operatic voice, is the sound of nineteenth-century sexuality. Of all the varieties of sexuality, homosexuality is arguably the most tainted by taxonomy, and is thus the most perverse and the most "sexual"; homosexuality is one of the few survivors of that fantastic penumbra of perversions that no one takes seriously anymore, such as fetishist, exhibitionist, and nymphomaniac. (Heterosexuality, too, is a category, though we often think it transcends classification.) Theories of how to produce a singing voice obliquely allude to "homosexuality"—term of travel, exoticism, charnel house, Sodom, Times Square, pathology, cure. Even if you're not queer, you live next door to homosexuality and can't prove that your property-line stops short of HOMO, syllables I sing repeatedly and truculently to exorcise their aura of taint: homohomohomo.

· *Throat* ·

The throat, for gay men, is a problem and a joy: it is the zone of fellatio. Not everyone chooses fellatio: gayness doesn't depend on oral sex, and straightness includes it. But sexuality, as a symbolic system of checks and balances, measures and countermeasures, has chosen the throat as a place where gay men come into their own.

The opera queen's throat is inactive and silent while he listens; the singer's throat is queen. But the act of intense, grounded listening blows to pieces the myth that we can know precisely where an emotion or an experience begins. I am not a singer, but I have a throat, and I am using it to worship and to eat opera, to ask questions of opera so that opera might eat me.

You listen to an operatic voice or you sing with operatic tone production and thereby your throat participates in that larger, historical throat, the Ur-throat, the queen's throat, the throat-in-the-sky, the throat-in-the-mind, the voice box beneath the voice box. Homosexuality is a way of singing. I can't *be* gay, I can only *sing* it, disperse it. I can't knock on its door and demand entrance because it is not a place or a fixed location. Instead, it is a million intersections—or it is a dividing line, a membrane, like the throat, that separates the body's breathing interior from the chaotic external world.

The singer and the homosexual each appear to be a closed-off cabinet of urges. But the body that sings and the body that calls itself homosexual are not as sealed as we think. Nor are they as free. They are looseleaf rulebooks, filled with scrap-pages of inherited prohibitions: page after page of pain.

· *Manuals* ·

About voice, I only know what I have read: a few bizarre books, mostly from the nineteenth and twentieth centuries, written to teach the art of singing. These guidebooks codify and control the voice, and imagine it as friend and as enemy, as soul's ground and as trapdoor into netherworlds.

Like conduct books, voice manuals are full of social history. They intend to spread "culture," to civilize, and to protect secret skills from vanishing. Do the manuals have musical legitimacy? Lilli Lehmann and Enrico Caruso wrote manuals; so did a renowned castrato, Piero Francesco Tosi, in 1723. And yet I don't trust these texts to recount what actually happens inside a singer.

Like tracts against masturbation, singing manuals dictate how energy and pleasure should move through the body; they are eager to legislate conduct and to condemn mistakes; they help me imagine the voice box as a sorrowing, peculiar human capability that wants to be free and paradoxically seeks its liberation in an art of confinement.

Like many literary texts (novels of sentiment, eroticism, suspense), a voice manual exhorts and shapes the body of its reader. And the voice manual cares most about the nonsinger, the amateur, the onlooker. What gifted singer truly needs to read *How to Sing*? Only the loser turns to textbooks. Voice manuals address the aspirant who will never become a singer, and who requires a field guide to the unobtainable.

· *Singing v. Speaking* ·

Opera emphasizes the gap between speaking and singing. Is there a physiological difference? Some manuals say that singing is just intensified speaking; but diva Maria Jeritza warned, "So many girls do not seem to realize that the speaking voice is actually the enemy of the singing voice." (Jeritza warns only the girls, but I assume that the boys should take note, too.)

If you speak a secret, you lose it; it becomes public. But if you sing the secret, you magically manage to keep it private, for singing is a barricade of codes.

· *Coming Out* ·

Good singing consists in opening the throat's door so the secret goods can come out. Enrico Caruso insists that "the throat is the door through which the voice must pass," and that the door must be left open lest the breath seek other channels—morally dubious detours. Many writers insist that the passageway to the human voice's resonance rooms be left open, as if singing were mostly a matter of sincerity and the willingness to confess. The throat's door must be kept open, but no one is allowed to guess that such a door exists. Know too much about the throat, and you'll fall silent.

Queers have placed trust in coming out, a process of vocalization. Coming out, we define voice as openness, self-knowledge, clarity. And yet mystery does not end when coming out begins.

· *Bel Canto, the Castrato, and the Laryngoscope* ·

In 1854, singer-teacher Manuel Garcia II (brother to divas Maria Malibran and Pauline Viardot) invented the laryngoscope. Garcia was not utterly a pioneer in this matter. In the eighteenth century, scientist Antoine Ferrein had discovered the *cordes vocales* by experimenting on a cadaver's larynx. But intrepid Garcia experimented on himself. Seeking the cause of his cracked voice, he assembled a contraption, involving a dentist's mirror, and peered into his throat to see his glottis.

With my imaginary laryngoscope, with my mirror, I am looking into the queer throat to inspect the damage.

The laryngoscope's influence may have been limited, but its invention coincided with the rise of scientific vocal methods, and the fall of the castrato, who, by 1800, had begun to disappear. (In eighteenth-century Italy, up to four thousand boys a year were castrated.) With the castrato's demise, however, came a vague fear that vocal art was declining. These fears of decadence were given a name: *bel canto*. *Bel canto* means, literally, beautiful singing; and it also implies a foreboding that beauty is in decline.

According to musicologist Philip A. Duey, the term *bel canto* acquired currency only after the era it describes had ended. The phrase itself had been loosely used for centuries, but it found its present, fixed meaning in the 1860s in Italy, and was taken up by other countries in the 1880s; these significances only entered dictionaries after 1900.

So it appears that *bel canto* (as a discourse of nostalgia and retrospection) emerged in the 1860s. Another term was coined in the 1860s—in 1869, to be exact: "homosexual." Imagine for a moment that this is not a coincidence, and consider that *bel canto* and homosexuality might be parallel. Homosexuality and *bel canto* are not the same thing, but they had related contexts: they came wrapped in languages of control and cure. There were voice manuals long before *bel canto* and homosexuality were conceptualized; but the desire to describe the voice scientifically and to cure degeneracies of vocal art grew vehement after 1860, and produced a torrent of advice literature in the 1890s and early 1900s, including Julius Eduard Meyer's *A Treatise on the Origin of a Destructive Element in the Female Voice as Viewed from the Register Standpoint* (1895), Clara Kathleen Rogers's *My Voice and I* (1910), Charles Emerson's *Psycho-vox* (1915), and Nellie Melba's *Melba Method* (1926). Manuals of this period provide the theory and practice of "voice culture"—training and liberating the natural voice.

Observe voice culture's affinity with psychoanalysis. Both systems believe in expressing hidden material, confessing secrets. And both discourses take castration seriously: voice culture wants to recapture the castrato's scandalous vocal plenitude, while psychoanalysis imagines castration as identity's foundation—star player in the psyche's interminable opera.

Opera culture has always fantasized about a lost golden age of singing; accordingly, a central ambition of the voice manual is to preserve *cantabile* style against degeneration and newfangled vices. Francesco Lamperti in 1864 wrote that "it is a sad but undeniable truth that singing is to be found today in a deplorable state of decadence." (A century before, the castrato Tosi considered opera to be a decline from the "manly" church style into a "theatrical effeminate Manner.") Voice culturists long for lost days of glory, but none dares to say, "I want the castrato back!"

· *Looking into the Voice Box* ·

It is difficult to avoid noticing that the spookily genderless voice box has been clothed with a feminine aura. And it is difficult to know what to do with this information.

One major reason voice has been marked as feminine is that the

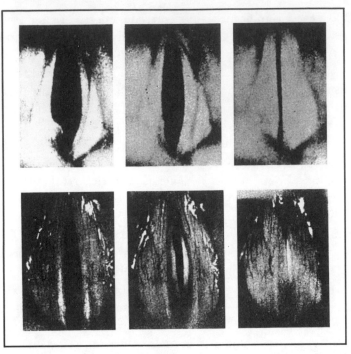

"If only I could see the glottis!"

organs of its production are hidden from view. A 1909 manual observes that the male instructor "has to teach an instrument which cannot be seen except by an expert, and cannot be touched at any time."

"If only I could see the glottis!" Manuel Garcia reportedly exclaimed, on the verge of inventing the laryngoscope. Modern scientific photographs of the singing larynx and glottis show us what Garcia might have seen: a lipped opening. Voice commentators describe the larynx as labial—based on visual analogy, and on the association between women and invisible things.

Jean Blanchet, in 1756, called the glottis "a horizontal cleft terminated by two lips." Robert Lawrence Weer, in 1948, called the vocal cords "two thick membranes," "two lips," "little shutters." But these are descriptions from outside. From inside, how does the voice box feel? Soprano Maria Jeritza compared stressful singing to "a strong rubber band being stretched out full length": divine Jeritza, thank you for precisely describing the approach to orgasm.

Though voice has been described as a duplicate of the vagina, the wily larynx can embody male and female characteristics, or neither. Some voice manuals make the larynx seem a vestige of an extinct, versatile, genderless species. In 1739, Johann Mattheson described the glottis as a "tonguelet" shaped like the "mouth of a little watering can." Other voice manual writers describe the epiglottis as an ivy leaf, or imagine the glottis surrounded by "ring-shield" and "shield-pyramid" muscles that can stretch or slacken, as if the glottis or the epiglottis (who can keep track of the difference?) were elaborate alternatives to our dreary genitals, genitals so slimy with story, so padlocked into history, that they will offer us freedom only if we rewrite them from scratch.

· *Punishing the Throat* ·

Voice culture loves, protects, and preserves the throat, but also scapegoats the insurgent throat for saying no to genital tyranny.

In the name of art, Greek tragedians slashed the backs of their throats to promote vocal projection. Diva Florence Easton commented in the 1920s that "you cannot make an omelet without breaking eggs" and you cannot make grand opera without "breaking voices." Opera pretends to dislike the broken voice but symbolically depends on it. Research into teaching the mute to speak (tuning-fork tests done on Helen Keller) illuminated the phonation and laryngeal movements of opera singers.

In lieu of injury, the singer's head and throat must vanish. Emmy Destinn said, in the 1920s, "When I sing I feel as if I have no throat." The female singer photographed in Millie Ryan's 1910 treatise, *What Every Singer Should Know,* has learned her lesson, for she has neither throat nor head: the picture stops at the neck, her head crudely cut off —as if the pose were compromising, and decapitation ensured anonymity. Without a head, she seems pure ground, deprived of mind and transcendence. As a cure for nervousness, the vocalist is encouraged to stand before an open window every morning, to take deep breaths, and to fondle her breasts and rib cage: she reminds me of Freud's Dora, a nervous case indeed, a girl whose sexual desires wandered out of control, toward women, toward the throat, and so Freud tried to shove her desires back down to the vagina, for he assumed that the vagina was the location of straightness and that movements away from heterosexuality were movements away from the genitals.

THE BREATH

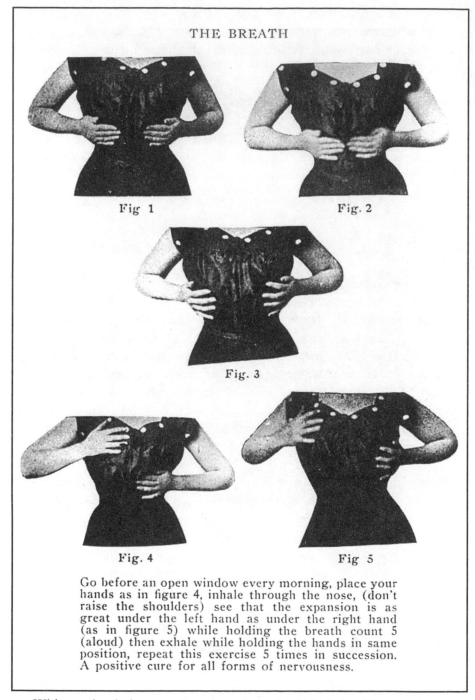

Fig. 1

Fig. 2

Fig. 3

Fig. 4

Fig. 5

Go before an open window every morning, place your hands as in figure 4, inhale through the nose, (don't raise the shoulders) see that the expansion is as great under the left hand as under the right hand (as in figure 5) while holding the breath count 5 (aloud) then exhale while holding the hands in same position, repeat this exercise 5 times in succession. A positive cure for all forms of nervousness.

Without a head, she seems pure ground, deprived of mind and transcendence.

Everyone understands that genitals are mythologized, but no one mentions the doctrines clustered in our throats, in our methods of singing and speaking. We lack a vocabulary for what the throat knows and suffers—perhaps because the throat is loath to speak about itself.

From the manuals, I learn that the singing throat is feminine, that it tends to wander and break, and that it has the mercurial ability to avoid gender. And so, despite my lack of a singing voice, I identify with the throat. I love to call it home, to skip the genitals for an hour and inhabit instead the moist vocal space between my mouth and lungs.

· *Mouth* ·

Recently I heard Jessye Norman live in recital. I sat in the front row. I looked into her open mouth and marveled at its self-disclosure, its size, its fearless capacity to open.

In a battered old voice manual, Herbert Witherspoon describes the mouth as a sexual organ, alive with easily excited "erective tissue," an organism containing "almost countless nerves": hence, "there is small wonder that things can go wrong very easily." Singing is *always* going wrong.

Is it unnatural to open the mouth? Composer Jules Massenet told soprano Alice Verlet, in a rehearsal of his *Manon*, "You have the ideal singer's mouth; it opens naturally!" But the mouth must not open too wide. Sir Charles Santley says that for the lips to "fulfil their office," the mouth "ought not to open more than sufficient to introduce the tip of a finger"—not even up to the knuckle. What severe regulation! Isaac Nathan in 1823 suggests that the "pretty mouths" of singers should "distend wide enough to admit a friend." The friend is not a penis but a finger: open the mouth wide enough so that "one can comfortably bring the little finger" between the teeth, writes Johann Adam Hiller in 1774. Other instruments—a spoon, a Popsicle stick—can take the finger's place. Lawrence Weer remembers his first lesson on "tongue control"; he was instructed to hold his tongue flat with a spoon while singing scales. The singer's open mouth grasps an imaginary object—sucks it, surrounds it. The object the singer sucks is space, air, blankness, hope: the cushioning condition for sound.

Voice has been described as feminine; but it is equally true that voice evades categorization. A singer wanders; a singer deviates. A voice begins in the body's basement, a zone that no one dares to name or authorize; and the singer sends the voice (or the voice sends the singer) to an *elsewhere*, a place outside of our knowledge, a verge I won't sketch or legislate except to say that I want to live there. Singing is a movement that never coalesces long enough for us to hold it. As soon as we can remark the moment of singing, it is gone.

Voice silently avoids the categories we bring to it. Voice is willing to be thrown, to disguise its source, to hurl itself out of sex-and-gender and onto the sands of a neutral, signless shore.

· *Finding the Falsetto* ·

Falsetto seems profoundly perverse: a freakish sideshow: the place where voice goes wrong. And yet falsetto obeys the paradigm of all voice production. Falsetto is a detour, and singing always imposes detours upon a blank and neutral surge of air.

Sing falsetto, now. (Are you alone as you read this?) Fill the room with a clear feigned sound, and ask yourself what act you have committed. Then produce the sound naturally, from the chest. Which of the two tones, chest or head, do you want your neighbors to overhear?

Singing is a matter of potential embarrassments. And falsetto is among the greatest of singing shames. Using falsetto, you perform an act deemed unnatural. But nobody is unnatural around the clock; a moonlighter, I am unnatural for an hour at night but the rest of the time I am natural. Pretend, for the moment, that homosexuality, like falsetto, is not an identity but a useful pleasure with a bad reputation: pretend it is a technique, a sideline, a way to outwit a taxing vocal situation.

Codified voice production has never been happy with the falsetto: sound of mystery, unnaturalness, absence. Isaac Nathan in 1823 called it the *fourth voice* (fourth dimension, fourth sex): "it is a species of ventriloquism . . . an inward and suppressed quality of tone, that conveys the illusion of being heard at a distance." Antoine Bailleux, in 1760, warns that a voice must emerge straight from the chest "lest in passing into the head or into the nose it degenerate into falsetto by its muffledness." No one dares to claim the falsetto, to say about that high, fine, exacerbated sound, "This is mine!"

The falsetto is part of the history of effeminacy—a compelling saga yet to be written. Long before anyone knew what a homosexual was, entire cultures knew to mock men who sang unconventionally high. Plutarch disparaged "effeminate musical tattling, mere sound without substance"; John of Salisbury discouraged "womanish affectations in the mincing of notes and sentences"; St. Raynard insisted that "it becomes men to sing with a masculine voice, and not in a feminine manner, with tinkling, or as is popularly said, with false voices to imitate theatrical wantonness." In the 1880s, after homosexuality's birth, a British physician described falsetto as a technique in which the two vocal cords push against each other "at their hinder part with such force as to stop each other's movement"; while chest tones emerge from the "natural aperture of the larynx," falsetto tones come through "an artificially diminished orifice, the chink becoming gradually smaller until there is nothing left to vibrate." Falsetto, bad news for civilization, is the decline and fall.

Though falsetto was scapegoated, and associated with degeneracy, detour, and artifice, it has long represented a resource: the castrato Tosi speaks of the feigned voice as something "of Use," particularly when it is disguised by art. If a modern voice culturist like Franklin D. Lawson in 1944 saw falsetto as a danger, causing a "white," "blatant," and "effeminate" sound in the adult male, and a "colorless, whistling hoot" in the female, the castrato Tosi considered it a treasure to be discovered by a knowing master: "Many masters put their Scholars to sing the *Contr'Alto*, not knowing how to help them to the *Falsetto*, or to avoid the Trouble of finding it." A sound at once false and useful, it may bring praise or condemnation to the singer who relies on it.

Falsetto is not a sin; the sin is breaking into it undisguisedly. Consistent falsetto, like expert drag, can give the illusion of truth. In 1782, when one "sopranist"—an uncastrated male who sang falsetto —broke accidentally into his real and robust tenor voice, Johann Samuel Petri observed that "my entire pleasure in his lovely soprano voice was utterly destroyed": a "loathsome harsh" note had interrupted the vocal masquerade, reminding listeners that the singer was a *he*.

I have always feared the falsetto: voice of the bogeyman, voice of the unregenerate fag; voice of horror and loss and castration; floating voice, vanishing voice. With a grimace I remember freak pop singer Tiny Tim tiptoeing through the tulips with his ukelele.

· *Puberty* ·

Puberty's onset: does it ruin or secure the voice? Does it destroy your life, or is it the moment your life begins?

Castration freezes the boy-voice before puberty can wreck it. But even for the uncastrated, puberty represents a moment of reckoning. When puberty hit, Caruso almost committed suicide (a headmaster wanted to profit from his prepubescent warblings); but he was rescued by a kindly baritone, who helped him place his voice. In puberty, the *real* erupts: acne, adam's apple, sperm, breasts, blood.

Diva Ernestine Schumann-Heink warns girls to postpone study until after their "physical development" is complete, and Isaac Nathan cautions males not to sing during "mutation." Only after puberty can a singer place the voice, discover where chest voice ends and head voice begins; only then can the singer balance the irreconcilable symbolic values of head and chest. The master must watch out for puberty's arrival in the student's body, and must teach the apprentice how to let the voice "pass" from one sexually allusive region into another.

Puberty can kill the choirboy's voice; but in most cases, singing begins after puberty, and so puberty casts its gruesome, enchanted shadow over all subsequent vocalizations.

· *The Registers* ·

Are registers a fact of nature, or a figment of voice culture? (It is not clear whether a register represents a zone of opportunity or of prohibition.) Some manuals say there are five registers, or one, or none. Some say men have two registers, and women three—or that each singable note is its own register.

There seem to be three bodily zones in which resonance occurs: chest, throat, and head. As the pitch ascends, the voice rises from one register to the next. The farther from the chest, the higher and falser the tone becomes, and the more one must take care to sing naturally. According to Domenico Cerone in 1613, "the chest voice is the one that is most proper and natural."

The break between registers—fancifully called "il ponticello" (the little bridge)—is the place within one voice where the split between male and female occurs. The failure to disguise this gendered break is fatal to the art of "natural" voice production. The singer schooled in *bel canto* will avoid eruptions by disguising the register breaks and passing smoothly over them. The register line, like the color line, the gender line, or the hetero/homo line, can be crossed only if the transgressor pretends that no journey has taken place. By coming out, gays provoke seismic shudders in the System-of-the-Line, just as, by revealing the register break, a singer exposes the fault lines inside a body that pretends to be only masculine or only feminine. (Or, by coming out, do we inadvertently reaffirm the divided world?)

· *Degenerate Singing* ·

Forgetting its dependence on the feigned, voice culture overvalues the "natural." Most theorists of voice would agree with William James Henderson, who wrote in 1906 that "singing is nothing more than nature under high cultivation." As long as singing is considered natural, however, some vocal techniques will be deemed degenerate; and "degeneration" was the rhetoric used in the nineteenth century to create the "homosexual" as a pathological identity.

Homosexual-as-degenerate: I embrace and impersonate the degrading image because there is no way out of stereotype except to absorb it, to critique it by ironically assuming its vestments. I'm already clothed with the mantle of degeneration; I can't refuse it. So I say: Degenerate, c'est moi.

A. A. Pattou's *The Voice as an Instrument* (1878) offers scientific methods to remove "the defects of an unnatural voice." An opponent of slurring, Pattou strives to reform the throat, manage the larynx, and eradicate "all the faults or vices to which the human voice is subject." He even includes his own case history: ignorant of hygiene, he sang wrongly and suffered an inflammation of the throat, leading to "mental depression and general distrust of society and all its belongings." Sir Charles Santley's voice manual, too, ends with a confession: his throat grew inflamed from singing in rooms decked with imported flowers (including the homoerotic hyacinth).

Degeneration discourse in the nineteenth century was also anti-Semitic and racist. Early, I swallowed anti-Semitism: no wonder that embarrassment flooded me when I first heard operatic plenitudes of sound. I dreaded the cantor's cry; I dreaded the expressivity of Jews, who seemed to open their bodies outward—scapegoats, hysterics, talking and talking. I remember the bad manners of the children in Hebrew school, and my fear of seeming like them. (The teacher told one garrulous, slavering, attractive brat that he had "diarrhea of the mouth.") Did I believe, as a child, that opera was a Jewish art, and that I, enjoying opera, might be coming into my own Jewishness—inherited, incurable, punishable?

Avoid excessive vibrato. Mozart criticizes a singer's vibrato as "contrary to nature." Antivibrato sentiment reached a peak in the nineteenth century (but so did vibrato itself); American laryngologist Holbrook Curtis observed in 1909 that vibrato is popular among the "Latin races," though frowned on by the Anglo-Saxons. I am not Latin but I am Jewish and I love to hear a note wobble out of control, shake and tremble until it seems our days of trim repose are at an end. . . . The trill, too, has been considered against nature or at least effeminate: voice culturist Francis Charles Maria de Rialp believes that though the trill was "very much in vogue" among nineteenth-century male singers, it should be confined to the female voice. Any affectation in singing is liable to be criticized as a symptom of degeneracy: Isaac Nathan warns in 1823 against lisping, drawling, or mouthing words so that "the singer appears dropping to the earth from the exertion."

Avoid unattractive gestures. According to Lilli Lehmann, "faces that are forever grinning or showing fish mouths are disgusting and wrong." You know the fish mouth. Singers look like freaks unless they control themselves, and this possibility of looking grotesque is immensely appealing if you choose (as I am choosing) to embrace rather than to reject a stereotypical freakishness. Many manuals recommend singing in front of a mirror to ward off fish mouth. Castrati were required to gaze in the mirror for one hour each morning while practicing; Tosi tells the singer that mirror practice will help him avoid convulsive grimacing. The singer staring in the mirror, practicing for a career, occupies a dubious, unsanctioned, pathologized position: the narcissist.

I knew Jewishness from looking in the mirror and from family sayings. I knew homosexuality from signs no mirror could catch. And yet I practiced for homosexuality as I would have practiced for a recital: slowly I memorized the notes. And I remember looking in the bathroom full-length mirror and wondering if my body was an optical illusion.

· *Some Speculations on Voice as Economy* ·

The categories "psyche" and "voice" do not simply record what naturally happens; they persuasively prescribe what *should* happen. The most important assumption about voice is that it moves upward, hydraulically, transcendentally. Like libido, voice wants out.

Voice aims to purify and to transcend; homosexuality is the dirt that singing, a detergent, must scour. In this sense, voice and homosexuality are adversaries: voice is evolutionary, homosexuality is devolutionary; voice is transcendent, homosexuality is grounded.

In its expenditures of breath, the singing body is either frugal or wasteful. Voice passes through a body as a toxin does, purgatively; to judge a voice's quality, we must ask, "Have all the poisons been flushed out?" Because voice is an essence, too fervid for storage, that escapes through whatever doors are open, falsetto is breath that took the wrong exit out of the body.

But we do wrong to place all the blame on falsetto. For there is something inherently suspicious about breath's movement from lungs to larynx to mask, something always digressive and errant about air's urge to exit the body. Though falsetto has the clearest links to homosexuality, all varieties of operatic voice are perverse. Within the logic of singing, air beguiled to a variant destination is as perverse as air that proceeds to the proper gate. Resonation *is* perversion.

Like bloodletting, singing is a drastic cure that restores internal equilibrium. John Gothard, in his *Thoughts on Singing; with Hints on the Elements of Effect and the Cultivation of Taste* (1848), opens with a case history of a neurasthenic man, afflicted with "continual sighing," who was cured by befriending young men who indulged in glee-singing. With equal optimism, Millie Ryan attests that "there is no tonic for the *nerves* equal to voice culture." Singing keeps the body, the psyche, and the moral apparatus in shape. Before training, the singer is tense, tight; afterwards, the singer unwinds.

But the unwinding is formulaic; the gestures of a singer are canned, and they are delectable because they are so easily imitated. Yvette Guilbert, in *How to Sing a Song,* offers guidelines for how to strike poses, and she includes photographs of her own face in dramatic, comic, and pathetic attitudes that look like Hugh Welch Diamond's photographs of Victorian madwomen: she labels her various expressions Ecstasy, Neutral Amiability, Moral Pain, Serenity, Gray, Red, Purple, and Vermillion. If I imitate Guilbert and make my face Serene, Gray, or Neutrally Amiable, will I have introduced new desires, or will I have restaged the old ones? Maybe old desires, when mimicked, become new: maybe there are no new desires, and all we can do is imaginatively and wittily reinhabit the old ones.

The voice manuals hardly encourage self-invention. On the contrary, they staple the singer into family morality: in 1839, H. W. Day writes that "singing has a refining effect on the moral feelings," and Lowell Mason, in 1847, comments that singing produces "social order and happiness in a family." A good voice originates in a childhood environment free from strain, in a family where the "natural voice" is habitually used, and where there is opportunity to hear good music. (I heard good music. But I never learned how to use the natural voice. I wonder if the natural voice is a repressive fiction, meant to keep us in line.) When a voice sings sweetly and successfully, it repeats the salutary childhood scenes that fostered it, and when it moves awkwardly between registers, or sings out of tune, it exposes a cloudy, unnatural past.

Like any conduct book, whether for Renaissance courtier or modern teenager, the singing manual instructs how to secure class position, how to "shun low and disreputable company," and how to indicate refinement. Discharging sound, voice turns desire into money. And singing bodies are prized for moving up: up the staff, up the social ladder. High notes are expensive: according to Benedetto Marcello in 1720, the higher a castrato ascends, "the greater is his price and reputation."

For the singer, wealth begins in stinting and in avoiding waste: and so the singer who wants to acquire vocal gold must learn to budget, and must learn, like a thrifty housekeeper or bookkeeper, the "correct management or the mis-management of the vibratory column of air" passing from vocal cords into mouth. The singer, according to Johann Mattheson in 1739, must let out the inhaled air "not at once nor too liberally, but sparingly, little by little, being careful to hold it back and save it." Caruso tells the singer to observe a similar economy over the career's whole length: the singer should limit the voice's output "as he does the expenses of his purse."

SERENITY

THE PRESENTIMENT OF DANGER

MORAL PAIN

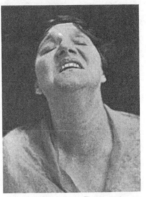

PHYSICAL PAIN

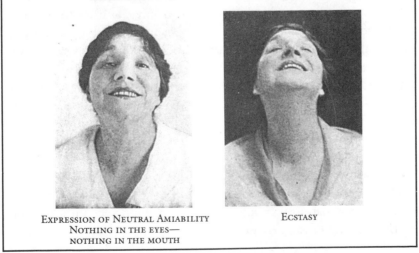

EXPRESSION OF NEUTRAL AMIABILITY
NOTHING IN THE EYES—
NOTHING IN THE MOUTH

ECSTASY

If I imitate Guilbert and make my face Serene, Gray, or Neutrally Amiable, will I have introduced new desires, or will I have restaged the old ones?

Save money, save air: prudences of homosexuality, prudences of voice. Homosexuality and voice are economies of spending, concerned with what might go wrong or what has already gone wrong, eager to manage the flow of vital stuff. The body called "homosexual" is one place where the sexual system sputters, digresses, leaks; where an error in bookkeeping (a wasted sum) comes to light; where housekeeping fails. Because Freud influentially asserted the connection between paranoia, homosexuality, and anality, we often assume that when homosexuality isn't an erotics of wasteful, promiscuous spending, it is, conversely, an erotics of cautious, retentive budgeting.

In a singer's training, the conduct of the entire body—not merely the voice—is subject to punitive budgeting. Singing requires purity from top to bottom. Pedagogues have long recommended sexual abstinence and dietary moderation: Aristotle's *Problemata* asks, "Why does it spoil the voice to shout after food?" In the twentieth century, Millie Ryan recommends dried prunes for vocal health; Herbert Witherspoon encourages the use of cathartics, and warns that "the mucous membrane of the pharynx and mouth is a 'tell-tale' of no mean value, and will often show clearly the troubles existing below." A voice announces whether the body's waste system is functioning. Of course, voice not only describes the system, but turns the system into sensations and sounds that we imbibe without guile and without analysis. We quiver as we hear a voice, and what we are hearing and learning to love is a theory of the body. I, who can't carry a tune, am caught within this economy of vocal production as surely as if I were a singer.

"Red lines denote vocal sensations of soprano and tenor singers," writes Lilli Lehmann in *How to Sing*. Look at Lehmann's diagram of the singer: a ghoul, a skeleton, a survivor, shorn of identity's specifics. Without hair, without skin, without history, Lilli Lehmann's anatomy lesson looks like the self before categories—the subject, waiting to be named. (Is this singer male or female? Does it matter, if tenors and sopranos, according to Lehmann, feel the same sensations?) Lehmann's shorn singer is a dreary model for self-invention; but I will take it for my own. A force emanates from the singer's mouth—an "I" as elastic, transparent, and continuous as the soap bubble that the youth in the Chardin painting has been blowing for centuries, a bubble that no viewer can ever puncture.

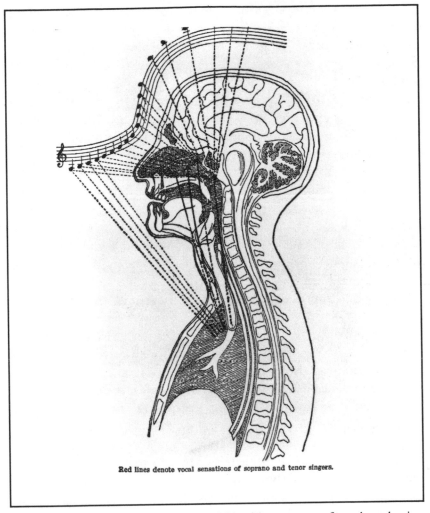

Red lines denote vocal sensations of soprano and tenor singers.

I, who can't carry a tune, am caught within this economy of vocal production as surely as if I were a singer.

· *Regretful Coda #1* ·

I wanted pleasure to suffuse this chapter. And yet the manuals rarely speak of pleasure. Rapture seems to have no more place in a voice manual than in a guide to auto repair.

It is a pleasure to sing, but it is also a discipline; it is sexy to be homosexual, but it is also a confinement (within an illicit identity). Free expression is a fiction: when I express a self I am pressing it out by force, as in *espresso*. Voice and homosexuality are industries that express what no body, left to its own devices, would care to produce. But bodies are never left to their own devices. And so my body produces homosexuality—sings it, expresses it. I don't have any choice. Homosexuality is the specific music my body makes. In retrospect I authorize the grand opera called "homosexuality," I forgive its dissonances and its outdated sentimental conclusions, I let the fantastic arias (The Sodomy Cabaletta, The Degeneration Cavatina, The Oral Scene, The Passive/Active Duet) purl uninhibitedly out of my mouth. Culture has called "homosexuality" the dirty X. The word we won't say. The word we mark in blood on doors. The sign of excommunication. The no-name of the outsider. In response, in retaliation, in revolt, I embrace the X; I plug my body into X; I ply X like a trade or a faith; I discover the beautiful, hardly audible overtones of X, which the world thought was a nightmare. I am X, I will always be X, the world can't rid me of X, the world can't rip X out of my body, I will write X wherever X has been erased.

Every unauthorized sexuality is an X. Hetero can be an X, too, if it tries.

Sexuality, whether homo or hetero, does not arrive only once, in that moment of revelation and proclamation that we call "coming out." Our body is always coming out. Every time is the first time. Every performance is a debut. Every arousal is a repetition of the first arousal. Every time you speak, you are coming out. Every time air makes the trip upstairs from lungs to larynx to mask, every time your body plays that old transcendental number, you are coming out. You *are* the OUT into which sexuality comes. Coming out is a way of telling a coherent story about one's sexuality, and it has worked political wonders, and it is a morally and psychologically cleansing process. But coming out is only one version of the vocalization underlying sexuality itself.

I have chosen to be vocal about sexuality (though many parts of sexuality—including my own—remain silent, inexpressible, resistant to category and phrase). And yet even if I didn't choose to be vocal about sexuality, even if I didn't come out, I'd already be vocalizing, for sexuality (as we know it) is always vocal, is ineluctably vocal, is structurally vocal.

Do we sing our sexualities, or do our sexualities sing us? Do we send sex out like tone into the air, or does sex send *us* into the air, propel *us* into repetitions and travesties we call "desire"?

Breath's excursion through the body to produce a voice is hardly a pleasure trip. These are slow, brutal, ardent processes, so arduous and so similar that I will put their names on separate, parallel lines:

training a voice;

voicing a sexuality.

· *Regretful Coda #2* ·

I've used obsolete manuals as a pathway into the throat that will never be mine—the singing throat. It is a pointless search. You can't find the queen's throat in a book. You can't learn how to sing from Lilli Lehmann's *How to Sing*—though if you already know how to sing, her manual might give you valuable tips. I remember trying to learn coitus by reading textbooks on human sexuality and studying diagrams of the four rudimentary positions: man on top, woman on top, man and woman on their sides, rear entry. I tried to learn the rules of football and baseball from the *Encyclopaedia Britannica*, so I wouldn't make a fool of myself in gym. On a cloudy day in the mid-1960s I looked up "Theaters" in the Yellow Pages and copied the names and phone numbers of cinemas in my first address book, red, pocket-sized, with alphabetical dictionary-style tabs. I copied down the words "Burbank Theater," and the Burbank Theater's phone number (which I would never use), solely because the Burbank Theater had recently shown or would soon thereafter show the silent movie *Wings*. I knew the list of theaters would do me no good. But I wanted to make the list. I had faith, then, in compilations.

I have always pursued magic in dry ways—in rulebooks, encyclopedias, directories. Dreaming that love might arise from borrowed incantations, I studied spells from a do-it-yourself witchcraft handbook. But the manuals teach nothing. Singing will not resolve into rules. I have looked for presence in the wrong places.

CHAPTER SIX

The Unspeakable Marriage of Words and Music

· Marriage ·

Shall I use the men's room or the women's room? Shall I seek my exaltations in music or in words? I enter the music room and find a string quartet's conversation, the crater vowels of a basso profondo. I flee the premises: I don't belong. In the words room, across the hall, I encounter the rigor mortis of meaning. I don't belong there, either. I dream of an undivided space, no W, no M, the M an upside-down W: and so I turn to opera, which promises double pleasure, a solution to the soul's rift. Private conditions—mine is homosexuality —are mirrored in cultural monuments. Curious why gay culture is operatic and why some gay people love opera, I conceive that opera's queerest feature is its divided foundation, its marriage of words and music.

It is not very queer to use the word "marriage," and yet I find marriage alluring. I do not wish to dispense with it as retrograde or useless. My parents were once married, and now in mock homage to them I wear a wedding ring. My matrimony to a man was never formally solemnized, but I still call it a marriage; I still believe in pairs and oppositions.

When I listen to opera, I dress up, inwardly, as the gender system, and as conjugality itself; I become bride and groom; I swallow the system because I dream that by taking it on, I might abrade and reconfigure it, just as a tenor, by vocalizing his maleness, makes it unfamiliar. Opera can change nothing in real life, but it alters our fantasies, and I can't draw the line between private wishes and public conditions, between opera-in-the-head and the bleeding world.

Words. Music. In English there is alliterative affinity between *words* and *woman*, and *music* and *man*, while in Italian, *parole* lines up with *padre*, and *musica* matches *madre*. We know that words and music are gendered properties; it's a commonplace idea that language is masculine and that music is feminine. Opera preaches this scheme—and helps us forget it. Listening, we forget the difference between words and music, masculine and feminine, because opera is a bastard genre, a hybrid, erasing distinctions.

Words and music are never neatly separable. Spoken language has pitch and rhythm; in vocalise a singer pronounces vowels (ah, ee, oh, you) which make rudimentary sense and are almost words. Furthermore, although we usually consider music to be abstract, Western tonality contains disguised narratives: the progressions of "absolute" music tell stories of seduction and consent, masculinity and femininity, power and weakness, deferral and climax. These tales are on the border of language: we could almost translate them into words, though music is supposed to be autonomous and unparaphrasable. At the opera, we must forget that language and music aren't mutually exclusive. *We want the border between music and words to exist, so that opera can erase the border in an act of apparent transgression.*

Opera may imitate a heterosexual marriage (with words as man, and music as wife), but because poets and composers have usually been men, it is difficult to imagine that music is really a woman, or that opera's marriage is really heterosexual. If words and music take on the gender of their authors and not their performers, then words and music in an operatic collaboration are both symbolically male. I am startled by the homoerotic implications of opera's male marriage. I hypothesize that opera's hypnotic hold over modern gay audiences has some connection to the erotic interlocking of words and music, two contrary symbolic systems with gendered attributes. I am an opera fan because I crave the soprano voice, but I could also trace my queer fandom to the nature of opera, which places words and music together and apart, always both at once.

Opera's task is to recombine words and music, the severed halves of a body once single and whole. We no longer believe in coherence: the idea of a unified body seems tyrannical, oppressive. We prefer to think that flesh is symbolically fragmented. And yet I, living in opera's shadow, sometimes experience *a desire for wholeness, and a simultaneous desire for fragmentation,* a contrary back-and-forth movement that has compelled me to write a book of fragments secretly wanting to form a married whole.

· *What Happened to Orpheus* ·

In Ovid's *Metamorphoses,* Orpheus takes up homosexual pleasure after he loses Eurydice, and the maenads, angry that he had rejected their amorous advances, tear him to pieces. The maenads cry, "Look at the pretty boy who will not have us!" and throw a spear at his singing mouth, as if his singing and his homosexuality were the same. Some of the first operas take Orpheus as hero and as symbol of the operatic enterprise, but these retellings omit his dismemberment and his homosexuality. In order for opera to announce itself as a genre and to take on imperial, entrenched stature, it must erase from our cultural memory what Orpheus did with boys in Thrace and what happened to his body as a result.

In two of the first operas, each titled *Euridice* (two composers, Jacopo Peri and Giulio Caccini, set to music the same poem by Ottavio Rinuccini), Orpheus rescues Eurydice from the underworld. And in the first great opera, Monteverdi's *Orfeo* (1607), the composer omits the angry maenads and makes Apollo descend from the sky to sing a duet with his son Orpheus. Apollo tries to make a man of Orpheus; father accuses son of effeminately yielding to emotion. Their duet might have convinced its first listeners that this new genre of *dramma per musica* would cure male fragmentation, harden the soft male interior, unify father and son, bind heaven and earth, and balance the oppositions seething in the listener's breast.

Operas are works of mourning; they repeat a task that failed the first time. They repeat Orpheus's struggle to cross over into the other world and rescue Eurydice; in every opera, language seeks its shadow-bride in music, and music crosses Lethe to find its echo in language. Neither quest succeeds, and so opera makes us melancholy. These sad quests for lost loves remind me of the explanation for homo- and heterosexuality that Aristophanes offers in Plato's *Symposium:* each man or woman, a lost half of a former whole, seeks the complement from which s/he was divided in the prelude to existence. No one believes this myth. But it explains opera, which no one believes either. It explains why words and music, once united, now separated, strive to regain their former bliss by moving through opera's Hell into an indissoluble embrace. But the reunion is a dream; Orpheus fails to rescue Eurydice, and words never clasp music so closely that we forget their difference. Opera can't achieve the coherences it seeks. This failure makes opera queer, because culture has cast homosexuality (like femininity) as the condition of loss, forgetting, and fragmentation. I don't mean that gay people are amnesiacs, or emotionally stunted; I mean that the discourse of homosexuality has defined gay desire as *operatic or Orphean*. We are supposedly possessed by the desire to cross the border and grasp lost creatures in the underworld, brides or grooms we will never find.

Always traveling downward to hell, haunting the J.O. clubs, skirting the grave: homophobic stereotype places me at a remove from procreation and from scenes of origin, and casts my erotic life in the shadow of the Xerox machine, every lover a shoddy copy of what I can't possess or incarnate. Supposedly a clone, I never possess the original, only the repetition, the remake, the reissue. To oppose these myths, I'll propose "homosexuality" itself as a port of embarkation, an origin, a First Scene. I am not a father, but I could be a father, and, anyway, paternity isn't the only method of moving toward that sacred territory of origins. When I trace my life's narrative back to "homosexuality," I am placing my faith in a world where sexuality excites wonder and awe because it holds the key to the beginning. Now I want to go backward and look at how opera began, even if the facts are shrouded in mystery. The more mysterious a scene, the more "gay" it seems to me, and the more I want to see if sexuality (which is always homo as well as hetero) was part of the story.

· *The Birth of Opera* ·

The surprise is that opera had a beginning. It was not a natural eruption. It was an invention. It arose from many sources and coalesced in the late 1590s, in Italy. One of its provocations was the fantasy of reuniting words and music after the long sleep of their division. The real facts of ancient Greek music and drama are inscrutable, but it seems probable that the identities of musician and poet overlapped, and that tragedies were sung. Some of opera's instigators wanted to remember and recompose this hypothetical Greek drama— as if it were a male body now sadly dismembered.

Though Laura Guidiccioni, a woman, wrote two pastorals which were predecessors of opera, primary-source accounts place opera's birth in a house of fathers, called the Camerata, in Florence. Music historian Claude V. Palisca admits that the Camerata was not "formally chartered or organized," and that "Camerata" is only a generic term for an "assemblage of people who live and converse together." Once it was easy to assign opera's origin to the Camerata, but now historians have realized that there were in fact *two* Cameratas, that other developments in Italian theater were leading toward opera, and that by the time opera was actually invented, Bardi's Camerata was in decline. And yet the story of the Camerata is compelling. Even if the Camerata never existed, we would have to invent it. *I* need the Camerata; I need to imagine opera's first moment, blurry yet absolute. You'd believe that homosexuality had dignity, clout, and centrality if I told you that gay fans didn't parasitically leech onto opera, corrupting its nature (as if opera were a child that gay fans were accused of "converting" to homosexuality), but that opera was queer from the start.

What was the Camerata, and what was its dream? The Florentine Camerata, in the 1580s and 1590s, was a group of scholars and musicians interested in ancient Greek musical theory; according to one member, they were noblemen "in the habit" of passing their time together "in honorable recreation, with delightful singing and praiseworthy discussions." The Camerata prepared young men for the university; a "delightful" academy, the Camerata "kept vice and every sort of gambling in particular at a distance." (I have no proof, and yet I imagine that in the Camerata's gatherings there was no distinction between intellectual and sexual intimacy, no law governing what men did in chamber, no punishment for erotic pleasure as they stared back to ancient Greece and assembled Orpheus's body.) The Camerata tried to realize its dream of resurrecting the ancient Grecian practice of sung tragedy by inventing recitative (*stile recitativo* or *stile rappresentativo*); without it, opera couldn't have been born. The *stile recitativo* has been described as "a harmony surpassing that of ordinary speech but falling so far below the melody of song as to take an intermediate form": between song and speech, recitative is a style of the borderline.

Memorials written by Camerata members and onlookers paint the fellowship as a body now divided and scattered, which the survivors must strive to reconstitute. The Camerata's patron, Giovanni Bardi, recollects the lost academy, after its dissolution, in a letter to the composer Caccini: "I collect one by one the countless discussions concerning music we have had together . . . into what I would regard as a little bouquet gathered from the field of your genius. I shall do it in such a way that you may seize them at a glance and thus understand and consider them as if they were a unified and well proportioned body." Bardi collects one by one the pieces of the Camerata's dispersed body so that Caccini may *seize them at a glance*—Orpheus's glance, the glance that recomposes, the glance that severs. Opera wakes up in the middle of its night and cries out, "I once was whole."

For opera to have a "unified and well proportioned body," a solid, original body, not a copy or a second-best, then someone must reconstitute it. In 1634, well after the time of origin, Bardi's son Pietro describes the mythical moment of opera's conception: "Vincenzo Galilei, the father of the present famous astronomer, was . . . the first to let us hear singing in *stile rappresentativo,* in which arduous undertaking, then considered almost ridiculous, he was chiefly encouraged and assisted by my father, who toiled for entire nights and incurred great expense for the sake of this noble discovery. . . ." Opera was born *at night.* Nocturnal toil: were these men like Dr. Frankenstein, graverobbing, putting together a body from pieces? These fathers worked together, without the assistance of mothers. The younger Bardi says that Giulio Caccini began singing in the *stile rappresentativo* "entirely under my father's instructions." These men compete, imitate each other, and remain under deep obligation ("Caccini and Peri were under great obligation to Signor Ottavio"): the work of inventing opera and remembering its origin gathers the men together in a daisy chain. Opera crosses generations and it crosses genres: opera is a secret put together *in camera,* and the labor of recollection required to resurrect opera's moment of origin also puts that moment (and the genre of opera itself) in doubt.

Opera could say, "I am a unique genre, I exist in a world of my own," because its words (bolstered by music) hit listeners with lightning force. To inspire the listener, words must be clearly understood: early opera aimed its effects at an audience that wasn't participating and that wouldn't understand the words unless they were lucidly projected and unimpeded by counterpoint. Instrumental accompaniment, if allowed to obscure the words, was a "new allurement" that would "lead the soul astray" from the words and enfeeble the listener. Music's "excessive delicacies" had the potential to stun and effeminize, and so the task of words was to enforce meaning and maintain the listener's maleness.

Opera was born with the astonishment of its first audience: imagine the original fan, the original blush, the first ecstatic response to opera! When *Dafne,* the Western world's first opera (story by Rinuccini, music by Peri), was "sung privately in a small room," Bardi the younger, a child at the time, was "speechless with amazement," he later recalls. Here are the sensations of all subsequent opera listeners: speechlessness, silence. And the listener must push against the mute tide to articulate the marvel, as I am trying to do; the fan must work against amazement and petrifaction to describe and recover a pleasure which will otherwise be smothered. Bardi writes, "There are few now living who remember the music of those times"; already, soon after opera's birth, its pleasures seem intrinsically evanescent.

About the first performance of *Dafne,* the very first opera, eyewitness Marco da Gagliano remarks that "the pleasure and astonishment which this novel spectacle produced in the spirits of the audience cannot be expressed. . . ." No one dares express what opera does to the body. Silence, a halo, surrounds opera to this day in honor of that first scene of pleasure and risk, the first Dafne, the first astonished moment; the listener, like Dafne, is frozen, trying to speak, trying to tell the dismemberment story, the story of the taboo against turning around.

Is opera a performance art—fluctuating, improvisatory—or is it an art of authorship, concerned with property and permanence? Since the most electrifying singers were often women and castrati, the emphasis on performance undid opera's masculinity. Jacopo Peri, in his foreword to *Euridice* (1601), gives credit to a female singer, Vittoria Archilei: she "has always made my compositions seem worthy of her singing," he writes, implying that a female performer has the power to make or break a composition. She adorns the opera with "those elegances and graces that cannot be written or, if written, cannot be learned from writing": the woman's improvisations exceed masculine writing—exceed the moment in which Peri, publishing *Euridice,* tries to transplant opera from performance into print, and thus prove that it comes from a father. Until it is printed, opera—or this particular first opera, *Euridice,* of which there are so many copies and rivals—doesn't have a verifiable origin or identity, but depends on its female performer.

Opera will pretend that it is written down, immutable, and immortal—that it has the status, the absoluteness, of law. But do not believe the ruse. Opera is an ideal, unattainable condition, projected on the culture's scrim like Oz above the poppies. Opera exhausts me just as heterosexuality used to fatigue me when I tried to feign it; it seemed that all the air in the universe was leaking, and that I was the puncture in the tire. To this day, I grow morose and lethargic when I contemplate opera's utopian task of uniting words and music, as if I were pushing against a mountain with my palm.

· Tickling the Ear ·

I'm not impregnated through the ear, but the "I" in me, the subject, streams out the ear: I emerge as soul, as sexual being, by declaring "I have heard this music, I have heard these words, I have heard them both at the same instant."

What if both were not simultaneously present? What if, at opera's nuptial scene, one of the pair were missing?

Two of the first operas, Peri's *Euridice* and Caccini's *Euridice,* were written to honor Maria de' Medici, who was marrying Henri IV, king of France. But he didn't appear at the wedding; he sent a proxy. When I hear that *the groom was missing* from this important historical occasion, the wedding where the first opera whose music and text survives was originally performed, I realize that opera is not the serene spousal bliss of words and music, but a flawed wedding, where the man is merely an absent symbol, not a present, breathing body.

The ear, too, has been a place of absence and loss—a culpable organ, a symbol of emasculation, and of music's undeserved supremacy. Opera culture blames the ear for loving music more than words. If opera's masculinity depends on the text's sovereignty, then the ear, by favoring music, unsettles opera's maleness.

The tradition of hating the ear's pleasure, condemned as "tickling," is ancient. Plato in his *Republic* says that listening to music is effeminizing, that music pours into the man's soul through the "funnel of his ears," and that the male listener's high spirit is "softened like iron"; after long devotion to listening, the man "melts and liquefies," and music like a dagger "cuts out" the "sinews of his soul." St. Augustine confessed that listening was effeminizing when the auditor cared more for the voice than for the song. The saint felt guilty when he was "more moved with the voice than with the ditty," and at those times wished "rather not to have heard the music." And critic John Brown, in his bizarre 1763 *Dissertation,* claimed that opera is virile only when

words and music are working together, but that when they are separated, *"unnaturally* put *asunder"* by "false Refinements," then opera
becomes the *"languid Amusement* of the *Closet."*

To avoid languor and effeminacy, the listener must care about the
words, and opera itself must make sure that words remain master.
Bardi of the Camerata believed that "text is nobler than counterpoint,"
and so he was "nauseated" when he heard singers who didn't care if
"any of their words were understood." He particularly disliked one
"wretched fellow" who cared so much for applause that he "broke the
lines, indeed shattered them to pieces." This vain and honeyed singer
commits violences against the phallic Word, which Bardi wants to
keep intact.

The ear and the castrato were believed to have an affinity, for the
castrato pleased the ear with music and paid no mind to words. Inat-
tention to language, impaired genitals: these flaws made the castrato a
contagion, actively spreading weakness with his "Emasculating
Voice." The castrato improvised and ornamented, substituted one aria
for another, ignored dramatic plausibility, and disrupted the fourth
wall separating performers from the audience. In Count Algarotti's
famous 1755 *Essay on the Opera,* he condemns virtuoso singers for
their "monstrous inversion of things"; these creatures "over do, con-
found, and disfigure every thing," and "pervert to a quite different
meaning and complexion from what was intended by the air," because
they are not "well instructed in their mother tongue." Algarotti accuses
all singers, not just castrati, of these errors: but sins against meaning
were quintessentially the castrato's crimes.

Over the centuries, opera commentators have criticized singers
for deranging language to accommodate virtuoso display, and have
criticized composers for catering to singers' whims. Opera culture fears
that singing can give pleasure *apart from language*. Why is this a fear?
Because pure music tickles the ear, and because it is effeminate to take
the ear's delight seriously.

· *Power Plays* ·

Opera insists its word/music marriage is a hierarchy, with text
dominating music, and yet opera is appealing because it overturns the
domination and reveals that music and words aren't located in two
bodies, male and female, but flourish within one listener. Opera's

marriage instigates an internal, autoerotic state: a trance in the listening body, like masturbation, introspection, or dreaming. Listeners love
when opera dethrones or kills language; the regicide, on these occasions, is the revolutionary, pleasure-seeking, penetrated, tickled ear.
Opera theory tells us that words master music, but we, in our secret
hearts, know music's superiority; and this destruction of language, this
reversal of hierarchy, makes opera a fit object for the enthusiasms of
sex-and-gender dissidents.

At the birth of opera, music was subordinate, the servant of text,
but music quickly stole power back. Note the anti-effeminate rhetoric
of the theorists who want language to remain in power. Count Algarotti in the eighteenth century calls the musical element in opera "effeminate and disgusting," a "despotic sovereign": the composer
"ought to be in a subordinate station," and music should be "the
handmaid to poetry." When music grows all-powerful, words "turn
about and recoil upon themselves," a movement "repugnant to the
natural process of our speech and passions." Music encourages words
to behave like sodomites—overturning "natural" sources of pleasure
and meaning. Benedetto Marcello, in his 1720 satire, *Il Teatro alla
Moda,* is angry that composers inflict "modern confusion" on language
by ignoring punctuation and taking apart words in their middles. This
degradation of language pushes it toward femininity and away from
masculinity, for (if we trust John Dryden) the recitative, which makes
language audible, is masculine, and the aria or the *"Songish Part,"*
which serves "to please the Hearing, rather than to gratify the understanding," and which rearranges words and pays no heed to their
integrity, is feminine.

I don't care about understanding; I want to be pleased by the
Songish Part. I care about an opera's words only because music has
garlanded them. I love the words "Ma il viso mio su lui risplenderà,"
from Boito's libretto to Verdi's *Falstaff,* because music has touched
them. In the 1957 Angel recording of the opera, soprano Elisabeth
Schwarzkopf slides the words "ma" and "il" together; I love to hear
words lose separateness and become a liquid amalgam. Even in this
silent room, the conjunction "ma" and the pronoun "il" remain suf-
fused with music, as a pavement retains heat after a scorching day. The
words "Ma il viso mio su lui risplenderà" have lived in a soprano's
mouth, and so music glows from the unimposing, plain syllables.

Do you blame music for erasing words? Libretti are so mythic
and vague that erasure seems justified. And even when words deserve

our attention, their disappearance contributes to opera's queer pleasure. I love the noble word that music robs of meaning, or the trivial
word that never had meaning in the first place. When the vowels and
consonants make no sense they also make no demands, thrust forward
no gruesome, normative particularity.

In the trio of tenor, baritone, and soprano from Verdi and Piave's
Ernani, act 1, scene 2 (an opera which has a literary origin, Victor
Hugo's *Hernani,* though few today will prefer Hugo to Verdi), the
three vocalists simultaneously sing different words to the same melody, so unless you have a fugal ear you won't hear all three words at
once: you will tune into one singer and then another. In an opera like
Verdi and Boito's *Falstaff,* the listener can pick out crucial words from
ensembles, but in *Ernani,* the singers flood the ear with too much at
once, and the listener must abstain from the desire to understand.

Occasionally, words emerge from the fray of a duet, trio, quartet,
or chorus, and whether or not I understand the words, I become their
advocate. In his first-act cavatina, on the 1968 RCA recording of
Ernani, tenor Carlo Bergonzi emotes the word "che" ("il primo pal-
pito d'amor *che* mi beò"), a word that glues together the syntax but is
not itself suggestive. I enjoy the word "che" because of its insignificance, and because Bergonzi colors it. By emphasizing it, Bergonzi
dwells in language's connective tissue and announces "language" as an
object of illicit love. (Bergonzi is my *che:* I can't forget elegantly suited
Bergonzi in stout middle age at a master class sending marmoreal tones
into Sprague Hall, Bergonzi the avatar of a lost art, Bergonzi the duke
of *bel canto,* Bergonzi born in Parma, Bergonzi singing *che* nobly and
tastefully around the world. . . .)

When Leontyne Price, in her rendition of the famous cavatina
"Ernani, involami," gives signature gestures, Price seals of approval, to
certain syllables, I respond by hearing more keenly, more privately; I
hear apart from structure and aim. I must choose which syllables to
love. I choose the "vi" in "vivere," the "vo" in "involami," and, most
of all, the endless play on the phrase "un Eden di delizia" repeated
again and again so that all the different D's, surrounded by vowels,
turn into a forest without viewpoint or center, an Eden of delight, an
Eden of the letter D, without a map or a motive to chastise the listener
who wants nothing in particular to occur, who wants glitter and im-
plication and no word said too loudly or too meaningfully. In her
cabaletta, I choose "gem" in the word "gemma," because it's hard to
articulate "gem" on a low F, and she does it nobly; and I choose the

second syllable of her lover's name, "Er-NA-ni," and the syllables "du-giar" in the phrase "è supplizio l'indugiar," because she lands on them so hastily. I love when unavoidable elisions destroy the walls between individual words, so that vowels collide and regroup, and "vola, o tempo, al core amante" becomes "volao TEM poal CO rea MAN TE." The cabaletta's speedy music damages words, and it gives them glossy new bodies.

One phrase the soprano sings in the trio is glorious because I can't hear the words. She sings "non conosce," but the tenor interrupts her and the bass drowns her out. And even when she sings "cadrò al vostro piè" by herself, I can't hear the separate syllables. Leontyne Price has no choice; she must cast the words aside. Who could enunciate "cadrò al vostro piè" at such high pitches, at such a swift tempo, against such a loud orchestra?

Homosexuality inverts meaning, diverts it: so goes the noxious myth. I succumb to this myth in sentimental moments. Listening to *Ernani,* I am perversely grateful for the libretto's words, for if opera had no words, there would be no meanings for the singer's mouth to distort.

· *The Love Affair of Composer and Poet* ·

I have emphasized the demise of language and the triumph of music, but opera's ideal (and obliquely homoerotic) condition is a marriage of the two properties. In an opera, words and music say "I love you" to each other. Richard Strauss wrote to his librettist Hugo von Hofmannsthal, "Anything I could tell you in words would be banal in comparison with what, as the composer of your wonderful poetry, I have already said to you in music"; and W. H. Auden believed that "the verses which the librettist writes are not addressed to the public but are really a private letter to the composer."

When men collaborate, on physics or poetry, on music or mathematics, they often imagine that they are doing the miraculous work of gestation together, homoerotically. (Von Hofmannsthal warned Strauss that "to be rent asunder, or not to come together, that would be a major disaster, a festering wound, or even a permanent crippling of our joint child.") Every opera is a coupling: not an affair of actual flesh, but an abstract romance of words and music.

Anxieties and delights surround the collaboration of poet and composer, a "friendly intercourse" (according to Count Algarotti). Not usually so friendly: when men get together, they try to figure out who is on top. Opera culture imagines coauthorship to be a scene of tyranny: Italian librettist Giuseppe Salvadori in 1691 considers composers to be "men of power whose textual changes it is useless to resist," and Gluck reformed opera by protesting, in his dedication to *Alceste* (1769), that music should restrict itself to "its true office of serving poetry." Tyranny, however, can be a kind of love: S/M, or service, or sodomy—imprecise terms for men submitting, men inverting. For example, in E. T. A. Hoffmann's story "The Poet and the Composer," the poet refuses to write a libretto because composers "cut out our finest lines and often mistreat our grandest phrases, turning them in the wrong way, inverting them, even drowning them in melody." *Turning them in the wrong way:* music reverses, inverts, and sodomizes language.

If words and music are both masculine, it might be unnatural for one to serve the other in a culture that homophobically fears the erosion of masculine primacy and vantage, and that despises men who play the role of "bottom." Wagner's solution to the problem of male service, the problem of keeping both poet and composer in the "top" position, was to take care of words and music by himself, and to turn opera composition into a divinely autoerotic act. Wagner would wish for poet and musician to be separate bodies, two men who had the strength to "rouse each other's powers into highest might, by love"; but Wagner could not see successful collaboration taking place in his era. And so he took hold of the whole production. He wrote the libretto and he composed the music. Making opera by himself, dissolving words and music into his solitary bloodstream, Wagner hoped to attain an amniotic and patriotic mysticism. He is the Jekyll-and-Hyde of opera's history: like opera itself, Wagner was "thrust forward by *two* artistic forces which he cannot withstand." Diagnosing opera, he inadvertently describes his own gender crisis. He took the word/music schism personally but he also pretended it was the sole problem of European culture and of aesthetic history. He solved these dilemmas by somatizing opera, stepping into opera as into a bodysuit.

I do not appreciate Wagner's endless quest for masculinity. Dreamer, he believed that opera was the land of manhood! Wagner thought that Beethoven, by including words in the last movement of his Ninth Symphony, was stretching out his hand toward a "brotherly Prometheus"; looking for music-drama, the artwork of the future, he had to "gird his loins about, and start *to find out for himself the country of the manhood of the future*." The dread of homosexuality and the desire to drown in it are often indistinguishable impulses.

Wagner detested music's golden rod. He hated composers for inflicting "painful torments" on their librettists and catering to the whimsical "throat dexterity" of singers; he couldn't countenance the *"naked, ear-delighting, absolute-melodic melody"* of Rossini, a "narcotizing melody" which "glides into the ear—one knows not why." Such ear-tickling music was obviously effeminate. That is why Wagner deplored it. Though he feared effeminacy, he borrowed the language of female reproduction to bolster his aesthetic program and make it seem divinely ordained. He used metaphors of procreative intercourse, but with a difference: intercourse and delivery occurred *inside* his male body. Music may be "child-bearing" and text may be "procreating," and opera may be "the glorious marriage of poetry's begetting thought with music's endless power of birth," but can we call opera's marriage heterosexual if its rituals all occur inside one man's body?

Søren Kierkegaard, like Wagner, used the rift between words and music as a metaphor for his own existential condition: in his novelistic treatise *Either/Or* (1843), he renders the unquenched desire of a man of words to cross over the border into the inaccessible fairyland of music. The narrator loves the opera more when he stands outside in the corridor than when he is a proper, seated member of the audience: "I lean up against the partition which divides me from the auditorium, and then the impression is most powerful; it is a world by itself, separated from me; I can see nothing, but I am near enough to hear, and yet so infinitely far away." The listener is always leaning against the partition. The partition will never fall down. If music or language ever crossed the border that separates them, opera would lose its allure. Sex-and-gender dissidents succumb to the charm because we are divided, and in a homophobic age we like to hear our schisms sung, replayed in public, so our "condition" might no longer seem private, so we might erode the wall between public and private realms, and imagine that our bodies are theaters for world-shattering coups.

· *Implicitness and Its Enemies* ·

Forbidden sexualities stay vague because they fear detection and punishment. Historically, music has been defined as mystery and miasma, as implicitness rather than explicitness, and so we have hid inside music; in music we can come out without coming out, we can reveal without saying a word. Queers identify with shadow because no one can prosecute a shadow.

Oscar Wilde, writing during an era of coalescing homosexual identity, used "music" to evoke a sexy suggestiveness that, with hindsight, looks gay to us. In "The Critic as Artist," he observed that music can create in the listener the illusion of "terrible experiences," of "fearful joys, or wild romantic loves," even if this listener seems to have led "a perfectly commonplace life." In Wilde's novel, *The Picture of Dorian Gray,* Lord Henry Wotton's "musical words said with musical utterance" awaken homoeroticism in the inexperienced Dorian because they evade explicit meaning. Wilde might have learned to worship music's mystery from his mentor Walter Pater, who wrote in *The Renaissance* that all art "constantly aspires toward the condition of music." Did Pater mean that all art aspires to be sung, that all art "aspires"—exhales, moves like breath through the body? And why did he use the word *condition*? A "condition" implies a malady, a state (like homosexuality or hysteria) that settles, for well or for ill, on the unsuspecting soul.

Wilde and Pater used "music" to symbolize a homosexuality they could not state clearly in words; they loved what they were unable to say. Writers like Max Nordau and Friedrich Nietzsche, on the other hand, saw music's connection to the queerness around them, but they didn't salute the rising queerness: they tried to quell it. Nordau, in *Degeneration,* criticizes Wagner for opera's intrinsic trait—its dependence on text *and* music—and thus implies that opera, because it is a hybrid form, is always morally tainted. Degenerates aren't satisfied with one artistic medium: they want words and music at once. "Moonstruck" and "somnambulous," they "transgress the most firmly-established limits" of a genre and push art back to a primitive state; they love Wagner's music because it is an opiate, a "hot, nervously exciting tone-bath" that is "incapable of profiting either normal fish or normal birds."

Nietzsche, too, detested Wagnerian opera for its appeal to moonstruck abnormals, somnambulous queers, and perverse fish. Although he celebrates Wagner in *The Birth of Tragedy,* Nietzsche later treats him like the subject of a case history: a diseased and feminine hysteric. Nietzsche writes *The Case of Wagner* to "take sides against everything sick in me, including Wagner," a contagion who "makes sick whatever he touches." According to Nietzsche, Wagner's use of instruments has the seductiveness to "persuade even the intestines (they *open* the gates, as Handel put it)": it seems ironic that Nietzsche should borrow an anal metaphor from queer Handel to perform a homophobic critique of Wagner. Wagner is an infection that enervates young male listeners: "Just look at these youths—rigid, pale, breathless! These are the Wagnerians: they understand nothing about music—and yet Wagner becomes master over them." Nietzsche's dual movement, first espousing and then repudiating Wagner, produces homoeroticism (I love what Wagner does to me) and homophobia (I hate what Wagner does to me). Homophobic energies in Western culture dislike opera for what it does best—confusing the distinction between words and music. Homoerotic energies enjoy the confusion. The tug-of-war in Nietzsche's heart between loving and hating Wagner is symptomatic of the nineteenth-century fascination with realms of ambiguous feeling it will also condemn as degenerate.

Nietzsche has homoerotic things to say about opera, even apart from his troubled relation to Wagner. According to Nietzsche, the marriage of Apollo and Dionysus, not of man and woman, gives birth to tragedy and opera. He places two god-bodies, two men, at the origin of opera: oscillation between two male primacies, each sexy, each prehistoric, engenders opera. You need to imagine Apollo and Dionysus naked to appreciate this story of how opera began.

Though Nietzsche's scheme is based on an alternation between opposite divine male principles, he prefers music to language. Music gets more metaphysical credit. Because music is an "immediate copy of the will itself," not an imitation, Nietzsche criticizes opera's founders for wishing to make words more powerful than music: the men of the Florentine Camerata were fops who had abandoned themselves, with "diversion-craving luxuriousness," to the "dream of having descended once more into the paradisiacal beginnings of mankind." From its beginning, opera has gazed backward, like Orpheus, to an inscrutable past; Nordau thought this desire to seek origins was degenerate (the "effort to return to beginnings" is "a peculiarity of degeneration"), but I savor the power of words and music, when joined, to sweep the listener far into the past.

· *The End of Opera #1* ·

If I die a peaceful death, I want to have an opera record playing in the room. Or maybe, as a terminal splurge, I will be able to afford a live singer, a student singer, a singer interested in the dying. It's likely I will be too distracted by pain. But sentimentally I imagine that opera is well suited to ends and terminations—because of its scenes of dying and departure, and because singing uses the body so exorbitantly and ultimately that I want to be reminded, when I leave my body, that even when I lived inside it I never completely used it.

Opera's dream of marriage rarely succeeds; words and music infrequently cohere. And yet I feel I am murdering opera when I take pleasure in the music *against the words*. Or at least I am performing an autopsy, an elegy; peering into opera's corpse, I am mournful and coldly curious, with my gloves, tools, and formulae.

The end of opera is now: my moment of attentive, melancholy listening. My ear is the melody's mausoleum: when I listen to a phrase of a dated but priceless opera (a moment from Maddalena and Andrea's first-act love duet in Giordano's *Andrea Chénier,* sung by Beniamino Gigli and Maria Caniglia), opera's ambitions and utopias seem to terminate in my ear, because the recording is crackly and from the 1940s, because the hackneyed, untranslated words don't match modern life, and because the music can't contain my response to it, nor can my response attain the music's height. And the words are left far behind.

· *The End of Homosexuality* ·

Long ago opera's founders (my imaginary Camerata) wanted music and words to cohere, and they also wanted the body to cohere. See flesh's border disperse; where we want the body's line to be solid, it is composed of Morse-code dots and dashes. I listen to opera—with its dreams of wholeness and reunification—in order to pretend that the body has an outer edge. But isn't opera a dead form, and am I not moribund to treasure it? In opera's demise, I hear echoes of another end: the obsolescence of "homosexuality," the departure from our guidebooks of that lovely, poignant category, "homosexuality," a limited term I still inhabit.

Farewell, homosexuality. You left the world before we effectively defined you, and yet some of us are still imprinted with your traces, and we will be lost until we can wholly circumscribe and narrate you.

Entropy: I live in a system—opera, homosexuality—that has already shut down, like the once marvelous carnival premises in the B-movie *Carnival of Souls*. The funhouse of opera and the funhouse of homosexuality are closed, though their Ferris wheels are still turning, still circulating a cargo of startled riders.

· *The End of Opera #2* ·

Strauss's last opera, *Capriccio* (1942), composed in the shadow of the Nazis, seems to mark the nearly final stage of opera's prolonged termination. *Capriccio* asks the question that inspired the invention of opera: which is primary, words or music? The listener must choose. And Strauss invites us to refuse the choice, to say, queerly, "I choose ambiguity."

The heroine is the Countess, whose first name is Madeleine. "Madeleine, Madeleine!" she says to herself in the mirror. The name brings to mind Proust's madeleine, and a Proust-derived homoerotic poetics of tasting and connoisseurship. When Marcel tasted the madeleine, he was deluged with sensations and memories; when we listen to Madeleine sing, when we taste her timbre, we remember the history of opera. And when I taste opera, when I listen to an aria's feathered phrase, I remember the history of homosexuality: it all comes flooding back, the sodomy trials, the secrecy, the passing, the invisibility, the urgent iridescent instants of speech.

My body asks: *words or music, which is primary?* That is a question on which homo and hetero sexualities depend. It is opera's question. And it fuels the delicate plot of *Capriccio*. Madeleine must choose between two men who represent words and music—a composer and a poet. The poet, a baritone, recites a love sonnet, and then the composer, a tenor, sings it, and the Countess must choose between the spoken and the sung rendering. Which would you choose? The sung version, of course. We know that music will win, in part because the higher voice penetrates our ear with greater fire and vibrancy. We will be pleased, at the opera's end, to hear Madeleine sing the sonnet to herself, so we can experience words rising from low baritone to high tenor to highest soprano, a transcendence, a movement upward in pitch and in purity, from masculine mire into feminine ether. The lesson? All words naturally wish to rise in pitch; all words inevitably aspire to the condition of the soprano voice.

In the final scene, the Countess Madeleine stares into the mirror and tries to decide between the men. They are offstage, forgotten, unnecessary. We have no emotional involvement with them. We care only about Madeleine, who, in trying to plumb her own heart, brings the opera to its melodic climax. On the plot's surface, the word/music contretemps seems a male rivalry. But it is really a question of what Madeleine feels, or of what the listener feels; and "the listener" is always a woman or a femme, always submissive yet secretly the arbiter of the entire operatic system.

Elisabeth Schwarzkopf, queen of text, famed for her exacting attention to the word/music marriage, sings the part of the Countess on the opera's first complete recording. Her husband, record producer Walter Legge, usually gets partial credit for her acute treatment of text, as if words and music were most successfully married in the throat of Schwarzkopf the wife. Schwarzkopf-as-Madeleine recapitulates the long erotic rivalry between words and music, which this opera nostalgically reopens only to affirm its undecidability and to close it forever: she decides that any choice is trivial, and exits without resolution. The glory of her performance makes us forget the rivalry entirely. The feminine or effeminate throat (castrato, tenor, soprano) is more compelling than the question of words versus music, so the poet and composer disappear, leaving the prima donna in the spotlight.

· *Saints* ·

Words and music are a male rivalry because men have written and composed opera throughout its history. (We assume these men were straight, because we are willing to import the category of heterosexuality back into history, though unwilling to do the same with homosexuality.) But what happens when the librettist is lesbian and the composer is gay? If Western culture associates music with femininity and words with masculinity, then the collaboration of Virgil Thomson and Gertrude Stein on *Four Saints in Three Acts* (1933) and *The Mother of Us All* (1947) reverses that crude paradigm by putting a woman in charge of the "masculine" realm of language. Stein's words disrupt the W/M division—and I think that opera has always striven to do the same, though under cover of our unconsciousness. (Few men would admit that they go to the opera to rid themselves of masculinity.) Stein's paradoxically *musical language* resolves the question of words versus music; she achieves what opera's founders and reformers wanted—language's supremacy over its musical setting.

I end with Stein because she helps me find a place in the alien land of opera. I can use the "saints" in *Four Saints in Three Acts* to describe my own shut-in opera love. Even if you don't love opera, you might feel shut in. You might feel this queer condition, quite holy, quite grim, which Thomson has called "inner gayety"; gayety, or queerness, happens *inside* institutions, systems, laws—and inside the imagination.

A repeated refrain in *Four Saints* is the flat question, "Who settles a private life." Stein's *Four Saints* traverses the boundary between private and public, and makes me feel that though I am separate from the regime of opera, I am, in my privacy, in my obliqueness to opera, also *inside* of it, just as I am inside the institution of marriage though I am legally outside of it. (Emily Dickinson knew that the mind's interior is "full as Opera," and that one needn't go to the opera to feel operatic or to participate in opera's symbolic system.) Stein's *Four Saints* suggests that a solitary soul, a shut-in, can be considered married, and that opera is the wedding ceremony for two parts of the listening soul; the saint is her symbol for that individual who balances interiority and exteriority, who lives in the cloister's isolation but also is married (to God, to privacy, to other saints). *Four Saints* steals the figure of the saint for queer purposes, reminding us that the saint, like the early premodern queer, is an exception, whose eccentric nature only later generations understand.

Virgil Thomson intended the opera's subject to be "the inner gayety and the strength of lives consecrated to a non-material end." What is inner gayety? Do I, who am gay, live inside the structure of gayness, or do I build my own sexuality from scratch, apart from regulation and terror? Stein's libretto plays with the word "in," rich with queer meaning: "Saint Teresa in in in Lynn," writes Stein, making me wonder whether Saint Teresa is in the town of Lynn, or whether she is in "interiority" itself, or whether Lynn is another woman that Saint Teresa is momentarily inside. . . . When I am *in*, am I closed, shut, closeted? Or am I proceeding toward inclusion, openness? *Four Saints in Three Acts* performed one major inclusion: Virgil Thomson insisted on casting only African-American singers because he admired their "clarity of enunciation" and possibly because he wished to subvert the whiteness of opera and of canonical saintliness. The African-American singer who plays the saint is also incommensurate with the role, not quite snugly inside it. Nor is there room for all the saints in a single opera's confines. Four Saints IN Three Acts: what happens to the fourth saint, the saint without an act?

I circle around the word "in" because I want to ask some pointed questions of opera. Am I extraneous to opera, an interloper? Do I necessarily skew opera's meanings by intruding my particular historical queerness into opera's majestic interior? *Four Saints* is a counting opera (it counts its saints and its acts, repeatedly asking, "How many saints are there in it?"), and I use its theme of counting to ask: do I—the queer fan—"count," do I matter, do I fit into opera's cloister, is there a space for my queer response inside the monolithic institution of opera? The acts that Stein's libretto obsessively counts are acts of an opera, saintly acts, and sexual acts. If there are more saints (four) than acts (three), then maybe saints exceed their frames, subjects exceed their representations, queers exceed the sexual acts that identify us as queer, and a listening experience exceeds the opera that occasions it.

Stein wrote her libretto without characters: just a collage of sentences. To make it singable, Thomson had to invent personae, including a "Commère" and a "Compère"—mother and father narrators, who turn this abstract drama of inner solitude into a family plot. But I don't think the parts of Commère and Compère straighten out the opera's queer bent. Commère and Compère have a marriage of convenience: as stand-ins for Stein and Thomson, they supervise the opera from a queer throne.

Thomson was passionately interested in opera as a marriage. He noted that "nowadays poetry and music live apart," but he wants to see them live together again. He says a phrase of "Old Folks at Home" is well-adapted to the text because "its elements are mated, not just living together." But Stein and Thomson maintain a *mariage blanc:* separate bedrooms. His folk idioms make her words behave, communicate, tell a story straight; but they don't interfere with her language's erotic meandering.

If we must choose between words and music, we will choose both. That is the operatic way to vote. Stein's second libretto, *The Mother of Us All,* tells the story of Susan B. Anthony, who worked to earn women the vote; the opera's subject is choice, voting, autonomy. Is sexuality mine to choose, and can I choose the stories that the larger world will tell about sexuality? Stein writes, "I must choose I do choose, men and women women and men I do choose. I must choose colored or white white or colored I must choose. . . ." Stein hops between opposites, just as opera does, for opera protects the listener from making the choice between words and music: opera eroticizes the moment *before* the choice, the instant of exile and indecision, outside the men's room and the women's room. Opera prolongs the vertigo: again we linger outside the well-marked doors, and we remember how dizzy and free we felt when we had not yet chosen our narrow path through the sexual world, or when we had not yet been introduced to paths.

I love opera because it is never (to quote from Stein's libretto) "once in a while" or "one at a time." I turn to opera for its marital structure. I don't believe in marriage as it takes place in city halls and synagogues, but I believe in marriage as a fantasy. I claim "marriage" for the listener whose mind is torn in two by opera's dual articulation —words, music—and who wishes to resew the seam.

I have written too much about marriage, not enough about solitude. It is impossible to listen to opera without thinking about solitude, but I avoid the subject because I dread the specter of the "lonely homosexual."

· *Dream* ·

Last night I dreamt that I sang in an opera. How velvet the theater! How ultimate the challenge! Or maybe it was a straight play with demanding incidental music. One phrase especially frightened me: a leap from a D in the treble clef to a G above the staff. I wondered how I would find the stamina to project the phrase to the theater's last row.

I used to dream about marriage: towering wedding cakes, and Jordan almonds wrapped in fake lace, favors for the guests. Now I dream about opera.

CHAPTER SEVEN

A Pocket Guide to Queer Moments in Opera

Listening speaks.
—ROLAND BARTHES

For three dark winter months I studied opera scores and salivated as I beheld sharps, flats, naturals: the concrete materials from which singers conjure song. As I held the *Carmen* score aloft, I pretended that I was Callas or even just a dull upstart preening before a hallway mirror, a nobody, practicing for an impossible role.

Here I present a sequence of soundings, responses, retrievals—composed in the space between the score and the stereo. An album of impressions. Twenty-eight opera highlights, queerly ventriloquized. What do these impersonations prove? Only that I have listened, queerly.

I model this mini-encyclopedia on modest compendia like the 1913 handbook *The Story of a Hundred Operas,* which gives synopses for forgotten operas like Hérold's *Zampa,* Leoncavallo's *Zazà,* and Paderewski's *Manru.* Such guides leave out details and muddle the already discontinuous plots. The author of *The Story of a Hundred Operas* confesses that "something had to be sacrificed for the convenient format which fits so handily in milady's handbag or causes scarcely a bulge in mimaster's coat pocket."

I have sacrificed objectivity. In its place, I give you objectivity's opposite: gush, abandon, naïveté. In retelling these arias and phrases, I hope to release *listening,* a fairy prince or princess, from its mute spell.

· 1 · Entrances

BUTTERFLY'S ENTRANCE

Listening to Puccini's *Madama Butterfly* (1904), I unwittingly participate in a history of racist imperialism. And yet at moments the opera works against its pernicious frame; the music's schmaltz overwhelms me and I forget my reservations. When Butterfly enters, I drift away from fixed vantage-point; the noose of gender loosens, and I begin to breathe.

American Lieutenant Pinkerton, on duty in Nagasaki, has purchased a bride, Butterfly, who is about to enter, and whom I crave: I've bought a ticket, and I wait with horny Pinkerton for the purchased presence to appear. But before Butterfly enters, her offstage companions intone a meaningless, pleasing "Ah," and amidst a gouache of harps, the offstage Butterfly sings, "Aspetta" ("Wait"). Because I find ecstasy through sound and not through sight, I don't want to see Butterfly; I want her to remain offstage, surrounded by an orchestra that has so thoroughly impersonated her floral and oceanic imminence that I pay no attention to Pinkerton anymore.

Or does Butterfly's entrance please Pinkerton-in-the-listener? No. I can listen *apart* from his values. I do not applaud Pinkerton's imperial system; I applaud the emotions released by Butterfly's voice, emotions to which no words in the libretto do justice. I rise above rapacious Pinkerton ("That fool doesn't understand Butterfly") and identify with the diva's exposure. I experience coming out or entrance as tasks of power, performed *serenamente:* the diva must exercise a tasteful rubato and must abstain from vulgar effects. She is supposed to be fifteen years old. She drips with pathos. Pathos is supreme among the showoff's bag of tricks. Later she will sing violently but now she must sigh and diminuendo on a high D-flat (Callas can't).

Opera kills the things it loves. Like Butterfly, if I enter opera, I will die, so I linger on its border to prolong and never complete my moment of entrance. I long to remain outside the frame of opera, immune to its dangerous charms, but I also feel narrative's seduction: I want to enter the story and I want the plot to proceed.

It is a pity that Butterfly abandons her girlfriends and ascends the stage-set hill to reach Puccini's (and our own) idea of climax. How much better if Butterfly never climaxed, never ascended! But then we would lose the pleasure of opera; we would never find sounds to correspond to our own regret at having reached puberty, a trompe-l'oeil backdrop. When heterosexuality unveils itself as *sumptuous* and *delusional,* the libretto shatters, and shadow-knowledges speak: by loving Butterfly's entrance more than her death, by isolating a moment that passes too quickly, by replaying her entrance on my imagination's Victrola, I can hear Butterfly as the emissary of sex-and-gender ambiguity. By listening sentimentally and interminably, by never outgrowing this entrance phrase, I can speak a different Butterfly.

TOSCA'S ENTRANCE

Tosca's entrance helps me say, "I'm alive."

So far the sounds in Puccini's *Tosca* (1900) have been masculine —Mario's aria ("Recondita armonia"), the sacristan's mumblings, the fugitive Angelotti's terror—and so I am glad when diva La Tosca sings her first offstage "Mario!" Sublime presences, like Butterfly, begin singing offstage to emphasize that our pleasure is aural, that we desire not a body but a voice. Coming nearer to visibility, the diva cries "Mario! Mario! Mario!" as if it were Mario's identity we needed to unveil and verify, when it is, in fact, hers—and our own.

As Mario opens the door for Tosca, he says "I'm here" ("Son qui"), and holds his note, without orchestral accompaniment, for as long as he wants: Jussi Bjoerling warms up the syllable with a tremor that almost upstages the entering diva. And then the Tosca theme arrives, a tune that symbolizes her secret vulnerability. Because I respond to Tosca's theme by unlocking my own deviations and sentimentalities, her theme seems to emerge from *my* heart, to articulate *my* love for the diva who has just appeared on stage, and to express, with sappy orchestral coloring, my hopeless identification with Tosca. When Tosca enters, Tosca returns: loved objects can never appear for the first time, they can only *re*appear, dragging with them a prehistory. When Callas returned to the Met in 1965 as Tosca, WELCOME HOME, CALLAS said the banners outside the opera house, and WELCOME HOME, TOSCA say the banners in the listener's imagination whenever Tosca enters, whenever queerness or obliquity wants to speak and uses opera as its medium.

The schmaltzy orchestra, accompanying her entrance, does not insist that I take sides, that I identify exclusively with male or with female, with composer or with singer. Released, my emotions swim toward the inspiring object and unite with it, and so I can't specify where the music places me. I wouldn't worship Tosca without this theme's assistance; it marks her as the object of adulation even before the diva sings to earn my love. I'm Tosca because my body contains the sympathetic orchestra's vibrations and because my nervous system, loving her A-flat-major perfume, produces Tosca-sensation as an unconscious reflex. The thrill of apprehending Tosca *always as if for the first time* is the pretense of abandoning borders and of saying, "I can't be contained by gender," though my body, through which Tosca's theme circulates like blood, has borders, limitations, codicils.

ELISABETH'S ENTRANCE

I don't participate in the heterosexual system and yet I worship schematic and artificial representations of it. Moments of high heterosexuality, such as Elisabeth's entrance in Wagner's *Tannhäuser* (1845), indirectly redeem my lifelong distaste for masculine activities and emotions. Listening to Elisabeth's "Dich, teure Halle," I inexplicably feel —and inexplicability is opera's charm—that I am eleven years old again watching my best friend's mother make crêpes, which she called "French pan-a-cakes." (I think she was a foreigner.)

Elisabeth runs onstage, into the Hall of Song, to await the arrival of her beloved Tannhäuser. If she is Leonie Rysanek, applause obscures her first notes. Strange, how Elisabeth gets so excited about a mere room. She arrives onstage only a measure before she starts to sing: a dangerously improvised, last-minute entrance. What if her gown's train got caught on a backstage nail?

She salutes the Hall of Song because her voice fills it. *Dear voice, I missed you! When Tannhäuser was gone, I couldn't sing to you, because women aren't permitted to address themselves—but now that he's returned, I have an excuse to fill my body's hall with vibrations.*

Elisabeth cheerleads for heterosexuality. Her joy is camp because it exceeds plausibility: is Tannhäuser worth this exuberance? And yet in her aria's rueful minor-key section, when she expresses doubt, Rysanek goes nearly flat, as if she were deliberately falling off the ship of joy, as if she were so perplexed she can't keep up appearances. Her gloomy accents redeem my own tendency to digress from heterosexuality, to wander away from permitted passion.

She'll rise to a triumphant high B on her final "Halle": Rysanek spends so long on the note the orchestra almost loses her. The moment is queer because her joy surpasses reason, and because she wants a place within an inexorable and punishing sexual system. But does she really desire Tannhäuser? She apostrophizes not her absent lover but her vibrating larynx and her electrified fans. Singing "Dich, teure Halle," the diva pretends that we, the listeners, are her soul's apogee. And I, listening to "Dich, teure Halle," think of inexplicability, and of gender, and of my decision to listen to music indoors rather than to hike with the French pan-a-cake artist's husband (she cooked crêpes, he led the Boy Scout troop) up a path compromised by poison oak.

OTELLO'S ENTRANCE

The entrance phrases of sopranos bless me with the illusion that my queerest desires are authentic, sanctioned, and rooted. But when men enter, I get another kind of thrill: I experience masculinity as mask—a costume, glorious for certain occasions but hardly a creed.

In Verdi's penultimate opera, *Otello* (1887), I savor Otello's entrance, which captures the paradoxes of appearing male. He enters with a stentorian phrase to prove that he is still capable of singing and that Verdi is still capable of composing. The chorus thinks that Otello has drowned. But then suddenly they exclaim "È salvo!" His ship is saved!

I'm saved! I can experience the return of the ruler, the hunk, the hero, the tenor! The strings, cooperative and sycophantic, diminuendo to silence. Otello has ascended the dock, and he can take a breath and enter whenever he wants.

Silence surrounds the male exclamation. So far I've heard crowds, thunder and lightning, anxiety. Now I hear the pulse of the individual man who pushes his strength beyond the border into unconventional identities. Otello's primary announcement is "I'm male"—or, "I'm still male." The tenor's vocal prowess proves Otello's fitness to rule, and fulfills the chorus's fantasy. Why pray for Otello to be saved unless a man of warm massiveness appears onstage?

When Butterfly, Tosca, and Elisabeth enter, a complicated, contraband experience of gender overwhelms my body with an aura of flowers, vulnerability, and risk, but when Otello enters, I hear masculinity's staged, tragic nature: it swells, it sobs—excessive and endearing as a fallen civilization. Otello doesn't sentimentalize maleness: he turns it into a performance, a test. Imagine the soul of the tenor, fearing failure, longing to seem a monolith, a spear, a novelty. Extreme dramatic and vocal peril underlies his phrase. When Plácido Domingo sings Otello I hear him stretch his nice-guy lyrical voice to try this brutal Little Caesar part so that he can steal the world's heart away. James McCracken's voice once broke in the part, and he returned to the Met to sing Otello only after years of absence and exile.

The orchestra and the crowd cooperate with Otello by falling mute before he sings "Esultate!" They pretend to listen to him in awed silence, but they have actually abandoned him, left him outside to die of exposure. Will he collapse? No: the last word of his entrance phrase is "l'uragano"—which means the "storm" he has just escaped, but it also anticipates the "storm of applause" from voracious fans at curtain-call time, and the blast of "Evviva!" from the cheering chorus.

When I hear "Esultate!" I applaud by experiencing a single, slow shiver, a harmless electrocution, as if my pinkie had just grazed a socket. While Otello enters, I bask in a display I couldn't predict, an unveiling that is completed (it only lasts twelve bars) as soon as I have the wit to acknowledge that it has started. I cannot set up shop inside Otello's phrase; it is too brief, nearly as fleeting as Tosca's "Mario!" In his entrance phrase I hear a presence I could clasp forever, but then it departs.

Singing "Esultate," tenors indulge in hysterical excesses and eccentricities. Free from the conductor's totemic commands, Jon Vickers erotically opens his vowels into a warmth that verges on the alien— particularly the "te," which he pronounces "ta." He nudges the text to suit his mouth's peculiarities: he flaunts his regal power to sing the way he likes. Vickers warps his vowels most in the phrase's last word: he sings the "ga" of "l'ura*ga*no" as if his entire body were caving in. And the unsubtle but stirring Mario del Monaco trumpets the "go" in "l'or*go*glio," and sobs on "gloria."

A public figure, fatally willing to expose his heart, Otello speaks a dialect of flaws and phlegm in which I hear a tone color that could belong to no one else—only Vickers, only del Monaco; I hear the man's quintessence, his irreducibility. In Vickers's vowels I hear 1968, I hear a space between my own listening experience and the silence into which I pour these sentences of quest and imploration.

Otello exits immediately after his "Esultate!" appearance; neurasthenic, he can't bear to remain onstage. Our applause fatigues him. Shouting "Evviva," we have beguiled him away from manhood, as a storm's premonitory gust turns a weathervane away from its prior north.

· 2 · *Gaiety*

JULIETTE'S WALTZ

Down the page I waltz, trying to match Galli-Curci's "pansy" tone, trying to imitate the mechanistic, ethereal heartbeat of her virgin song. . . .

I question the relation of sexual desire to happiness, and yet I am forced to say "gay" and hear the word's cork-pop effervescence. The dictionary says: "GAY suggests a lightness of heart or liveliness of mood that is openly manifested." Open manifestations deceive: sometimes they manifest merely *the desire to manifest*.

Opera characters openly manifest. Juliette, for example, in Gounod's *Roméo et Juliette* (1867), bursts into her coming-out party, the Capulet ball, with a saucy "Écoutez!" Listen to me! Her show-off waltz, a "gay" melody, contains a covert melancholy. Is Juliette a virginal debutante, or is she mortality's emissary? What, finally, is gay about coupling?

On a meaningless "Ah!" (I am opening up!) she sings a brilliant descending chromatic scale: and yet by diminuendoing, by making the transition from freedom into strict tempo, from cadenza into the waltz's opening melody, she proves herself polite and socialized, a well-behaved soprano: "I know how to fit my huge 'Ah!' of pleasure and willfulness into the social world of waltz, duet, family obligation, and heterosexuality (a tomb)."

This aria is her libidinal declaration of independence, like Susan Hayward's *I Want to Live!* But Juliette also expresses grave reservations. She dabs each measure's first beat with a grace note, and then lets go. Stuttering, she doesn't yet participate in the world of ballroom merriment and sanctioned intercourse: her grace notes distance her from the downbeats which nonetheless determine her vocal behavior.

I heard Cecilia Gasdia sing Juliette at her Met debut. Her "Je veux vivre," attenuated, hesitant, controlled, sought me out, where I sat, in Family Circle's second-to-last row. I imagined she was suffering debut tremors, and I sympathetically held my breath during her phrases so she wouldn't fall apart.

Juliette imagines that by singing she can retain her secret self and not carelessly emit it to the crowd. Nameless to Roméo, she wants to keep this debut day "comme un trésor" ("like a treasure") in her heart forever. But by singing a waltz she invokes Roméo's response; and by singing a showpiece, she surrenders her vocal treasure to the listener. The aria, adrift from its dramatic context, replayed on records, holds the diva spellbound, as she holds the audience captive. In a 1917 recording of "Je veux vivre" (transposed up from F to G major, for flair's sake), Amelita Galli-Curci avoids all consonants, and slides between notes with a portamento that seems noblesse oblige. On the final high D, held for eleven seconds, she proves herself a stratosphere-shatterer: I arrest my life to contemplate her aberrant and athletic physiology, her D. She gives her jewel to us ("Listen to my high D!") but she also retains it, for by awe-striking us, she remains her throat's powerful proprietor.

Callas, recording "Je veux vivre," manages the scales, but we hear the struggle, the masochism. When Callas murmurs, on pain-evoking harmonies, "Laisse-moi sommeiller" ("Let me sleep"), I know that I imprison the diva by listening too intently.

I play and replay Galli-Curci's "Je veux vivre" because I want to believe in life-force as a girlish phenomenon that I might borrow. Her prelapsarian coloratura drips like sucrose into my veins. And I don't ask whose grave I am standing beside.

VIOLETTA'S "SEMPRE LIBERA"

A sick, sad woman sings, "I'm gay, I'm bursting with joy": Verdi's Violetta Valéry, the lady of the camellias, from *La Traviata* (1853). Tubercular, she projects a fast showy cabaletta to stun the house at the first act's end. As coloratura was falling out of style, Verdi resurrected it for this one moment in *La Traviata;* coloratura, no longer the soprano's natural gift, is a sign of her recidivism—a talent she turns on when pushed to the edge. Coloratura is Violetta's problem, her last resort, a sign that she has abjured bourgeois sexual arrangements and has returned to a scapegoated social position. When she proclaims free love and goes gay ("Gioir!"), these liberating decisions force her into archaic modes of routing air through her body, virtuoso techniques for which her recompense is an audience's love.

The phobic logic that frames AIDS today and that framed TB and syphilis yesterday locks Violetta in a jam. By living for pleasure she commits suicide. Coloratura will kill her, but it thrills us. And though she, too, takes pleasure in courtesan delights, with each repetition of the gay yet lumbering main theme the soprano grows more dolorous, the downbeats more ponderous, as if this cabaletta were a totentanz.

In a 1955 La Scala performance, Maria Callas's "Sempre libera" has the deliberateness of a girl about to swallow Seconals. She says she wants to flit from pleasure to pleasure ("Sempre libera degg'io folleggiare di gioia in gioia"), and her melody lands on the downbeat's blossom, sucks it, and rebounds. She rises to a high C, slides down, and continues, with effort, the self-consciously gay melody. The slide and the slowness convince us that her illness is showing, that she can no longer afford to live it up. Ha ha ha! No one believes operatic laughter: horrid, hollow. Offstage, Alfredo serenades her, but she repeats her cabaletta, she returns to coloratura's seraglio.

Her initials are V. V.: the V of Verdi, vortex, virtuoso, violet, venereal, and voice. (She began to spill and display on the syllable "vor" of "vortici.") In "Sempre libera," Violetta warns: *Lose yourself in my voice's vortex, and you'll die of consumption.* The song we love for its own sake, the soprano we love because she turns away from Alfredo and domesticity, and pumps us with coloratura: these are deadly delights. It kills her to sing, and it kills us to listen. She is contagious. From Violetta, we catch the opera bug.

I first heard "Sempre libera" in a listening library: 8:45 P.M., autumn 1980. The library would close soon. I couldn't stay to hear the second act. The soprano: Anna Moffo, the 1961 recording. Outside, the moon poured down its own somber "Sempre libera," the color of a silver crayon. Nothing gay about "Sempre libera," though I used it as the portal to a gay tomorrow.

· 3 · *Vengeance*

DONNA ELVIRA'S "AH! CHI MI DICE MAI"

I devoted my twenty-first winter to Mozart's *Don Giovanni* (1787) and to the search for a boyfriend. In my dorm room, I listened to Donna Elvira's "Ah! chi mi dice mai" again and again; I wanted the boy next door to hear it, through the thin wall separating our bedrooms, while he slept and studied.

Jilted Donna Elvira wants to claw Don Giovanni's heart out. But she only shovels out her own vocal muck. She extracts most silt, or gold, from the word "cavare": to dig out. Vengeful desires harm the throat before they reach their intended object, the rake: sing "vengeance," and you will be doomed to find it in your own larynx. Kiri Te Kanawa purrs, like a goblet vibrating, on the syllable "tor" in the word "torna" ("return"). She rolls the "r" and finds a veiled, covered sound for the long B-flat: the rolled "r" of the celibate, the rolled "r" of the woman who wants to occupy the center of a vengeance opera but becomes a quaint, comic, imitable refugee from opera seria—only one of Don Giovanni's many sexual conquests.

Churchgoer Donna Elvira has the gall and confidence to fall straight down the B-flat-major chord when she sings "Ah! se ritrovo l'empio" ("Ah! if I find the traitor"). No ambiguity in her descent. She says, "I'll give you the key you want, I'll bravely plumb the depths of my degradation." I love Donna Elvira for her complacency, upright uptight woman expressing a botched and illegal love affair in a countenanced, forgiven key. And then in the next phrase she shows her Jack-the-Giant-Killer ability to leap whole octaves: "vo' farne orrendo scempio!" ("I'll kill him most horribly!").

Queer vengeance: to identify with wronged women, to desire erotic impossibilities. Donna Elvira expresses queer vengeance not as pining lyricism but as juridical confidence: *I sit at the center of a sexual discourse because a rake abandoned me.*

During my days of "Ah! chi mi dice mai" I feared that my love affair with the boy next door would end any moment and that I would become Donna Elvira, crying on the streets. Only the abandoned are entitled to speak of their reprobate loves, and so I placed the discourse I wanted to occupy, *boy meets boy,* like a nested box inside a larger, more authoritative discourse: *the wronged woman.* In order to speak to myself about *boy meets boy,* I entered the vocal consciousness of a woman who can sing boldly about her erotic life only because she's been deserted.

PRINCESS EBOLI'S "O DON FATALE"

The love affair didn't end, but I retained the discourse of wronged women, and graduated from Elvira to Eboli.

Princess Eboli, in Verdi's *Don Carlo* (1867/1884), curses her own beauty, and trusts that we'll find her beautiful, and knows, with the confidence of the mezzo, the underdog, that we won't say, "Drop it, Eboli; you're homely." She uses the aria to gestate a new way of perceiving an old wound, and to convince us of her wound's centrality to the world. I call her cries for vengeance "queer" because she attains vocal triumph by addressing herself as a monstrous enemy, finding a "you" inside the castle of her "I."

Suddenly the madwoman remembers how to be lyrical: she declares sostenuto loyalty to her rival, the Queen. Eboli hides vintages of sapphic mellifluence in her angry body's cellar, as if she had a prehistory of sweetness and light before erotic accident doomed her to maledictions. Repentant, Eboli vows to bury her shame in a convent. The aria might have ended with this change of heart: *Surrender to the Queen and brainwash yourself into believing that gorgeous royal soprano women are so intrinsically superior that you must bow your outcast body down before them*. But iron Eboli returns to combat. She quickly remembers Carlo, doomed to die the next day. Horrified, on an orchestra-enforced high G-flat, she vows to save him! And this turnabout lends her a queasy masochistic joy: in Callas's Hamburg concert, 1962, available on videotape, the diva's face lights up as she sings "la speme m'arride" ("Hope smiles on me"), and she raises arms to her bosom and embraces herself as if she were the Heavenly Empress Who Smites, as well as the Empress's Abject Victim. (After Callas sings "O don fatale," a woman steps onstage with a bouquet, and holds Callas's hand a few seconds too long.) Eboli's campy, deluded conversion reminds us that Eboli is possibly lesbian for loving the Queen and for savoring the Queen's sentence. Time's up, but mad Eboli repeats "un dì mi resta" ("one day remains for me"), blind as Violetta in "Sempre libera": women exclaiming, at the ends of gloomy acts, that acres of time remain for erotic vindication.

Eboli's "O don fatale" undoes the mezzo's subordination to the soprano: the low-voiced woman steals the show. Embracing self-sacrifice ("I'll live in a convent forever just like Queen Elisabeth ordered") and masochistic altruism ("I'll save Carlo with my one remaining day and Heaven will smile on me"), Eboli rushes offstage with the confidence, bolstered by applause, that Verdi's opera orbits around her. But Elisabeth's sober, philosophical aria, "Tu che le vanità," highlight of the last act, will reverse Eboli's victory. How narcissistic and chest-voiced Eboli seems, in retrospect, as we rise to Elisabeth's soprano height! Eboli stands queerly beyond the pale of exonerated passion, though she sings as if the law upheld her.

RIGOLETTO AND GILDA'S "SÌ, VENDETTA"

In tenth grade I watched a druggie undress in gym, and I covertly imagined grazing my curious hand over his mature thighs while he lay flat on his back on the locker-room floor (I'd touch him as experiment, not as eroticism): this epiphany is no different from what I imagine Gilda feels in a crowd of men, the Duke of Mantua's palace, whose intrigues will kill her, but not before she learns to express herself.

Men's voices fill the court until helpless, degraded Gilda, the hunchback's kidnapped daughter, starts to sing. Her soprano, and my desire for her voice, throw wrenches in the vengeance works, the mill wheel of Curse that fuels Verdi's *Rigoletto* (1851).

With a hurdy-gurdy melody, fortified by chthonic triplets, the hunchback Rigoletto calls for vengeance ("vendetta"), and then Gilda choicelessly repeats her father's phrase. Thus her vocalizing seems pre-programmed: exhalations of a zombie lyric soprano. And yet Gilda contradicts her father's intent: she uses his melody to plead for clemency, not vengeance.

Yes, I am a sneaky gay voyeur, and inside my erotic imagination, littered with pictures of naked men and women-in-the-presence-of-men, I am Gilda, my voice a reclamation agent stealing what I can't own. If you choose to be drugged in your vocalism it will be a delight only if your voice is high enough, because then you will ascend, invincible and superior, above the men you mimic, and no one will disturb your meditation.

Anna Moffo, in the 1964 Georg Solti recording, uses subtle rubato to express Gilda's resistance: she seems to say, "Bend, don't break, when patriarchy's storm assaults you." Her perturbed triplets delay the downbeats, and yet she always attains them; the vengeance maelstrom never leaves her lagging. Moffo rushes and almost ruins the game of meaning; she participates in "Let's go!" fervor but she also abstains by keeping her words half-inaudible.

The queerest moment: Gilda crescendos on the syllable "te" (of "Perdonate") into a vigorous restatement of the vengeance theme—louder this time, including a high B-flat that Moffo hits with astonishing purity and directness, the outsider finally leading the carnival that had excluded her. Gilda is speaking to Gilda, and doesn't wish to be overheard. She follows her father but thinks of the Duke. She echoes her father's vengeance music but demands its opposite. She behaves like a good daughter but she is not.

She ends the duet in unison with her father: incest disguised as "closeness." She assumes his wound, licks it, identifies with it.

I have listened to this vengeance music countless times—mostly attending to Moffo's/Gilda's reluctant yet rhythmic collaboration, barely in time, as if Gilda had shrunk her voice to fit her father's warped scheme, and this accommodation or self-betrayal had diffused an implicit *sigh* over the ensemble. I listen for Gilda's part in the duet because I want to learn how to bend my soul as Gilda bends her line; I want to learn how to grovel and pretend to be subordinate. If I imitate Gilda, and use a serene, piercing soprano voice, then no one will obstruct my desires.

How coarse and male and extraneous I feel when Gilda's voice enters my room. My maleness seems a clumsy pocked moon in a sky of tender, enviable stars named Gilda, glints of light, Gilda-dots in the night, who are shocked to know what I think while I listen to their reluctant emanation. . . . By moving into a pornographic, puerile melancholy, do I outrage the voices I love?

· 4 · *Serenity*

THE COUNTESS'S "DOVE SONO"

I discovered serenity after the years of vengeance ended. Safely gay, permanently gay, I returned to C-major women: but now in the midst of my solidly queer life I remember with violent nostalgia a violinist I once loved saying that Mozart's phrases were "crystalline" —which meant that I, her accompanist, whom she nicknamed "Moose," wasn't crystal, but was clay, mud, or soot; to this day, Mozart's superior, icy phrases conjure for me a kingdom of women who are, like Botticelli figures, sheer outline, without pulp or interior. When I listen to these Mozartean women, to Mozart phrases which are always, figuratively, women, I hear homosexuality, or my gritty soul, fall away like dross, as if operatic serenity's purpose were to purge my queerness, rid the world of it. But queerness secretly returns, under the cloak of the Countess's phrases, though they pretend to be unperturbed, and though her sublime "Dove sono," from Mozart's *Le Nozze di Figaro* (1786), is resigned to dwell within C, E, and G—pitches that form C major, the key of promise and bier.

I take the Countess into my body as she sings—or, when she sings, she peers into my interior; she exposes me. And so I associate my inward-looking moments with the sound of a woman thinking serenely aloud.

I thought this opera was a divine joke, but when the second act begins with the Countess musing mournfully in "Porgi, amor," I suddenly find my point of tragic identification: the oversensitive woman, on whom no slight is lost, and who has the cathedral-capaciousness of soul to contemplate her condition while she endures it. Singing about her life as if it were already over, she gives the illusion of musical naturalism: the texture of introspection as it really occurs.

And after the first part of "Dove sono" she repeats the sublime melody I will avoid describing; repeats it, with one poignant alteration. The first time, a rest bisects the phrase ("Dove sono [REST] i bei momenti"); but the second time, the Countess fills in that rest. I take the Countess to be *one state, never changing,* but when her aria alters, I realize that I have underestimated her, and have underestimated my own will to forgive, with a liaison, a melody that once was prison.

In the final, allegro section of the aria, the Countess exclaims (I paraphrase), "I still have time to change the world!" The furious, trilling soprano has acquired, through the medicine of the aria's serene moments, the fortitude to fight for her man, as well as the moral righteousness to accuse him, rather than to ponder the metaphysics of past and present.

But I haven't yet explained the uninterrupted sweetness of Elisabeth Schwarzkopf moving, without haste, through the central melody. And will I ever? Is it possible to describe what I love? "Dove sono," no showpiece, opens the soprano to humiliation if she reveals impure taste. She must exhibit fidelity to air, to C major, to a nostalgia permitted to speak because it is trained, socialized.

The Countess regrets the beautiful moments ("i bei momenti") of her early marriage; listening, I regret the beautiful moments of the soprano's performance (as if it were over already), and I regret the gulf between the modern soprano's rendition and the Mozart aria itself, each performance a bittersweet revisitation of a lost source. And so I remember my own mournful separation from ways of behaving that are now gone, behaviors I never liked, such as "boy meets girl," or "wife forgives husband": I am riven, suddenly, by *my* separation from the Countess, from this model (who dares to imitate it?) of *a woman enduring gender's martyrdom with fortitude.*

Listen to the Countess sing sweetly about events that usually provoke anger, and learn to forgive history's mutations, domesticity's interruptions. Listen to the Countess, and learn to sublimate your own abjection. The Countess *does a Mozart* when she sings; she does the inspiration trick. She drinks reality—foul air—and transfigures it.

NORMA'S "CASTA DIVA"

I love calling it *the* "Casta Diva," acknowledging the aria's iconic status within the soprano repertoire: in the "Casta Diva" from Bellini's *Norma* (1831), Norma goes serene (as in "goes under"), tranquilizing herself for the community's sake.

When Norma comes out on stage, in one of opera's great camp entrances, her head "encircled by a wreath of verbena," gazing around as if "inspired" (nervous about her number), none of the other Druids and Druidesses, who are calling for war against Rome, know that she has betrayed them by sleeping with the Roman proconsul and bearing two illegitimate children.

Norma comes out to preach serenity. Norma comes out to give the Druids and the Druidesses a voice lesson.

"You seditious voices, how dare you question my inspired words!" She speaks of herself in the third person—"alla veggente Norma." Norma is an ordinary name now, not glamorous as in the days of Norma Shearer, but Callas pronounces it grandly: Norrr-mah. Norrr-mah enters a trance. Serenity, a soporific, enters her bloodstream. We Druids in the audience need to be taught peaceful voice production. Norma, show us how to loosen muscles knotted for a lifetime's war against desire!

For Norma, as for the Countess Almaviva, vocal serenity compensates for erotic distress or calamity. To save her Roman lover, Norma must sue for peace; she must teach serenity, must spread it like obfuscation and propaganda over her listeners. Norma is not chaste ("casta"), and yet she must deliver her aria sublimely and serenely to fake chastity. She must escape lie detection. And if we notice mistakes —botched passages, missed pitches, a failure to be fluid—then *we've found Norma out.* Witness the case of Renata Scotto, who bombed as Norma at the Met, and was mercilessly booed.

Like "Dove sono," "Casta Diva" shows us a woman in the process of looking within: overheard introspection. But in Norma's case, on-stage beholders remind us that even amid a crowd, the singer is a narcissist in a trance, addressing herself not others: "Lunar counterpart, my other self, make me chaste, untroubled by sex. Let me calmly shine on the opera house and on the prairie alike." Callas drops all color from the word "vel" ("veil"), as if she, like the moon goddess, were unveiling, strip-searching her own instrument for weapons, and finding none.

Norma reigns over a female community of divas, moons, and handmaidens. Priestesses help Norma perform the ritual cutting of mistletoe before "Casta Diva" begins, and Norma adores her rival, the mezzo Adalgisa; in the last of their juicy, extended duets, the two women swear eternal friendship. If Norma is etiquette teacher for Adalgisa and the Druidesses, she must herself have a headmistress, a female superior. And so she turns to the moon as a vocal coach, a muse, a greater diva, to whom, in "Casta Diva," Norma indirectly prays, "Give me the strength to sing this difficult opera."

Norma's performance, like the cutting of mistletoe, is a rite that sublimates and conceals unsanctioned erotic behavior. In the serene aria, the singer channels air through the body to produce a socially desirable effect. To pass the trial of "Casta Diva," the diva must make it sound easy. But the role of Norma is surpassingly difficult. Sopranos assume Norma as divine mantle, maybe rashly, late in their careers. And so "Casta Diva" is the would-be Norma's test, an ascension into a brightness which might melt her wings.

Norma sings serenely to produce in the audience a momentary cease-fire. But we can't grant the diva this reprieve, because even her request falls inside the inexorable system of singing. We will treat her prayer as itself another pretext for criticism and condemnation —another place where the diva might go wrong and justify our wrath.

Ritual transforms the shaman's or the singer's introspection from mumble and rant into public, legato utterance. Norma is narcissistic for the commonwealth's good: because her introspection serves a social cause, she is permitted to render her thoughts serenely. She passes muster; no one detects her secret *déshabillé*.

Like Norma, I want to go serene, to retreat into a long, fluid line for the good of queers, without cloud, without veil. But I'm not the elected priestess; tremolo afflicts my line.

· 5 · *Serenades and Seductions*
COUNT ALMAVIVA'S "ECCO RIDENTE"

Writing these meditations, I am serenading opera itself: "Opera, cold beloved, open yourself to my interpretation and affection."

In Rossini's *Il Barbiere di Siviglia* (1816), Count Almaviva serenades Rosina, locked in a palazzo. She hasn't yet appeared. He aims to seduce her, and so his voice must shine. The count, a lyric tenor, convinces us that manhood is a caress, not an army; that never until this moment have we understood manhood's intrinsic affability and earnestness; that a tenor, unlike a baritone, sympathizes with women's secret needs because his voice, like a woman's, is elevated; that a tenor has something virgin and unexampled to reveal.

Why does the Count sing? Because he has been wounded by a love-dart. His wound takes the form of coloratura, a cadenza marked "a piacere": the tenor may pursue his own pleasure. And yet his showy, sense-stopping repetitions limn a love-wound, a St. Sebastian gash connected to his voice's dangerously antimasculine height. He sings high and he sings fast because he has been pierced by love's arrows: "Oh, istante d'amore! Felice momento!" *Happy moment of singing! Instant of warbling, without object or hesitation!*

A present, palpitating man opens his mouth to invoke a woman. But the woman fails to appear, and the aria, retroactively, becomes queer: the woman appears not in person but in his timbre. He sings for the pleasure of singing, for no woman, because he loves to linger in the land of wounds.

Tenor Tito Schipa's timbre makes me optimistic about maleness: his restrained rendering of this serenade avoids sleaze. He adds ornaments. The quiescent orchestra lets him delay. And Schipa unpredictably jumps an octave to a high B on the word "speme." Time, and the orchestra, stop for this leap.

What are the poetics and politics of a man's rubato? When a man takes liberties with a phrase, when he sings "a piacere," is he stretching the walls of his masculine identity, or is he becoming Don Juan, making a pass at tempo, taking liberties with music as he is free to take liberties with women? Masculine identities usually feign impermeability, but Schipa's maleness fluctuates when he bends a phrase's time, when he vibrates, when he pitches his voice so high that he almost qualifies as an exception. And yet there's nothing freakish about his tone. We expect these thrills from lyric tenors.

The Count's ardency lacks militancy: voice without the bone, without the hammer. He purveys the masculinity of "Ecco!"—of annunciation, exclamation, and surprise. What takes the Count and the audience by storm is not the arrival of Rosina; she doesn't show up to hear the serenade. We're surprised, rather, by this new *dolce* sound entering history: sound of a different maleness, which passes as heterosexual but also displays itself, falls prey to rallentando, doubt, vacillation—the tremors of a rubato that saves the man from strict tempo's regime. The Count tries to wake Rosina up. Instead, he wakes in me (and in other listeners?) an optimism: I didn't know men could sound like this, I didn't know masculinity could reveal itself.

"Ecco ridente" introduces the noise of male vanity, male rapture: a man permitted to sound excited. Anywhere outside of the opera house this tone might lead to tragedy: gaybashing.

It is dawn. We dwell now in the land of stereotype. In Tito Schipa's rendition of "Ecco ridente," I hear the hope of empathizing with a nice, sincere man. The voluble Count opens his heart. Will I open my window? I either take pity on the serenading tenor or I feel —for the first time in my life?—that maleness wants my cooperation and response, that maleness includes me and beckons.

WERTHER'S "POURQUOI ME RÉVEILLER"

Werther has blue balls. His "Pourquoi me réveiller," from Massenet's *Werther* (1892), is hydraulic: he sings to let off steam, because he aches and needs release.

I identify with Werther's sadness but not with his relentless desire to reach climax. I seek a Werther waylaid by passion, unable to progress, unable to find closure. I want a deathless Werther who won't urge Charlotte to have sex against her will. Listening, I say, *Werther, if you elope with me, I'll rescue you from singing's stranglehold.*

Goethe's Werther taught Europe a new, glamorously riven masculinity: the discourse of the sensitive man, virile because he hysterically exposed his wounds. A manipulative poseur, Massenet's Werther wants Charlotte to pity him, to take his ardor's measure. Performances of vulnerability earn sexual favors. His self-revealing aria, his fit, works as erotic blackmail, extorting a kiss from a married woman.

In the aria he serenades his lungs: "Pourquoi me réveiller, ô souffle du Printemps?" ("Why wake me, o breath of Spring?") The song's geyser-force belies his death wish; or else he resents singing's involuntary, instinctual nature. *I'm singing again, and yet I want to die! Breath of spring, why wake me, why enter me? Phrase of Massenet, why possess me?*

The audience sits up, attention renewed, as the aria—the most familiar bit in *Werther*—commences: this zephyr of inspiration awakens us, as spring's return rouses unwilling Werther. For three minutes, we may take uninterrupted pleasure in the singer's throat. Only the vocal line is the subject here: only the ability to measure out breath.

The second verse of the aria reveals Werther watching himself, pitying the spectacle of his own imagined obsolescence. A traveler will come tomorrow into the valley and look for Werther's former splendor and find no traces of it. This traveler is the operagoer: the listener who loves "Pourquoi me réveiller" posthumously gratifies Werther by considering him an Ozymandias, a stone eminence worth touristic attention. Werther loves to dream that his body is turning dusty and anonymous.

Tito Schipa slays me with the word "gloire." I am not Charlotte, but Werther's aria seduces me with a principle I never before believed: suddenly I trust the man who looks backward, the man who regrets springtime, the man with a nostalgic *idée fixe*.

Male vocal suffering is unusual, and contrary to patriarchal expectation; and so I, like Charlotte, am tricked by his display. Like Charlotte, I succumb to Werther because he dares to go so far over the edge into effeminacy and self-exposure. Against my judgment I enjoy the subsequent love duet, when Werther forces himself on Charlotte —urging her to kiss him though she sings "Pitié," have pity on me, "Je vous implore," I implore you to leave your hands off me! Unison, in opera, implies unanimity and consent: but Werther forces Charlotte up the scale to their shared orgasmic "Ah!" He declares that his love is a divine principle ("le mot divin") though she cries out "Save me, Lord!" ("Défendez-moi, Seigneur!"). But the only god in the house is Massenet, who rules that the man and woman must sing one impassioned phrase on the same pitches. I no longer pity Werther, who has now "come" all over Charlotte. He has released his passion; I regret the mess. And yet because Werther's masculinity is sweetly vocalized, I make allowances; the high notes convince me that the tenor has suffered enough to earn my love.

I've never seen a man, in public, behave as Werther does in "Pourquoi me réveiller." Imagine a man exploding in an elevator: "Listen to my wound!" The other passengers are embarrassed, titillated, terrified. I count myself among the titillated.

DALILA'S "MON COEUR S'OUVRE À TA VOIX"

Usually, men serenade women; but in Saint-Saëns's *Samson et Dalila* (1877), Dalila does the serenading. Her big aria, "Mon coeur s'ouvre à ta voix," ostensibly praises the power of Samson's voice to open her up. But Dalila opens *me* up: a ravishment I don't consider ruination.

How does she open me up? By descending. When, slowly, this mezzo's melody moves down to a low C, my body expands to accommodate her bottomlessness. What does she say to Samson while she descends? No narrative. Only pure plea: the kind of exclamation (like "I'm coming!") that announces pleasure already at hand, though it pretends to want response and reciprocation. Dalila asks for Samson's body: but by plumbing the depths of a woman's tessitura, she declares her own strange commitments and self-sufficiencies. When she sings the tenderness phrase ("tendresse"), the drunkenness phrase ("ivresse")—accept my stumbling terms for pleasures I'll never otherwise capture for you—her solitary body becomes a bridge spanning more miles than two bodies in sex can cover. Tonally generous Rita Gorr takes a breath smack in the middle of the drunkenness phrase, so she can find a silty C embodying the "ivresse" she wants from Samson. If Dalila masters legato, if she holds the air to sing this phrase, if she can chromatically, deviously, and ineluctably descend to a low C that seems a natural depth, like dying in one's sleep, then she deserves to be subject and object, surpassing man: only Dalila could give Dalila this deep and narcotic a welcome.

I played this aria—transcribed for trumpet—in fifth grade. Blaring "Mon coeur" with no regard for its history, I didn't know that I was performing a siren's song. Thus the melodic line depends on its harmonic and operatic context, and doesn't intrinsically emit erotic perfume.

My heart opens to *your* voice, says Dalila, but who can believe in the separation of "I" and "you" after fording through "Mon coeur"? The aria is queer because its love scene happens inside the mezzo's body, and inside the listener's body—not between Samson and Dalila.

Dalila asks for sex and for response; but all the mezzo wants is a solo. "Mon coeur" is the voice-voluptuary's favorite moment: the aria advances the drama of our interest in Dalila as Queen of Openness, She who opens the closed places in history.

· 6 · Duets

SOPHIE AND OCTAVIAN:
PRESENTATION OF THE ROSE

In Richard Strauss's *Der Rosenkavalier* (1911), Octavian, a mezzo dressed as a man (a role Mary Garden refused to create, because of its lesbian implications), presents a silver rose to the soprano Sophie, and the two women seal with a duet their instant infatuation. Drugged by this music, I overvalue passion; I don't ask its name.

When the silver rose arrives, Sophie falls in love with a woman. This lesbian moment depends on roses, which exceed and baffle nomenclature (a rose is a rose is a rose). Duets usually speak the number *two;* but Gertrude Stein's conundrum suggests that a rose introduces a third term, a third sex, into the two-pronged gender system. The silver rose—and opera itself—carry the charge of an unspeakable and chronology-stopping love because a connection arose in the late nineteenth century between *tampering with time* and *tampering with gender*.

Disturb gender, and you disturb temporality; accept the androgyne, and you accept the abyss.

Einstein, Freud, Bergson, and Proust took time apart. They demonstrated that past doesn't precede present, that the two states create each other. And queerness, as a sensibility, a conceptual category, and a subculture, has benefited from these radical underminings of linear time. In such "deviant" and metaphysically exceptional states as homosexuality, gender loses its confidence, and reality abandons its claim. The queerest gift of opera is its ability to torque time, to stretch it, to create pockets—momentary, unending—of sacred or divine duration.

When Octavian enters, Sophie knows that time will soon be bending, and so she exclaims, "This is so lovely, so lovely!" ("Denn das ist ja so schön, so schön!"). Sophie speaks for the listener. "This is so lovely!" I sigh, hearing the soprano's excitement and the orchestral explosion announcing Octavian's arrival. The music provokes my exaltation and also comments on it; this vocal and orchestral climax justifies my devotion to swooning and obliteration. Smelling the rose (listening to Schwarzkopf-as-Sophie, in 1947, sing the word "Paradies"), I become clandestine, insurmountable. The listener may well ask: who am I, and what is my gender, if this vocal outpouring elects me as its recipient?

Sophie's and Octavian's lines finally come together to describe ecstasy in a double movement that hypnotizes the police. After the eeriness ends, time resumes its waltz, and courtship commences. Though we learn that one of Octavian's many names is Hyacinth, and that his secret nickname is "Quinquin" (Schwarzkopf sings this code word with a warm tone that passes "Quinquin" from the gay margins into acceptability), Sophie forgets the damage done to gender in the duet, and agrees to believe in manhood. Sophie thinks Octavian is a man! That is why Sophie can dip her voice into the risk-reducing honey of A major when she sings, "Er ist ein Mann" ("You are a man"). Ambiguity gives way to truce, hygiene, closure. Let Sophie believe in gender, if it makes her happy. Let her sway obediently to waltz time. In the ecstatic duet, a few moments before, she stared into runic secrets of erotic bliss and eternity that now she forgets so that the drawing-room comedy can proceed. If *Der Rosenkavalier* were consistently ambrosial, we might perish from ecstasy, or tire of it, or learn to distrust it.

NADIR AND ZURGA'S "AU FOND DU TEMPLE SAINT"

When a tenor and a baritone share a melody, one octave apart, I am relieved, as if a declaration of war has been called off, or as if a fist threatened to slug my face and then it retreated and turned into a rose. Progress, not apocalypse! No reason to be lugubrious! The baritone, blending with the tenor, admits his affiliation with lightweight, head-toned men, while the tenor transcends the merely personal, and annexes the masculine themes of politics and paternity. Together they take apart masculinity by exhibiting vocal difference within one gender: some men sing high, some sing low.

In Bizet's Orientalist *Les Pêcheurs de Perles* (1863), Zurga and Nadir (baritone and tenor) join in duet to salute a mystical heterosexual experience they vowed to forget: long ago, in Candi, they spied the lovely virgin princess Leila in a temple. . . .

The men salute an absent woman, a distant scene; but in their bodies they bring woman and locale to life. Who would want the past unless it returned in tuneful form? When Nadir sings the word "Candi," the orchestra rewards the deluded singer by bodying forth the lost place with the lowing of a mournful clarinet. And then the tenor himself impersonates the missing woman: my Nadir, Alain Vanzo, has a high, nasal, hollow, French voice, close to falsetto, and so when he sings the phrase "A woman appears," a "femme" enters his voice. On the word "femme," a high A-flat, his head tones become Leila's simulacrum.

Two men singing together hope to restore a melancholy, remote object: their own subjectivity. This duet is their cloister. In its walls, they seek refuge from the contemporary, as I hide, in opera, from life's failure to be operatic. No baritone will materialize from stage left's mist and crush my dissatisfactions under the heel of his ample, courtly vibrato.

When tenor and baritone sing Leila's theme, virtually in unison, the melody is so catchy and simple that they repeat it, even though the flute has already done so. The tune instructs us to *memorize* Leila. And I willingly perform the work of memorization, inspired by the clarion voices of Jussi Bjoerling and Robert Merrill, who recruit, at top volume, for an unnamed cause. I'll name it: narcissism, the joy of doubling. Leila's absence can't move Bjoerling; grief leaves him bullheaded. Alain Vanzo sings "Une femme apparaît" nostalgically, introspectively, while Bjoerling, the greater singer, is ramrod, not numen.

I, too, worship the memory of a distant, exotic princess—but she is Bizet, or Bizet's melodies: inaccessible *Carmen,* risqué as porn, boxed set I didn't have the cash or effrontery to buy when I was nine years old! And now this *Pearl Fishers* duet persuades me to believe in the time-line's revocability, like a measuring tape that automatically rewinds into a tight coil.

SANTUZZA AND TURIDDU'S DUET

"Santuzza, credimi!" Believe me, singers, you keep me alive.

"Battimi!" Beat me, melody; strike me dead with your impetuous wish to embrace the next measure.

Why does this duet from Pietro Mascagni's *Cavalleria Rusticana* (1890) pummel me? Though a duet between a man and a woman, why does it drip with queerness? Because it is corny, and because it portrays masochisms, abjections, and fulfillments that sober art won't

risk. Two bodies sing, but the music advances only one point of view
—Santuzza's. Through a failed heterosexual scene, the duet expresses
one soul's impossible emotional predicament. Musically it is an ulti-
matum: *weep*. The codes of female and effeminate conduct demand
that I react hypersensitively, that I identify with both soprano and
tenor, and that I let their doubleness speak my divided solitude.

Easter Sunday, the church steps: Santuzza begs Turiddu to stay,
to listen to her pleas, and Turiddu denies his affair with Lola, and
callously demands to be left alone. Santuzza grovels. Turiddu spurns.
Miraculously, their quarrel leads to celestial unison. We "get off" (catharsis) by listening to Santuzza extract consonance from a man who
no longer loves her.

So many women sing "ascolta" in opera. "Turiddu, ascolta!" Turiddu, listen to me! And she will make him hear.

Renata Tebaldi is Santuzza in a bygone recording; I attend to her
sorrow. But in a more recent set I expend my devotion on the Turiddu, Luciano Pavarotti. I accept what his larynx bestows, and I
understand the soprano's paradoxical love for the masculinity that
hurts; his seductive voice—announcing itself as a force of nature—
promises that maleness, a cruel substance, also contains its opposite, a
guilcless paradisiacal stream that never flows while Santuzza watches,
only behind her back.

Santuzza achieves, with Turiddu, the utmost ecstasy opera permits: a duet in unison, top volume, the highest altitude, the most
expensive pitches. Opera can offer no more piercing reminder of our
emotional penury than by suddenly flooding us with sentiment we
must suppress, though we vow to live henceforth for the sake of this
moment, to revise all future conduct to accommodate this phrase's
bounty. But the opera ends, and I forget my impossible vow to take
operatic emotion seriously as a guide to conduct.

The second half of the nineteenth century produced most of the
standard-repertory operas. And we still love and listen according to
their patterns. They advance an operatic Bill of Rights, which proposes
the inalienable right to melody: each heroine and hero demands and
deserves a divine tune. The more empyrean the melody, the more
justified and genuine the utterance. If you sing a sensational melody,
the listener will vote you "not guilty," no matter what your crime.

I imagine queer identity as a violence against structure and nature,
and so Santuzza and Turiddu's shared melody absolves me of all my
willful wanderings. Blessed by it, I feel once again in the swing of

nature. I don't believe in nature. But opera makes me swoon, and persuades me that swooning *is* my nature.

· 7 · *Ensembles*

TRIO: ANTONIA, VOICE OF ANTONIA'S MOTHER, DR. MIRACLE

Are there any among us who would refuse the chance to sing a duet with absence, with a voice that rises from an oil painting's nook and beseeches, "Sing!" This wish is queer. Not only queers harbor it. But it goes against the grain of commonplace sexuality—this desire to experience vocal unison with an implausible partner. Opera gives its listeners what their secret, refractory, "sick" souls crave.

I'd die to sing a duet with the past. Antonia, in Jacques Offenbach's *Les Contes d'Hoffmann* (1881), gets my wish: she dies by singing a duet with a portrait of her dead mother, brought to life by Dr. Miracle.

The portrait wakes up and sings "Antonia!" Antonia occupies our position—we, drowsily passive, waiting for our strangest desires to be given melody's papal seal. Male composers traditionally impersonate female authenticity, and so the mother's melody bears no internal stigmata that brand it as fake: her phrase sounds surpassingly genuine. I know she's real because her line's 12/8 time stretches my body out: a pleasant, mystifying rack. Each measure, the mother rises one pitch; but at the melody's conclusion she returns to ground zero. Will she ever reach the scale's top? Her implacable movement upward presses Antonia, against her will, higher. Correspondingly, when she responds to her mother's melody, Antonia's notes tend downward, escaping the elixir of altitude.

The mother is barker to the freakish sideshow of her own voice: listen to the Dead Lady sing! "Dear child, whom I'm calling as in former times, this is your mother, listen to her voice!" Repeating itself, the melody signifies "remembrance," and urges us to memorize it. But when I first heard *Les Contes d'Hoffmann,* I left the theater haunted by this melody, which I couldn't exactly recall. I knew it courted and evaded obviousness; I knew it was associated with the night's obscurity and with my forgetfulness. I could have borrowed a score or a record to verify the melody. But I wanted a more absolute retrieval.

Illusions dupe Antonia; melodies dupe me. I, too, would choose to sing and to die, if a portrait serenaded me. As a gay listener, I adhere to Antonia because she embodies *the power of fantasy*. I resemble Antonia when I do not dismiss the mother-daughter duet as sentimental, when I drink its climax-refusing phrase, when I lift up the tone arm and return to the duet's first groove. . . . Opera is a sonic portrait whose tints are fading, though the auctioneer promised me that they were immortal. Antonia's love scene with her mother's portrait satisfies me because it crosses the summit of sickness (didn't I learn, at the beginning of time, that queer desire was "sick"?) and exposes the pleasure gardens on the other side of trauma.

"MISERERE": LEONORA, MANRICO, AND THE MONKS

I remember a children's biography of Giuseppe Verdi; I think it was called *On Wings of Song*. The word "wings" promised that opera was an art of magical transportation. I'd fly on opera's wings, but where would I land? At dawn, in my rocking chair, reading *On Wings of Song*, I learned that Verdi's wife, daughter, and son died within the span of two years. Forever, opera will seem the compensation for a first and fabulous loss.

Whatever the lost trace, I regain it by listening to "Miserere," in Verdi's *Il Trovatore* (1853). The troubadour Manrico, condemned to death, rots in a tower; Leonora (who stores poison in her ring—she'll drink it soon) waits outside; a chorus of monks prays for mercy on Manrico's doomed soul. Illicit eroticism clashes against authority; the voices of Leonora and Manrico throb against a drab monastic monotone, all-male, *a cappella*, somberly praying, "Lord, thy mercy on this soul." Forward movement halts: we've entered the monastery's *nature morte*. Here, as in Matthew G. Lewis's novel *The Monk* (1796), holiness is a front for sadism, sexual excess, and hyperstimulation of the prurient reader/listener.

Only Leonora is visible. The voices of the unseen monks provide miasma; to make an impression, Leonora needs their somber chant as backdrop. If you're deprived of erotic freedom, imitate Leonora. Banish comedy from your body. Dive below the staff to summon chest notes, and quickly reascend to your head.

From his tower, which looms on the stage like an abstract, harmless phallus, Manrico delivers a real melody, more lyrical and arching than Leonora's separate spasms of distress. Hysterical Manrico spills outward, displays his symptoms, forbids containment. Because we hear Manrico before we see him, he represents "voice" itself: singing confines him, as it confined Antonia in *Les Contes d'Hoffmann*. Dear Manrico lacks an onstage body: he is just a tower, a tower that warns, in its stiff salute, that a man will soon be missing.

Listening to Manrico, Leonora exclaims, "Oh, ciel! Sento man-carmi" ("Heavens! I feel faint"). Whether she is singing "I want to die" or "I want to live," whether she says "I" or "you," "Leonora" or "Manrico," it all sounds the same: she settles her entire vocal body behind any proclamation, without stint. I must give you the Italian words, because Leonora expresses so much self in singing

> Di te, di te scordarmi!
> Di te, di te scordarmi!
> Di te scordarmi! di te scordarmi!
> Sento mancarmi!

> Forget you, forget you!
> Forget you, forget you!
> Forget you! Forget you!
> I feel faint!

Opera grows no more sublime, no more tautological, than Leonora's repetition compulsion: "Forget you, forget you, forget you...." Though the word "te" ("you") is her passport to vocal altitude, her attainment of the high A-flat implies "me," not "you." She controls the bar's rhythm. The monks are meek with their "miserere" now—hushed suppliants, huddled in the middle of the measure. A dazed ballerina, she twirls. The listener who still cares about drama asks: does she have time to be detailed? Isn't Manrico in danger? Or is she singing these measures for her own pleasure, for the joy of expressing her hunger?

Baltimore, 1981: two nights in a row I stood to see *Il Trovatore*, starring Gilda Cruz-Romo and Ermanno Mauro. Men in standing room authoritatively praised Cruz-Romo: "You won't find a better Leonora today." I envied their savoir-faire, their familiarity with many Leonoras. On the second night, at the end of the last act, when the curtain tried to close, it collapsed and fell on the stage. This lapse in stagecraft, harming no one, explained Baltimore, Gilda Cruz-Romo, *Il Trovatore,* and the crazies in standing room, whose enthusiasm justifies opera.

· 8 · *Solitude*

LUCIA'S MAD SCENE

My wedding day, *my* performance, *my* body, *my* voice, all mine, no one can interrupt or stop me: I sing because I want to come out, to express my horrid and fascinating loves, but the voice in which I seek liberation is a body I'm forbidden to kiss wholeheartedly, a body divided from itself, a body that doesn't know its meanings and that will die at the end of the scene; and so though I try to use my voice to tell you "I am having an orgasm!" or "Save me from this burning house!" the voice itself is the executioner and the crime and so cannot take sides or embody revolutionary ardor. Every time I sing of my pleasure you must listen for a *rip*, like cloth tearing.

Lucia is not just a victim. A performer paid to sing, she likes to make a show, to exaggerate. She demonstrates how to scream, defile, delay, draw blood, go high, grab attention, startle a crowd, break up family parties and town meetings. Her coloratura signifies joy's explosive force, a pleasure that's socially irresponsible, suicidal, and seemingly directed toward a man, though it is really aimed at a phantom and at paying customers. Who wouldn't identify with Lucia, the wandering voice, careening from impulse to impulse?

Hearing various divas try Lucia's mad scene, I find it hard to pay attention to the music or the words. I can pay attention only to the voice. How does this particular diva manage madness? The aria serves us a woman's vocal apparatus. Even when shallow practitioners—the nightingales—attempt this setpiece, it remains tragic, for the scene's depth consists in Lucia's body. Her gender isn't stationary or stable; it moves, through musical syntax, somewhere, and then somewhere else. We listen to Lucia's mad scene for the noises anatomy makes when it migrates.

Forced to marry a man she doesn't love, Lucia kills him, and in her bloody nightgown (maybe she holds a knife) she wanders onstage, where the wedding festivities continue. Her gown is voice-stained. Singing demands blood: vocal display can't occur until gender endures laceration. A few generations before Donizetti, would a castrato have sung Lucia's part?

Raimondo has already spilled her story, so Lucia enters to hushed, prurient anticipation. Audience pulse quickens: she's out of control! Raimondo's cry of "Eccola!" ("She's here!") announces a seismic shift in my gender, my erupting joy that the mad scene, structurally the opera's center (though it pretends to be going haywire), is about to begin.

Throughout the scene she converses with the flute. It speaks first, and she responds to its initiatives. Lucia has knifed Arturo and now in turn a shard of Edgardo's voice, in the guise of flute, stabs her: "Il dolce suono mi colpì di sua voce!" ("The sweet sound of his voice struck me!"). The flute is not—except in shape—a particularly masculine instrument, so how can Edgardo be a flute? Lucia's association of "flute" with "Edgardo" confounds our map of male versus female sounds, just as her ascensions from chest to head make her seem schizoid, androgynous. "Il fantasma!" she sings, loudly, on a low G-flat, and then for "ne separa" she jumps to the staff's ceiling: "Edgardo, Edgardo! Ah! Il fantasma, il fantasma ne separa!" ("Edgardo, Edgardo! Ah! The phantom, the phantom separates us!"). What phantom separates the lovers? Sexual difference. She can chase after echoes of Edgardo, she can try to imitate his fluty presence, but she can never move beyond impersonation: she can never actually *become* Edgardo. And yet her flashy attempts make it seem that she has swallowed or introjected her nemesis/innamorato, that Edgardo is now lodged in her larynx.

Just now I listened again to Callas's 1953 studio recording of this "il fantasma" passage: I chastise myself for misinterpreting, misrendering. Her timbre's inexpressible loveliness transcends and damns everything I say about this scene. Now I am in Lucia's position: I am trembling, and I am saying, "Alas, I am separated from a desired voice!"

Over the flute's B-flat-major chord, a trampoline on which a stage victim must jump, unaccompanied Lucia sings, "Un'armonia celeste, di', non ascolti?" ("A celestial harmony, don't you hear it?"). Lucia's drama is the listener's: hearing what can't be verified—sound waves set off by inmost wounds. The mad scene renders the vertigo of self-listening: like Lucia, I'm always falling into the gulf between the "I" and the sourceless unvocalized sigh at the psyche's pit. Lucia denies voice's authenticity because her every phrase is a vain flawed imitation ("can't get it right!") of a prior, unrehearsed, unverifiable arabesque.

Lucia wants to make a point. When Callas explodes on "Oh gioia che si sente"—she spits out the pitches—I feel that Lucia has reason to be optimistic, or that, within episodes of alienation, within one's own private mad scenes, there are moments when wandering joy discovers a motive and a destination; moments, like the first orgasm I ever had (for some time I've been tempted to say that Lucia's mad scene is a wet dream), when I hallucinate that passion has a purpose, reaches a termination, has rituals only the self alone in her powder room knows. Alone with my climax, I knew I was alone; I also knew I was performing, and that I was entering a system through an unmarked, seedy gate.

Fioritura overtakes Lucia, and she finally joins the flute in soul-numbing, soul-restoring unison: but at this moment when Lucia catches up to the magic phallus, the missing memory, the flute that is the reverie and the regret, she sounds craziest. Once she enters coloratura we know she's dead already, and we don't feel sorry for her: we admire her as a specimen.

In the cabaletta, "Spargi d'amaro pianto," she buries herself. Here she has a newlywed's smugness. Lucia, once at the mercy of gender, now coyly collaborates with it. No more meandering. No more staying out past her vocal curfew. Her staccato attacks and grace notes (Callas sings them in slow motion) convey a self-curbing gift for living on pointe.

The second time around, Joan Sutherland ornaments "Spargi d'a-maro pianto" so floridly I think of Madame Tussaud, wax manners no one remembers: in the nineteenth century, Lucia's cabaletta might have been terrifying, each mordent the spur of a separate sadism, angry roulades hurled at an audience unable to predict the denouement. On each of the three *Lucia* mad-scene recordings I own, the last, climactic, high note is worn down from overplaying, so I can hear its pitch but not its size or resonance. And this depletion, this lost note, tells me it is impossible to vest mystery and truth in a vocal climax. The final stretch of the cabaletta, repeating and embellishing old material, seems a drive through the ghost town of gender; I register surprise that the formerly grand stores and hotels have been boarded up for years.

I want Lucia to be a symbol of sexual willfulness, erotic independence, madness Artaud-style (the mad are more profound than the sane); but I always turn off the stereo, after the mad scene, feeling disappointed.

SALOME'S FINAL SCENE

Listening to Salome's final scene, I indulge in lush, irresponsible fantasy: Salome loses her mythic resonance and becomes the kind of girl I could have known—say, a 1975 prom queen—and by a leap of faith *I* become the kind of girl I could have known, *I* become a Princess of Judea in the sheath of a prom queen, and suddenly the nineteenth century's thicket of "perversity" turns into a dance soon to end, just a corny scene without ethical claims, nothing to take seriously, nothing to commit suicide over. Loving Salome's ecstasies, I dream that an entire century, the twentieth, hasn't happened yet, or that I can refuse it.

In Richard Strauss's *Salome* (1905), based on Oscar Wilde's play, she performs the Dance of the Seven Veils for Herod and receives Jokanaan's head as a reward. Her monologue melts together the separate deviations (necrophilia, masturbation, homosexuality, fetishism, S/M) into one alluring advertisement. Listening, I respond to the ad; I buy the product, Perversion.

The soprano finds hard proof for her head tones in John the Baptist's head. The head helps Salome sing, just as Arturo's blood aided Lucia: husband's blood and prophet's skull are trophies that prove the soprano's victory and give her wings to soar in a solo. But unlike Lucia, Salome fights an enormous orchestra; her cries for erotic satisfaction are atavistic, and must succumb to the orchestra's civilizing force. Until the orchestra subdues her, however, Salome dominates it; her head tones rise above the modern din, like a pastoral flute over Sodom.

What does Salome want? To give head, to kiss a severed head, to masturbate, to love someone of another religion and race. If in the violent and dissonant moments Strauss's orchestration calls these wishes perverse (while exploiting their spectacular effect), then the tonal, romantic moments legalize her hungers. Alternately the orchestra condemns Salome and clothes her in grace.

After her scene, the orchestra and the soldiers' shields crush her ("Kill that woman!"). *Salome* is a cautionary tale directed at voice culture. Its grim moral: *Head tones, and the men and women who produce them, are perverse. Those who love head tones are perverts, and should be killed.*

Do you see how Salome's music erodes my ethics? Tasting her tones of repentance and candy, I imagine that Salome doesn't know better: "Well, if I must," says Salome, no pervert, capitulating to the newfangled dissonances around her. The timbre of Ljuba Welitsch's voice on "Jokanaan" ("Yes, I will kiss thy mouth, Jokanaan") makes me want to be John the Baptist, even if I must then lose my head.

For her final, whispered conversation with the head, Ljuba Welitsch presses her mouth too close to the mike, so I hear cistern reverberation. And when the orchestra rejoins Salome for the climax, Montserrat Caballé sounds as if she has left the room, as if violent emotions engulfed her and she needed to sing unobserved in a distant lounge. Salome confesses her crime: "I have kissed thy mouth." This moment is the diva's triumph: she ends on a brash, high, summarizing phrase. When the soldiers rush forward, and the orchestra slays her, we will still remember when tonality cloaked Salome's desires in decency's raiment.

I heard Jessye Norman sing this scene at Tanglewood. I admired her carriage: head proudly elevated, as if she were separating it from the body. How do I hold my own head? Bent down. An old habit: I look at the ground when I walk, hunting for coins.

After hearing Jessye Norman sing Salome's death, I drove through the night: death everywhere, "no vacancy" signs, closed gas stations. I was alone with the state of Massachusetts, an unseeing immensity. I wanted to transform Salome into conduct; I wanted to "practice" Salome, as one practices advanced yoga, or Christian charity. But in what venue could I apply Salome's lessons?

Recently I dreamt of a severed head. It was opera's head, lying on a silver charger. I will recognize this head, if it returns, by its wispy beard—the beard of a dandy—and by the aura of uselessness surrounding the ears.

TATYANA'S LETTER SCENE

Stern aesthetician Adorno condemned gay Tchaikovsky for sentimentality; but ignore Adorno, for Tchaikovsky at his most purple, in Tatyana's "Letter Scene," from *Eugene Onegin* (1879), justifies "sick" emotions. How can my sexuality be sick if lush violins reinforce it?

Tatyana comes out by writing a love letter to Eugene Onegin: "I drink the magic potion of desire!" Alone in her bedroom, she composes the letter, breaks off, resumes. The indecisions of closeted composition: "I really should stop writing, I should tear up this manuscript."

Tatyana sings her melody once, and then a prolonged pause, like guilt ("I shouldn't come out of the closet after all"), arrests her, astonishing the strings, too, into silence, and with renewed force she repeats her theme;

in slower tempo (depression, after mania?) she goes to the writing table to transcribe the ecstasy she has just sung to the audience, and she complains, like a self-critical singer, "No, that's all wrong, I'll begin again";

then, with a speculative, hypothesizing sweetness, she punishes herself by imagining a life without Eugene Onegin;

and she opens her mouth wide again for the full-throated declaration, singing her emotions directly to the audience, not bothering to write them down in a letter (and I love this phrase because—how to explain the beauty?—it begins C major, immediately travels into sentimental chords, and as the melodic line *rises,* the harmony develops complications, and at the point of maximum congestion the soprano holds the note and then, regrettably, wilts, sinks, only to discover that she has returned to C major and the melody has recommenced: thus Tatyana's melody expatriates her and sends her home again, and this effect of detour-and-return bestows on Tatyana's sentiments the luster of the real, the autobiographical);

at the climax of the scene, Tatyana declares her solitude but the orchestra proves her wrong (when she sings "I am alone" *she is not alone,* an orchestra surrounds her with corroboration and blossoming);

and finally, after her climactic high note, the orchestra keens some unnamed plight, maybe Tatyana/Tchaikovsky's revolt against the human condition or the gay condition or the condition of having a "condition."

Finished! She says the letter is too frightening to reread but I will play this letter scene again and again to remember the excitement of saying "I'm queer" or "I'm in love with Eugene Onegin" or "I've confessed it all."

Queerness isn't a private condition. It occurs in public. Tatyana divulges, divulges, divulges. If only I could sing her signature phrase, that traverses me, and won't release me from its hold. . . .

Maybe I'm jealous of Tchaikovsky: another gay man, breathing life into Tatyana, while I stand on the sidelines, I a secondary, latter-day gay man, envious of the great Slav's hold over this vocalizing loner, Tatyana, whose throat he infused with ore.

· *9* · *Backward Glances*

DON JOSÉ AND MICAËLA'S DUET

From the beginning of memory I have wanted to know *Carmen*, and I presumed, also from the beginning, that it was too late for knowledge. I sought to revive an early, imaginary chapter in my life: the period of opera. How could I have believed, at age ten, that my life was already over, that my opera years were finished, when they had not even started? A package from Gotham Records arrived a week before my tenth birthday and waited unopened on the fireplace: it was the boxed set of *Carmen*, whose "Toreador Song" I knew from a grand-opera kiddie record. The distinctive smell of the Richmond/London *Carmen* set, the way Janine Micheau, the Micaëla of the moment, pronounces the "J" in "José": where can I place that odor, where deliver and expunge it? As I cream butter and sugar for a dessert in 1982 (I am always cooking when *Carmen* relocates my body), suddenly Micaëla sings to Don José about the village he has left behind, and I stop, afraid to enter the stereo room, because if I move, the music will mitigate a wound I want to keep intact.

Carmen, lewd-voiced mezzo almost outside opera's pale, has just sung to Don José her seductive "Habanera." Then Micaëla, hometown soprano, enters with a message from José's mother: a letter, some money, and . . . a kiss! Micaëla sings a seraphic melody while repeating the ailing mother's words: "Go find my José and give him this kiss!" (I may be the only living listener who considers this melody the world's most ineffable.) When Micaëla's lips meet José's, he suddenly sees his mother, and Micaëla participates in his delusion, overjoyed to be a go-between and steal a kiss in the process. But he grows distracted and stares at the flower Carmen threw him. Evil sorceress! Requiring once more the anodyne of melody, he repeats the entrancing tune that Micaëla delivered like a message from the grave, though he will postpone for another act his engagement with her timbre (it can't compete with Carmen's) and with soprano virtues: one chaste no-tongue kiss, a melody that brims with the forgotten.

Micaëla repeats the mother's message but converts it into her own soprano. Only a *mediated* mother delights the ear: if she came onstage and sang to José herself, her melody would not evoke nostalgia, but might threaten the operagoer's pleasure. In Micaëla, I love the mother's absence—the specter replaced and purified, turned into quotation, and into melody, the one principle I still believe is transcendent.

Listening to Micaëla, I experience Don José's nostalgia for hetero-sexuality, as if I once lived there: Eden I might have stayed in, had I tried, had I decided, had I said yes to Micaëla's sonority, had I not met Carmen. . . . Nostalgia for heterosexuality: a wish—paradoxical—to possess a body I do *not* typically wish to possess: a wish to stand inside Don José's silence and hear the mother's message infuse Micaëla's soprano frame. The possibility of joining Micaëla and recollecting the past! Better to listen to the recollection than actually to follow Micaëla out of the opera and into a country a few miles north of Bizet's *Carmen,* a province (I see and smell its trees) where Micaëla and the absent mother dwell.

If Micaëla entered my life I might travel backwards in time with her; I might embark on the voyage of retrieval she promises the lis-tener. Or I might ask her if she prefers women, if she courts me only because she knows I'll refuse her, if her timbre's hospital purity ex-presses her indifference to masculine tones. Maybe Micaëla's first love is the mother she impersonates, whose steadfastness she celebrates, whose kisses she receives and passes on.

AMONASRO AND AIDA: "PADRE!"

During a recent immersion in *Aida,* I dreamt Montserrat Caballé, a great Aida, was locked in a hotel room adjacent to mine. Through the wall, I could hear Caballé stumble, like a caged lion, or blind Audrey Hepburn bumping into furniture in *Wait Until Dark.* The soprano had flown here to perform in a festival. I was the festival.

Outside the moonlit temple of Isis, Aida must choose between lover and father. Will she extort a military secret from Radames, while her father, the exiled Ethiopian king Amonasro, eavesdrops? Aida the abased, the exhausted, the enslaved, the ignored, kneels on the stage, crying "Pietà!"

When Herva Nelli, on the Toscanini recording of *Aida,* sings "non imprecarmi" ("don't curse me"), her voice catches. I know her pain isn't real, and so I can enjoy it, borrow it. Herva Nelli's imperson-ation of Aida is *not* the best—in fact, experts call it mediocre—and so I can entrust it with secrets.

My favorite part: Aida goes as low as she can go on "della mia patria degna sarò" and then the long "o" of her last word meets the up and up and up of her father's melody, which Giuseppe Valdengo sings with gymnasium vibrato to prove he has the whole country behind him. Praising patriotism, he lifts Aida off the dirty floor. Why is the father melodic? Why do his hot harmonies shift, pool after pool of mirage in the desert?

Verdi wants us to hear the father from Aida's abject point of view, to imagine the father as the source of favors. Only when Aida has ruined her life will ruthless Amonasro dispense a noble phrase; Aida thinks she deserves no better. I, too, would throw myself on the floor and lap Amonasro's melody like milk. His cerulean melody, and the harmonies which gird it, reflect how badly Aida wants him. The extent of her desire is queer: Aida's abjection is my gay *arc-en-ciel,* my covenant, its spectrum promising I'll go somewhere with my desires, and not perish from them, unsatisfied.

Our passions drape purple over unkind objects. When you are crouched at your father's feet, anything he sings will sound divine. And Verdi, too, interprets the world from the daughter's groveling vantage; by investing Amonasro's "Okay-Aida-you-may-stand-up-now" gesture with a melody I'd swim ten miles to hear, Verdi tells me that even a curse sounds sweet as a blessing if you are a girl prone on the ground wanting her father's body and her lover's body and able to possess neither.

DIDO'S "WHEN I AM LAID IN EARTH"

Death can have a queer flavor, particularly when the dying lady speaks her last words to a girlfriend: as in Dido's lament, from Henry Purcell's *Dido and Aeneas* (1689), composed for Mr. Josias Priest's Boarding-School at Chelsey for Young Gentlewomen, a three-act opera that takes only one hour.

When Dido's lament begins, I think, "At last I've discovered a decorous, contained way to cope with immensities! I've found a position for my grief, somewhere between caricature and the Elgin Marbles!" Dido's Samothracian lament wards off the toxin of depth. She sings: "When I am laid, am laid in earth, may my wrongs create no trouble, no trouble in thy breast." First she moves upward on "When I am laid," carving *mobility* and *destination,* however glacial, from a grief that may have otherwise lacked a future: but then she turns into a frieze again, she gets stuck (broken record), "am laid—am laid" (hysterical tic, the double meaning of "laid"—getting laid—intruding, anachronistically), and she slides down a half-scale to the word "earth"; on "trouble" she appoggiaturas her body downward, signifying she *wants* trouble to be made, she wants Belinda and her audience of schoolgirls to weep forever because Queen Dido is gone from this world.

Monteverdi's Orfeo repeated "Rendetemi" ("Restore to me"), and Dido repeats "Remember me": "Remember me" first on a D, then again, repeated, on a D, then she sighs ("ah," I am taking my time, protracting my dying, turning it into gorgeous cortège), and moves, for another "Remember me," to a high G: REMEMBER ME!

One kind of self-pity is gay or girlish: another kind is restrained, stoic, has the smell of catharsis, and so can pretend to emerge, fat with homilies, straight from dominant culture. Lear and Brutus knew the manly ways of exhibiting sorrow. Dido's grief can *almost* be said to pass, to acquire Attic and Elizabethan dimensions, rather than to reek of the carnival and the women's room.

Dido's grief—her renunciation of life, her display of death wish in front of the dumbstruck Belinda—is queer because it is equally stiff and supple. She sings stonily. Then suddenly in the last high G "Remember me!" we believe that Flagstad, or Dido, or some woman existing between the diva and her character, wants to be remembered, and we believe in Belinda, standing there, loyal from the very beginning, nothing better to do in Carthage than hold the queen's hand . . . and my listening body's suspension between farce and tragedy, between stillness and plasticity, as if the statue were about to breathe and speak, is camp, and it is also operatic.

The opera lasts barely an hour. The entire tragedy seems a scene carved on a snuffbox: Purcell and librettist Nahum Tate make womanly tragedy miniature enough to fit the bloomer confines of a young girl's vocal body—the florid lines lying low, abjuring floridity. *Dido*'s girl-body proportions take the civilization-upholding legend of a "queen" *in extremis* and make it cute, tender, flaming.

Dido has a hard time expressing herself (coming out). At the beginning, Belinda extorts an erotic secret from the queen; by the end, Dido adores confessing, and bends Belinda's ear. When Dido reaches the stylized realms of plangency and lament, we are happy that at last she has earned the right to confess, that buried sadness has wormed its way out of her queen-stiff body. And so lament—that poker-faced, dignified mode—grows lavender, overcast with values that highbrows discountenance, pretending that opera is austere and mature.

The opera's message: confine your laments to the closet. At the brink of suicide, you'll have won the right to sigh. A girl will hold your hand and listen. Your queerness will have earned you just an aria, just the privilege, in the name of art and self-restraint, to expel your soul in front of amazed witnesses, schoolgirls who crave your scapegoat's part because, though the scariest, it is also the flashiest.

· 10 · Death

THE DEATH OF MIMÌ

Even before AIDS, I listened to death scenes so that I might identify with the dying woman and the bereft man, and so that I might produce "sentimentality" in my body: sighs, tears, extravagances I can never explain. Call by its proper name the pity and terror we feel when an opera mauls us, suffocates us with sentiment, makes no reasoned dramatic claim. Not camp, not bathos, not sentimentality: dignify queer emotion by saying *catharsis,* even if opera induces the wish, condemned as effeminate, never to reassemble the socialized self, but, instead, to remain in tears forever, to stay where Puccini's *La Bohème* (1896) places us.

Where does it place me? In self-pity; in the land of the choked voice; in the land of Jan Peerce's Toscanini-directed Rodolfo crying "Ah!" with cantorial wail as the orchestra resumes its reign of deception, its theme of Mimì the mirror woman—Mi Mi, she who knows but also questions her name, who lives to address herself, to designate or denote her emotions (the narcissist). I pretend I don't know Mimì is dying so I can surprise myself with pathos when she finally dies.

For Mimì's death to forge in my breast a new, nightingale-quick worldview, Puccini must supply onstage voyeurs and sympathizers: the other bohemians—Schaunard, Colline, Musetta, and Marcello—who have no lives of their own, who are slaves to the cult of Mimì. Her suffering and vindication depend on this stadium of glances: Rodolfo watches her, and the others watch Rodolfo, so that he, too, becomes a Mimì figure, a public wound.

The bohemians exit, leaving the lovers alone, and now returns the first-act love-duet theme, from Rodolfo's "I'm a poet and your hands are cold" aria (I write, you freeze). Mimì reaches her hands out to supplicate Rodolfo, his back turned—his bachelor preoccupation leaving Mimì alone with the love theme, once her property, now her tormentor, reiterating her insatiable desire. What love theme ever quenches the thirst it describes? But finally Rodolfo notices Mimì's grief, and *con grande espressione* she enters her big, sad, ultimate moment. Orchestral heartbeats give her funeral-march proclamation the spaciousness of depression, forgiveness, and bodily injury:

> Ho tante cose che ti voglio dire,
> o una sola, ma grande come il mare. . . .
>
> I have many things I want to tell you,
> or just one, but it is immense as the sea. . . .

The immense wordless ocean she summons is our tendency to drown in *La Bohème* and in her death; melodramatic identification opens, wet and unnameable, in the collective body of opera listeners.

Again and again Mimì nearly arrives at her last moment, but Puccini delays it. She says "la mia cuffietta, la mia cuffietta!" ("my bonnet, my bonnet!") without accompaniment and then rises to an E (still naked) and then attains an F, like health, for B-flat-major mirage (harps in the background) and *this, this* is her last moment? No. The orchestra mimics her past: repeats her theme to rub our noses in her imminent departure.

She declaims her final words to background fragments of "Che gelida manina": the best moment in her life was when Rodolfo noticed her cold hands.

> Qui, amor . . . sempre con te! . . .
> Le mani . . . al caldo . . . e . . . dormire. . . .
>
> Here, love . . . always with you! . . .
> Hands . . . in the warmth . . . and . . . to sleep. . . .

Licia Albanese drifts off, pallid and fatigued. Renata Tebaldi clings to the notes, sliding downpitch, as if she were hanging off a high ledge, fingers gripping the uncertain stone.

Mimì is dead, but Rodolfo still stares ignorantly out the window; bad news can't penetrate a dolt. The last dramatic gesture of the opera: how can we keep this secret from Rodolfo? But finally he says, "Che vuol dire, quell'andare e venire . . . quel guardarmi così?" ("What does it mean, this coming and going . . . why look at me like this?"), and then, after a fateful pause, the death-declaring orchestra gives backbone to his embarrassing lament, "Mimì," at the top of his range: our newest diversion is hearing the man cry "Mimì!" We receive, as background information, the music that accompanied Mimì's statement, "I have so many things I want to tell you, or just one, but it is immense as the sea, profound and infinite as the sea," and the music is deceitfully nautical and shimmery, like Debussy's *La Mer,* particularly after Rodolfo stops crying. ("I may never recover from this experience," I say to myself as the opera ends; but I always recover.) When the orchestra repeats Mimì's "my love for you is immense as the sea," the strings seem her spirit-messengers telling us, from heaven or hell, *to batten on my death scene, to thrive on what can't be summarized or spoken.* The music, at the end, narrates and justifies our tears, and hides this embarrassing release in a social context: operagoing. Protocol determines that the performance will end and that, unable to find exact words to describe the strange experience, we will dismiss it, underestimating melodrama's power to bind the solitary listener to a collective mourning.

SIEGLINDE'S EXIT

Listening to Sieglinde's exit, I kneel like Aida on the dusty floor and say, "I give up my people for the sake of this music pouring its destructive fluency over me." The only way I can fully appreciate Sieglinde is to lip-synch her.

In Act Three of Wagner's *Die Walküre* (1870), Sieglinde discovers her transfiguring pregnancy just before she exits the *Ring* for good. One may marvel at the *Ring* but there are few moments when one naïvely identifies with the characters. But my own excesses speak with Sieglinde when she departs. I'm mild-mannered Clark Kent but I become queer Superman when Sieglinde stretches out her arms with astonishment and dupes herself into feeling reborn, when she trusts transfiguration and doesn't bite it, suspecting a counterfeit. The body, if you take it literally, can lead you far astray.

Before Sieglinde decides to live for the sake of the unborn Siegfried, she wants to kill herself. Her beloved brother/lover Siegmund is dead. She struggles between an E and an F. Should I rise? Should I fall? The phrase hurts, exquisitely: the space—the no space—between E and F! And when Brünnhilde says, "You're pregnant," Sieglinde experiences a renascence so abrupt it sounds camp. Suddenly she cries out, "Save my child! Shield me, ye maidens!" In these exclamations Sieglinde advances Wagner's cycle and embodies his vision of woman, but she also represents a joy separate from his plan—a pleasure that I can loosely wear, like a cape. She subscribes to her body: she votes for thrill over theory. In the oppressive context of Brünnhilde's exhortations and brass fanfare, which seem malignly to declare, "Trust the auguries, and march toward the Master Race," Sieglinde's lyricism offers a sticky, exempted hideaway.

Brünnhilde gives her sister a taste of the future, the Coming Hero, by undraping the Siegfried theme: I welcome the clear articulation of any leitmotif, particularly this one, because of its thematic centrality and its simplicity. Hearing an emotional postulate announced as if it were self-evident and not in need of proof, I hearken, I obey. But the Siegfried theme exudes a sinister hygiene. The tune rouses me to a program I don't support, so I shut out the leitmotif, and listen instead to Sieglinde's exultation.

Sieglinde lives wholly within her change of heart, and dreams only of the high G she circles as in a mordent: "O hehrstes Wunder! Herrlichste Maid!" ("O sublime wonder! Glorious maid!"). Speaking about Brünnhilde, she also praises herself—her function as womb, as mouthpiece. (Surprisingly the orchestra crescendos within each phrase, suggesting an emotion already at its saturation point but wishing still to expand.) Sieglinde simply sits on the dais of her rapture. Yes, she participates in the Siegfried theme, cooperates with the orchestra, and says, "I am mostly womb"; but I value Sieglinde's ability to waylay Wagner's tetralogy in a gushy eddy he can't afford or explain. To a certain listener, the woman's exhalations surpass the political ingot called Siegfried.

Sieglinde operates as the principle of melodramatic excess and imported lyricism within *Die Walküre*. She stops the opera to stare into her solitude and exclaim, "O holy wonder!" She loves what her body can do. She doesn't care what Wotan thinks. She wants to hide in a cove with her memories, to gloat and reminisce. She knows she has made a sensational exit. Pity Sieglinde but not too much. Rather, envy her confident ecstasy: Sieglinde who grabs rapture like a lost twin, who sleeps with her brother, who retreats from the world, who believes her body's evidence, who stretches time with her phrase of death and departure, who opens my throat. . . . Not literally. In Sieglinde's presence a listener will keep a respectful, awed silence.

ISOLDE'S "LIEBESTOD"

Inside my borrowed vocal score of Richard Wagner's *Tristan und Isolde* (1865), some anonymous, all-knowing hand has glued a Dorothy Lamour movie ad, clipped from a July 8, 1945, Kansas City news-paper: "THIS GIRL'S PROBLEM COULD HAVE BEEN YOURS!"

Isolde's most famous moment, popularly called the "Liebestod," self-consciously an aria, concludes an opera divorced from the retro-grade idea of contained song. Tristan has just died, moments after Isolde finally returned to him. Too late! She stares into the middle distance and sees her lover revive. In Lucia's mad scene, the flutes proved the heroine demented, but in Isolde's "Liebestod," the orches-tra corroborates her vision. (A harp scatters arpeggios on her head.) Her solo reveals the paradox of female or effeminate solitude: when a woman makes imaginary love to a dead body, or when a woman desires a woman, or when a man desires a man, the entire culture sings along. Strauss orchestrated Salome's scene to sound perverse. Isolde, in her transfiguration, possesses an enviable ground: everyone in the audience wants the waves of string tremolo that she has achieved.

Isolde's "Liebestod" depends on certain beliefs, some homopho-bic, sewn into opera and queer culture. (1) Taboo love leads to death and is only satisfied by death. (2) In an unsanctioned love affair, gen-der dissolves. (3) Declarations of love rebound: Isolde serenades dead Tristan, but Isolde also serenades Isolde. (4) A dead, wounded, or paralyzed male body is an erotic sight and will inspire a soprano to sing. (5) Gay love grows social, sublimated, and audible by passing through the soprano voice.

I can't describe what happens in the "Liebestod": conglomera-tion of my every lyric impulse, long postponed, finally sieved into a soprano's body. A complete harmonious society (an audience, an or-chestra) surrounds Isolde, and affirms her as power's mouthpiece, even while she performs the diminuendos of a scapegoat. She controls the tune and doesn't merely comment on a melody more prominently advanced by the orchestra. Singing fills her paranoid head with vibra-tions that equal the hallucinated breath she sees fluttering from Tris-tan's lips, and she says, "Do I alone hear this melody?" ("Höre ich nur diese Weise?"), but we hear it, too, so we want to tell her, "No, you're not alone." For Isolde and for the listener, the interminable opera has yielded funereal fruit. If I must pass through death to reach my love, will I renounce eroticism?

It is unsavory to end this book with death. And yet opera offers nothing else.

I imagine Jessye Norman girding herself for a phrase in the mid-dle of the "Liebestod": I call it *the vindication phrase*, simply because I require a private vocabulary to describe my opera pleasures. I imagine Jessye Norman saying to herself, "Now it is the end of the opera, the end of my long night. I must turn on the 'majesty' effect and relax, and spread out the powerful sound I've been saving, because when immortality arrives I want Isolde to be ready." As the "Liebestod" rises toward its ending, I close my eyes and feel torsion in my chest, as if I were a modern suspension bridge, a marvel of technological sophistication.

Isolde ends on the phrase "höchste Lust" ("supremest bliss"), and sinks into the arms of her female companion, Brangaene. The harmonic resolution at the end of this aria, the end of an opera that had postponed such satisfactions, excites me, but I prefer the vindication phrase in the middle, because gay culture, condemned to embody endings, resists them.

Where have I traveled in this pocket guide too bulky for a pocket or a purse? At thirty-three, old enough to know better, what inquiry have I advanced by repeating, five times a morning, the record of Isolde's "Liebestod," and struggling, against my own naïveté, to put into words the emotions that overwhelm me when I listen?

I invited myself into the opera house, and on the sacred premises I have spoken too loudly, chewed with my mouth open, revealed my own throat. I, who possess no special knowledge of music, have blurted out, in public, my experience of living inside a modern queer identity—just my own experience, not everyone's; I've dared to narrow the commonwealth down to my own body, and I've pinned these private, nonuniversal intimations of "queerness" onto opera arias that put me in a trance.

Isolde sings, "Do I alone hear this melody?" and I want to say to you, "Do you hear what I hear? When you listen to opera, do you hear your least sanctioned desires speak?"

Recently I dreamt I stood in an arena, beside an upright piano, its lid piled with scores to every opera I've tapped in this pocket guide.

I was finally a singer! And although I was performing *Werther* and *Lucia* next week, I decided to devote the weekend to muscle building. I walked from the arena to the gym, and lifted weights. And though at this point the dream was fading, I entered the steam room for a last few instants, and saw a gay guy with his towel protectively wrapped around his middle: to hide incipient arousal, or to hide plumpness? I knew he was gay because of his eyes, his haircut, his intensity. He opened his mouth. He was about to sing "Pourquoi me réveiller." Then the dream shut down.

This person exists, outside the dream. He is real. He is the opera queen: my shy reflection, my flamboyant ghost. I've seen him at the local opera and around town. We pass each other on Grove Street, by the secret societies and the cemetery, and we never say hello. But we know each other, with a complicated, abiding knowledge.

Notes

· *CHAPTER ONE: Opera Queens* ·

14   *"O throat!"*: Walt Whitman, "Out of the Cradle Endlessly Rocking," *Complete Poetry and Collected Prose* (New York: Library of America, 1982), 391.

14   "A tenor large": Whitman, "Song of Myself," *Complete Poetry,* 215.

14   "sodomy changes the voice": letter dated 1896, in J.-K. Huysmans, *The Road from Decadence: Selected Letters of J.-K. Huysmans,* ed. Barbara Beaumont (London: Athlone Press, 1989), 157–58.

14   "the voice is one": Earl Lind, *Autobiography of an Androgyne* (1918; New York: Arno Press, 1975), 11.

14   "At the opera": Ibid., 27.

15   "Call me a freak": Marcia Davenport, *Of Lena Geyer* (New York: Charles Scribner's Sons, 1936), 208.

15   "meant as much to me": Ibid., 203.

15   "fresh water pouring": Ibid., 232–33.

15   "gripped me": Ibid., 233.

15   "It was exactly": Ibid., 225.

17   "opened and expanded": Marcel Proust, *Remembrance of Things Past,* vol. 1, trans. C. K. Scott Moncrieff and Terence Kilmartin (New York: Vintage, 1981), 227.

17   "But while I was humming": Ibid., 870.

17   "I can remember seeing": Richard Edgcumbe, *Musical Reminiscences of an Old Amateur for Fifty Years, from 1773 to 1823* (London: W. Clarke, 1824), 16.

18   "As to the number": *Opera News* 4 (December 4, 1939): 19 (hereafter cited as *ON*).

22   "Miss Garden never knew": quoted in Mary Garden and Louis Biancolli, *Mary Garden's Story* (New York: Simon & Schuster, 1951), 186.

22   "I used to study": Mary Watkins Cushing, *The Rainbow Bridge* (New York: G. P. Putnam's Sons, 1954), 10.

22   "I no longer passed": Ibid., 11–12.

23   "I . . . felt my pulses": Ibid., 173.

23   photograph of Eby [and] Ponselle: Gordon M. Eby, *From the Beauty of*

243

Embers: A Musical Aftermath (New York: Robert Speller & Sons, 1981), 18.

23 "pyramid of bouquets": quoted in H. Sutherland Edwards, *The Prima Donna: Her History and Surroundings from the Seventeenth to the Nineteenth Century,* vol. 2 (1888; New York: Da Capo Press, 1978), 106.

23 "matinée girls": Nellie Melba, *Melodies and Memories* (Garden City, N.Y.: Doubleday, Doran & Co., 1928), 128–29.

23 "sixteen exquisite little bouquets": Ibid., 324.

24 Jenny Lind: Edwards, *Prima Donna* 2:22.

24 Sontag-guard: Edwards, *Prima Donna* 1:220.

24 "I abhor such practices": quoted in Edwards, *Prima Donna* 1:20.

24 "chosen friends": Melba, *Melodies and Memories,* 111.

24 "Callas's people gloated": Kenn Harris, *Renata Tebaldi* (New York: Drake Publishers, 1974), 30.

24 "the Tebaldiani that evening": Ibid., 28.

25 "stopped traffic on West 40th": Ibid., 29.

25 "Tebaldi, always glad": Ibid., x.

25 "on the first night": Ibid., 45.

25 "queen of the Met regulars": Patrick J. Smith, quoted in Rupert Christiansen, ed., *The Grand Obsession: An Anthology of Opera* (London: Collins, 1988), 132.

25 "originally mastered by": Harris, *Renata Tebaldi,* 118–19.

26 "Your devoted little friend": quoted in Winifred Ponder, *Clara Butt: Her Life-Story* (1928; New York: Da Capo Press, 1978), 144.

26 "search out every pirated": Dorothy Kirsten, with Lanfranco Rasponi, *A Time to Sing* (Garden City, N.Y.: Doubleday, 1982), 100.

26 "When the news": Ibid., 162.

26 "She is the sort": Clara Louise Kellogg, *Memoirs of an American Prima Donna* (New York: G. P. Putnam's Sons, 1913), 207.

26 " 'I've come to ask you' ": Ibid., 204.

27 "She studied my 'ways' ": Ibid., 206.

27 "Who knows what sympathies": Ibid., 216.

27 Monsieur de Saxe: Blanche Marchesi, *Singer's Pilgrimage* (1923; New York: Da Capo Press, 1978), 138.

27 "Let no one think": Ida Cook, *We Followed Our Stars* (New York: William Morrow, 1950), 214.

27 "private vindication": Ibid., 222.

27 "No doubt she needed": Ibid., 27.

27 "fierce violet shade": Ibid., 76.

27 "she was probably as moved": Ibid., 239.

28 "we passed the receiver": Ibid., 224.

28 Philothée O'Neddy: April FitzLyon, *Maria Malibran* (London: Souvenir Press, 1987), 77.

28 "fine people and gay": Willa Cather, *Youth and the Bright Medusa* (New York: Alfred A. Knopf, 1920), 205.

28 "was Paul's fairy": Ibid., 215.

28 "He felt now": Ibid., 227.

28 "horrible yellow wallpaper": Ibid., 218.

33 "appears to lead": quoted in Joe Morella and Edward Z. Epstein, *Judy: The Films and Career of Judy Garland* (New York: Citadel Press, 1969), 215.

33 "Photographs and posters": quoted in Morella and Epstein, *Judy,* 212.

37 "It's a shame": quoted in John Ardoin, *Callas: In Her Own Words,* broadcast on KUSC-FM, Los Angeles, February 1988, reissued on cassette by Pale Moon Music, 1988.

38 "I have been an unusual": Lind, *Autobiography of an Androgyne*, 116.
38 "It was the practice": Benjamin Lumley, *Reminiscences of the Opera* (1864; New York: Da Capo Press, 1976), 63.
39 the women waved handkerchiefs: FitzLyon, *Maria Malibran*, 45.
40 "It seemed to me that my love": Proust, *Remembrance of Things Past* 1:870.
41 "The Met's production": *Opera Fanatic*, no. 3 (1989): 85.
42 "A new world": quoted in Robert D. Faner, *Walt Whitman and Opera* (Carbondale: Southern Illinois University Press, 1951), 43.
42 "In the darkening sky": Willa Cather, *Lucy Gayheart* (1935; New York: Vintage, 1976), 11.
42 "he was sitting quietly": Willa Cather, *The Song of the Lark* (1915; Boston: Houghton Mifflin Co., 1988), 359.
43 "young Billy Crawford": *ON* 14 (January 16, 1950): 3.
44 "The friendships and enmities": Cook, *We Followed Our Stars*, 41.
44 "young divinity student": *ON* 8 (November 1, 1943): 23–24.
44 "For a super standee": *ON* 7 (February 22, 1943): 10.
44 " 'I prefer to stand' ": *ON* 10 (December 3, 1945): 12.
45 "an elaborate web": Terrence McNally, *The Lisbon Traviata*, in *Three Plays by Terrence McNally* (New York: Plume, 1990), 88.

· CHAPTER TWO: *The Shut-in Fan: Opera at Home* ·

For the phonograph's history, I am indebted to Roland Gelatt, *The Fabulous Phonograph: From Tin Foil to High Fidelity* (Philadelphia: J. B. Lippincott, 1955). See also Theodor Adorno, "The Curves of the Needle," "The Form of the Phonograph Record," and "Opera and the Long-Playing Record," *October* 55 (Winter 1990): 49–66; Thomas Y. Levin, "For the Record: Adorno on Music in the Age of Its Technological Reproducibility," *October* 55 (Winter 1990): 23–47; Roger Boar, Jacques Lowe, and Russell Miller, *The Incredible Music Machine* (London: Quartet Books, 1982); Brian Rust, *The American Record Label Book* (New Rochelle, N.Y.: Arlington House, 1978); Michael W. Sherman, *The Paper Dog: An Illustrated Guide to 78 R.P.M. Victor Record Labels 1900–1958* (A.P.M. Press, 1987); J. B. Steane, *The Grand Tradition: Seventy Years of Singing on Record* (London: Duckworth, 1974). Victor Records materials are in Historical Sound Recordings Collection, Sterling Memorial Library, Yale University; I thank Richard Warren for his assistance.

48 "with or without": Frederick J. Garbit, *The Phonograph and Its Inventor, Thomas Alva Edison* (Boston: Gum, Bliss & Co., 1878), 10.
49 "reproduce the sob": quoted in Gelatt, *Fabulous Phonograph*, 52.
49 "blind asylums, hospitals": Garbit, *Phonograph and Its Inventor*, 11.
53 "at a painting": Thomas Mann, *The Magic Mountain*, trans. H. T. Lowe-Porter (1924; New York: Alfred A. Knopf, 1946), 637.
55 "Heavens, it's *me*": quoted in *New Victor Records* (March 1918): 27.
55 "Ah, *mon Dieu!*": quoted in Boar, Lowe, Miller, *Incredible Music Machine*, 81.
55 "A mirror may reflect": *New Victor Records* (July 1920): 27.
55 "some tone on the hills": Walter Pater, *The Renaissance: Studies in Art and Poetry*, ed. Donald L. Hill (Berkeley and Los Angeles: University of California Press, 1980), 188.
55 "Into every life": *New Victor Records* (October 1918): 2.
57 "if you could stretch": *New Victor Records* (September 1917): 39.
57 "It would seem superfluous": Victor Records, *The New Complete Catalogue* (1933), 3.

57 "If you desire": *Victor Record Review* 2 (April 1940): 2.
58 "The recommended method": *Victor Record Review* 1 (August 1938): 11.
59 "if a record": Hans Fantel, "Record Hygiene–II," *ON* 29 (March 6, 1965): 32.
61 "More good music": *New Victor Music: List of New Records* (January 1926): 31.
61 "Like the concept Love": Karl F. Reuling, "High Fidelity," *ON* 21 (November 19, 1956): 24–25.
63 "Searching for that one": *New Victor Records* (October 1918): 14.
63 "curious voyagers": *Victor Record Review* 1 (May 1938): 2.
63 "living organism": *New Victor Records* (October 1918): 14.
63 "Since recording standard": *ON* 26 (October 28, 1961): 30.
64 "instead of learning": Manuel Puig, *Betrayed by Rita Hayworth,* trans. Suzanne Jill Levine (New York: Vintage, 1981), 76.
64 "Color the illustrations": "How to Get Ready for an Opera Broadcast," *ON* 12 (January 5, 1948): 30.
65 "No sooner was the historic": *ON* 11 (December 9, 1946): 14.
65 "the smooth and graceful": *ON* 10 (February 11, 1946): 31.
66 "An amazing number": *New Victor Records* (November 1911): 2.
66 "trashy," "refining influence": *New Victor Records* (December 1907): 10.
66 "The music of the second": *ON* 8 (February 14, 1944): 32.
67 "ruefully started rubbing": *ON* 7 (November 23, 1942): 11.
67 "In the final temple": *ON* 6 (December 8, 1941): 16.
67 "Miss Traubel's costumes": *ON* 8 (December 6, 1943): 22.
67 "study the pictures": "How to Get Ready for an Opera Broadcast," *ON* 12 (January 5, 1948): 30.
72 "Their Feet Are Young": *ON* 16 (November 12, 1951): 8.
72 Lee Foley: *ON* 6 (January 19, 1942): 24.
76 "We're all 'shut ins' ": quoted in *New Victor Records* (May 1917): 13.
77 "blind," "an earnest listener," "ardent opera lover": Cedric Hart, "Opera in the Sick Room," *ON* 7 (November 9, 1942): 18–20.
77 "I am lame": *ON* 8 (March 6, 1944): 3.
77 beside her idol Risë Stevens: *ON* 13 (April 11, 1949): 4.
77 "Chin-Up Girl": *ON* 9 (December 4, 1944): 2.
77 "When Helen Keller": *ON* 14 (March 13, 1950): 2.
77 "led backstage": *ON* 9 (April 2, 1945): 11.
77 Eleanor Steber: Leslie Rubinstein, "Improper Diva," *ON* 55 (October 1990): 11.
78 "In Atlanta if I spoke": *ON* 7 (November 16, 1942): 32.
78 "I was so entranced": *ON* 9 (December 25, 1944): 32.
78 in Betty's memory: *ON* 11 (October 21, 1946): 31.
79 "Every day she": *Favorite Records Review* (October 1922): 5–6.
79 "gorged his sensitive": *Victor Record Review* 2 (July 1939): 15.
79 "make contact": *Victor Record Review* 2 (September 1939): 3.
79 "Bampton, Moscona, Novotna": *ON* 11 (December 23, 1946): 31.
80 "starry-eyed over the mere": *ON* 11 (March 10, 1947): 31.
80 "beautiful natural bass": Jan Popper, "Anyone Can Be an Opera Lover," *ON* 15 (January 29, 1951): 30–31.
80 "A Loving Opera Fan": *ON* 10 (December 3, 1945): 31.
80 "I am the only person": *ON* 21 (February 18, 1957): back cover.
80 "I am an opera-lover," "found anyone": *ON* 20 (December 19, 1955): 33.
80 "I actually do not know": *ON* 20 (March 19, 1956): 31.

82   "much more thrilled": Ellen R. Silvers, "Wishbones for Opera," *ON* 16 (January 28, 1952): 26–27.
82   "red velvet, sequin-trimmed": *ON* 12 (December 22, 1947): 29.

· *CHAPTER THREE: The Codes of Diva Conduct* ·

85   "At any rate": Melba, *Melodies and Memories,* 73.
86   "I became, in": Frances Alda, *Men Women and Tenors* (Boston: Houghton Mifflin, 1937), 118.
86   " 'My,' I would say": Garden and Biancolli, *Mary Garden's Story,* 252.
86   "I, Mary Garden": Ibid., 253.
86   "I always had my audience": Ibid., 154.
86   "it left Melba's throat": Ibid., 94.
86   "All my creations": Ibid., 125.
86   "I have a horror": Ibid., 276.
86   "had to come out": Kellogg, *Memoirs,* 92.
87   "open secret": Cather, *Song of the Lark,* 409.
87   Marian Anderson felt apprehensive: Marian Anderson, *My Lord, What a Morning* (New York: Viking Press, 1956), 78.
87   Mrs. Price: Hugh Lee Lyon, *Leontyne Price: Highlights of a Prima Donna* (New York: Vantage Press, 1973), 27.
88   "dollies": Emma Eames, *Some Memories and Reflections* (1927; New York: Arno Press, 1977), 11–12.
88   "little bit of a doll," "Wonderful Child": Herman Klein, *The Reign of Patti* (New York: Century Co., 1920), 18, 34.
89   "Here, little one": quoted in Klein, *Reign of Patti,* 19.
89   "first sensed the psychic": C. E. Le Massena, *Galli-Curci's Life of Song* (New York: Paebar Co., 1945), 180.
90   "Was there a hidden": Ibid., 155.
90   "Of course I was": quoted in Mary Jane Matz, *Opera Stars in the Sun: Intimate Glimpses of Metropolitan Personalities* (New York: Farrar, Straus & Cudahy, 1955), photo insert, 240–41.
90   "dressed like a man": Mary Lawton, *Schumann-Heink: The Last of the Titans* (New York: Macmillan, 1935), 27.
90   "There is Nature": quoted in Ponder, *Clara Butt,* 19.
90   "MARY GARDEN, SUPERWOMAN": Garden and Biancolli, *Mary Garden's Story,* 111.
90   "even at the risk": Le Massena, *Galli-Curci's Life,* 27.
91   "In thirty seconds": Melba, *Melodies and Memories,* 247.
91   "I shall be one": Le Massena, *Galli-Curci's Life,* 30.
91   "Personality is the most": quoted in Emily R. Coleman, *The Complete Judy Garland* (New York: Harper & Row, 1990), 7.
92   "voice is personality": Cather, *Song of the Lark,* 318.
92   "Oh, Mamma": Eames, *Some Memories,* 13.
92   "Living with her": Kirsten, *Time to Sing,* 44.
92   "which in her native": Harris, *Renata Tebaldi,* 14.
93   "I am not afraid": quoted in FitzLyon, *Maria Malibran,* 184.
93   "Mary Garden, this": quoted in Grace Moore, *You're Only Human Once* (Garden City, N.Y.: Doubleday, Doran & Co., 1944), 112.
93   "Salvatore, j'ai enfin," "Alors": quoted in Melba, *Melodies and Memories,* 35.
93   "everybody who heard": quoted in Melba, *Melodies and Memories,* 35.
93   "My bed was covered": Moore, *You're Only Human Once,* 135.
94   "The crown that was Mary": quoted in Eby, *From the Beauty,* 64.

94   "Mary, Thaïs must": quoted in Garden and Biancolli, *Mary Garden's Story,* 45.
95   "Dorothy, that first": quoted in Kirsten, *Time to Sing,* 64.
95   "The evening was over": Kirsten, *Time to Sing,* 13.
96   "I believe that I owe": Ponder, *Clara Butt,* 217.
96   "I sang what my mother": Lawton, *Schumann-Heink,* 4.
96   "mother the insistent": Le Massena, *Galli-Curci's Life,* 303.
96   "seductive vision": Geraldine Farrar, *Such Sweet Compulsion* (New York: Greystone Press, 1938), 56.
96   "Thursday 9th": quoted in Kellogg, *Memoirs,* 167.
97   "I often think that the art": Kellogg, *Memoirs,* 93–94.
97   "tenors are queer creatures": Ibid., 71.
97   "I must have been a rather queer": Ibid., 8.
97   "queer silence": Ponder, *Clara Butt,* 50.
97   "so lovely, so": Moore, *You're Only Human Once,* 157.
97   "in flaming headlines": Farrar, *Such Sweet Compulsion,* 139.
98   "very queer, extraordinarily": Blanche Marchesi, *Singer's Pilgrimage* (1923; Da Capo Press, 1978), 39–40.
98   "During my entire career": Eames, *Some Memories,* 133.
98   "Such pretty girls": Ibid., 33.
98   "Men (as such)": Eby, *From the Beauty,* 11.
98   "various shades": Moore, *You're Only Human Once,* 15.
99   "You are my goddess": Ibid., 28.
99   "To be a buffer": Cushing, *Rainbow Bridge,* 119.
99   "This she tweaked": Ibid., 124.
99   "flat and heaving bosom": Ibid., 113.
99   "Put your hand down": quoted in Cushing, *Rainbow Bridge,* 184.
99   "handsome, tremendously charming": Garden and Biancolli, *Mary Garden's Story,* 9.
99   "The surgeon went to Lily's": Ibid., 84.
99   "a shiver of freedom": Ibid., 144–45.
100 "I never feel": quoted in FitzLyon, *Maria Malibran,* 85.
100 "I think a theatrical": quoted in FitzLyon, *Maria Malibran,* 89.
101 "fried brown and curled": quoted in Henry C. Lahee, *The Grand Opera Singers of To-Day* (Boston: L. C. Page & Co., 1912), 79.
102 "If I were near": quoted in Rupert Christiansen, *Prima Donna: A History* (Harmondsworth: Penguin Books, 1984), 72.
102 "elephant that swallowed": quoted in Henry Pleasants, *The Great Singers: From the Dawn of Opera to Our Own Time* (New York: Simon & Schuster, 1966), 224.
102 "at every performance": Carl Van Vechten, *Interpreters* (New York: Alfred A. Knopf, 1920), 48.
103 "The cords of my": Melba, *Melodies and Memories,* 208.
104 "an asp, a fury": quoted in Pleasants, *Great Singers,* 108.
104 "features horribly disfigured": François Joseph Fétis, quoted in Pleasants, *Great Singers,* 215.
105 "ugly habit of pressing": Ellen Creathorne Clayton, *Queens of Song* (New York: Harper & Brothers, 1865), 157.
105 "slight squint perceptible": Clayton, *Queens,* 72.
105 "I adore the unusual": quoted in Ethan Mordden, *Demented: The World of the Opera Diva* (New York: Franklin Watts, 1984), 236.
105 "wanted to be a surgeon": Anderson, *My Lord,* 25.
105 "small, ugly": Henry Scott Holland and W. S. Rockstro, *Jenny Lind the Artist, 1820–1851* (London: John Murray, 1893), 12.

105 "perverse, unreasonable": Signora [Regina] Mingotti, *An Appeal to the Pub-lick* (London: the author, 1756), 2, 4.

106 "Negroid sound": quoted in Rosalyn M. Story, *And So I Sing: African-American Divas of Opera and Concert* (New York: Warner Books, 1990), 38.

106 "negro blood": Edmond Cottinet, quoted in FitzLyon, *Maria Malibran*, 230.

106 "little brown throat": quoted in Klein, *Reign of Patti*, 38–39.

106 "born exponent": Klein, *Reign of Patti*, 86.

106 "tawny Tuscan": quoted in Clayton, *Queens of Song*, 17.

107 "dignity of a dusky": quoted in "S. Hurok presents Marian Anderson," publicity flyer, James Weldon Johnson Collection, Beinecke Library, Yale University.

107 "She's a rosebud": quoted in Farrar, *Such Sweet Compulsion*, 105.

107 civil rights: FitzLyon, *Maria Malibran*, 125–32.

108 "My mother was almost": quoted in Edwards, *Prima Donna* 1:300.

108 "marched to her ordeal": Cushing, *Rainbow Bridge*, 115.

108 "Never mind": quoted in Edwards, *Prima Donna* 1:106.

109 "sang *Mimi, Nedda*": Lahee, *Grand Opera Singers*, 212.

110 "made her début": Ibid., 59.

110 "Madame Butt": quoted in Ponder, *Clara Butt*, 239.

111 "Remember, wherever you are": Anderson, *My Lord*, 11.

112 "the smell of flowers": quoted in Cushing, *Rainbow Bridge*, 172.

112 "la bataille des fleurs": Cushing, *Rainbow Bridge*, 15.

112 "Like most prima donnas": Lyon, *Leontyne Price*, 131.

112 "Adelaide, tu canti!": quoted in (Mrs.) R. C. Waterston, *Adelaide Phillipps: A Record* (Boston: A. Williams & Co., 1883), 32.

113 "What a dreadful": quoted in Garden and Biancolli, *Mary Garden's Story*, 92.

113 "I am sure": Farrar, *Such Sweet Compulsion*, 140.

113 "these artists sing trifles": quoted in Cushing, *Rainbow Bridge*, 106.

114 "Giulietta Simionato": quoted in Lyon, *Leontyne Price*, 140.

117 "*Either Alda or myself*": Alda, *Men Women and Tenors*, 72.

118 "I would sit there": Cushing, *Rainbow Bridge*, 102–3.

119 "my white silk": Garden and Biancolli, *Mary Garden's Story*, 3.

119 "A small trickle": Ibid., 107.

119 "her pet cat": Le Massena, *Galli-Curci's Life*, 139.

119 "like a new-born": Marchesi, *Singer's Pilgrimage*, 223.

119 "dog's breath": Ibid., 291.

120 "Gertrude Stein": Gertrude Stein, *The Autobiography of Alice B. Toklas* (1933; New York: Vintage, 1961), 89.

120 "At last I was dressed": Alda, *Men Women and Tenors*, 29.

120 "flowing folds": publicity flyer, James Weldon Johnson Collection.

122 "a law unto herself": Ponder, *Clara Butt*, 204.

122 "In the second part": Le Massena, *Galli-Curci's Life*, 79.

122 "Surely no one": Eby, *From the Beauty*, 11–12.

122 "costume possibilities": quoted in Eby, *From the Beauty*, 6.

122 "I have never forgotten": quoted in Alda, *Men Women and Tenors*, 51.

123 "altered for personal use": Eby, *From the Beauty*, 42.

123 "compatible with the grandeur": Ibid., 20.

123 "Informal portrait": Rosa Ponselle and James A. Drake, *Ponselle: A Singer's Life* (Garden City, N.Y.: Doubleday & Co., 1982), 212–13.

124 "Is she not divine": quoted in Marchesi, *Singer's Pilgrimage*, 140.

126 Desmâtins: Edwards, *Prima Donna* 1:70.

126 "an extremely original medley": Ibid., 211.

126 "Suddenly the bejeweled": Lyon, *Leontyne Price,* 103.
126 "Gerster cakes": Marchesi, *Singer's Pilgrimage,* 36.
126 "if a person": Ibid., 280.
127 "I have advised": Ibid., 201.
128 "I didn't sing well": quoted in Lawton, *Schumann-Heink,* 217.
128 "Poor Nordica": Lawton, *Schumann-Heink,* 218.
128 "internal derangement": Clayton, *Queens of Song,* 135–36.
128 "a remote part of her house": Ibid., 23.
128 Francesca Cuzzoni: Edwards, *Prima Donna* 1:52.
128 *"Enfin j'ai retrouvé":* quoted in Melba, *Melodies and Memories,* 333.
129 "I wish to tell you": Eames, *Some Memories,* 303–4.
129 "I thank you": quoted in Holland and Rockstro, *Jenny Lind,* 197.
129 "Goodbye is of": quoted in Brian Adams, *La Stupenda: A Biography of Joan Sutherland* (Richmond, Victoria: Hutchinson of Australia, 1980), 183.
129 "I have never made": quoted in Cushing, *Rainbow Bridge,* 256.
129 "dissolved in tears": Moore, *You're Only Human Once,* 91.
129 de l'Épine: Edwards, *Prima Donna* 1:15.
129 "I almost wish": Lawton, *Schumann-Heink,* 191.
130 Cuzzoni came back: Clayton, *Queens of Song,* 60.
130 "prodigy of the stage": Gustav zu Pulitz, quoted in Edwards, *Prima Donna* 1:241.
130 "Of course she did not sing": Cushing, *Rainbow Bridge,* 301.
131 "heavy and dull": Clayton, *Queens of Song,* 174.
131 "It was marvelous": quoted in Story, *And So I Sing,* 167.
131 "I am Melba": Melba, *Melodies and Memories,* 247.
131 "I began my career": quoted in Eby, *From the Beauty,* 85.
131 "Tell Mr. Simpson": Marchesi, *Singer's Pilgrimage,* 166.
132 "Do you call": quoted in Waterston, *Adelaide Phillipps,* 47.
132 "Ah, how I dote": quoted in Edwards, *Prima Donna* 2:103.
132 "a clearer vision": Kellogg, *Memoirs,* 62.
132 *"Ma chère* Nellie": quoted in Melba, *Melodies and Memories,* 51.
132 "Isn't that nice": quoted in Cushing, *Rainbow Bridge,* 213.
132 "It is the end": quoted in Cushing, *Rainbow Bridge,* 236.
133 "You forget, *maestro":* quoted in Alda, *Men Women and Tenors,* 86.

• *CHAPTER FOUR: The Callas Cult* •

I am indebted to John Ardoin, *Callas: In Her Own Words;* John Ardoin, *The Callas Legacy: The Complete Guide to Her Recordings* (New York: Charles Scribner's Sons, 1991); John Ardoin, *Callas at Juilliard: The Master Classes* (New York: Alfred A. Knopf, 1987); Evangelia Callas, with Lawrence G. Blochman, *My Daughter Maria Callas* (New York: Fleet Publishing Corp., 1960); Jackie Callas, *Sisters* (New York: St. Martin's Press, 1989); a video documentary, *Maria Callas: Life and Art,* produced and directed by Alan Lewens and Alistair Mitchell, Picture Music International, 1987, released by Kultur; David A. Lowe, ed., *Callas, As They Saw Her* (New York: Ungar Publishing Co., 1986); Giovanni Battista Meneghini, with Renzo Allegri, *My Wife Maria Callas,* trans. Henry Wisneski (New York: Farrar Straus Giroux, 1982); Pierre-Jean Rémy, *Maria Callas: A Tribute,* trans. Catherine Atthill (New York: St. Martin's Press, 1978); Nadia Stancioff, *Maria Callas Remembered* (New York: E. P. Dutton, 1987); Arianna Stassinopoulos, *Maria Callas: The Woman behind the Legend* (New York: Simon & Schuster, 1981). The example of Richard Dyer's *Heavenly Bodies: Film Stars and Society* (New York: St. Martin's Press, 1986) helped me write this chapter.

135 "Come on, men": Catherine Clément, *Opera, or the Undoing of Women,* trans. Betsy Wing (Minneapolis: University of Minnesota Press, 1988), 28.

136 "Callas? She was pure electricity": quoted in Stassinopoulos, *Maria Callas,* 121.

137 "flapping high C": Ardoin, *Callas Legacy,* 100.

139 "I want my art": quoted in Meneghini, *My Wife,* 62.

140 "Don't come to us": quoted in *Time* 68 (Oct. 29, 1956): 62.

141 "When you are summoned": Meneghini, *My Wife,* 215–16.

141 "I'm afraid he's": quoted in Ardoin, *Callas: In Her Own Words.*

142 "Don't you just love": Tennessee Williams, *A Streetcar Named Desire* (New York: New American Library, 1947), 83.

147 "little girl": Ardoin, *Callas Legacy,* 70.

148 "There was a lawsuit": quoted in Lowe, *Callas, As They Saw Her,* 157.

148 "dear colleague and friend": quoted in Lowe, *Callas, As They Saw Her,* 140.

148 "Rivals I have not": quoted in Ardoin, *Callas: In Her Own Words.*

149 "straitjacketing": quoted in Ardoin, *Callas: In Her Own Words.*

150 "Every time a taxi": quoted in Lowe, *Callas, As They Saw Her,* 152.

151 "Only my dogs": Charles Ludlam, *Galas,* in *The Complete Plays of Charles Ludlam* (New York: Harper & Row, 1989), 731.

151 "a monstrous phenomenon": quoted in Stassinopoulos, *Maria Callas,* 133.

· CHAPTER FIVE: *The Queen's Throat: Or, How to Sing* ·

For singing physiology and technique, I depend on Philip A. Duey, *Bel Canto in Its Golden Age: A Study of Its Teaching Concepts* (New York: King's Crown Press, 1951); Edward Vaught Foreman, *A Comparison of Selected Italian Vocal Tutors of the Period Circa 1550 to 1880* (Ann Arbor: University Microfilms International, 1985); Brent Jeffrey Monahan, *The Art of Singing: A Compendium of Thoughts on Singing Published between 1777 and 1927* (Metuchen, N.J.: Scarecrow Press, 1978); Robert Rushmore, *The Singing Voice* (New York: Dembner Books, 1984); Sally Allis Sanford, *Seventeenth and Eighteenth Century Vocal Style and Technique* (Ann Arbor: University Microfilms International, 1979). On castrati, see Angus Heriot, *The Castrati in Opera* (1956; New York: Da Capo Press, 1975). On the discourse of homosexuality, see Eve Kosofsky Sedgwick, *Epistemology of the Closet* (Berkeley and Los Angeles: University of California Press, 1990). See also Sander L. Gilman, "Opera, Homosexuality, and Models of Disease: Richard Strauss's *Salome* in the Context of Images of Disease in the Fin de Siècle," in *Disease and Representation: Images of Illness from Madness to AIDS* (Ithaca: Cornell University Press, 1988).

154 "singing is an art": Millie Ryan, *What Every Singer Should Know* (Omaha: Franklin Publishing Co., 1910), iv.

157 "So many girls": quoted in Frederick H. Martens, *The Art of the Prima Donna and Concert Singer* (New York: D. Appleton & Co., 1923), 195.

158 "the throat is": Enrico Caruso and Luisa Tetrazzini, *Caruso and Tetrazzini on the Art of Singing* (1909; New York: Dover Publications, 1975), 52.

159 "it is a sad": quoted in Duey, *Bel Canto,* 5.

159 "manly": Piero Francesco Tosi, *Observations on the Florid Song,* trans. John Ernest Galliard (1743; New York: Johnson Reprint Corp., 1968), 76.

160 "has to teach": Sir Charles Santley, *The Art of Singing and Vocal Declamation* (New York: Macmillan, 1908), 11.

160 "If only I could": quoted in Rushmore, *Singing Voice,* 177.

160 "a horizontal cleft": quoted in Duey, *Bel Canto,* 135.

160   "two thick membranes": Robert Lawrence Weer, *Your Voice* (Los Angeles: the author, 1948), 49.
160   "a strong rubber": quoted in Martens, *Art of the Prima Donna*, 202.
161   "tonguelet": quoted in Sanford, *Vocal Style*, 58.
161   "ring-shield": Salvatore Marchesi (1902), quoted in Monahan, *Art of Singing*, 136–37.
161   Greek tragedians slashed: Herbert Witherspoon, *Singing: A Treatise for Teachers and Students* (New York: G. Schirmer, 1925), 1.
161   "you cannot make": quoted in Martens, *Art of the Prima Donna*, 69.
161   Helen Keller: see Monahan, *Art of Singing*, 270.
161   "When I sing": quoted in Monahan, *Art of Singing*, 30.
163   "erective tissue": Witherspoon, *Singing: A Treatise*, 25.
163   "You have the ideal": quoted in Martens, *Art of the Prima Donna*, 286.
163   "fulfil their office": Santley, *Art of Singing*, 56.
163   "pretty mouths": Isaac Nathan, *An Essay on the History and Theory of Music; and on the Qualities, Capabilities, and Management of the Human Voice* (London: G. & W. B. Whittaker, 1823), 63.
163   "one can comfortably": quoted in Sanford, *Vocal Style*, 94.
163   "tongue control": Weer, *Your Voice*, 5.
164   "it is a species": Nathan, *Essay*, 47.
164   "lest in passing": quoted in Duey, *Bel Canto*, 108.
165   "effeminate musical tattling": quoted in Duey, *Bel Canto*, 29.
165   "womanish affectations": quoted in Duey, *Bel Canto*, 34.
165   "it becomes men": quoted in Duey, *Bel Canto*, 41.
165   "at their hinder": Sir Morell Mackenzie, quoted in Monahan, *Art of Singing*, 149–50.
165   "of Use": Tosi, *Observations*, 24.
165   "white," "blatant," "effeminate": Franklin D. Lawson, *The Human Voice: A Concise Manual on Training the Speaking and Singing Voice* (New York: Harper & Brothers Publishers, 1944), 46.
165   "Many masters put": Tosi, *Observations*, 23.
165   "my entire pleasure": quoted in Sanford, *Vocal Style*, 43–44.
166   "physical development": quoted in Martens, *Art of the Prima Donna*, 265–66.
166   "mutation": quoted in Monahan, *Art of Singing*, 21.
166   "the chest voice": quoted in Sanford, *Vocal Style*, 34.
167   "singing is nothing more": quoted in Monahan, *Art of Singing*, 33.
167   "the defects of an unnatural": A. A. Pattou, *The Voice as an Instrument* (New York: Edward Schuberth & Co., 1878), 4.
167   "all the faults": Ibid., 28.
167   "mental depression": Ibid., 58.
168   "contrary to nature": quoted in Rushmore, *Singing Voice*, 190.
168   "Latin races": quoted in Rushmore, *Singing Voice*, 190.
168   "very much in vogue": Francis Charles Maria de Rialp, *The Legitimate School of Singing* (New York: the author, 1894), 76.
168   "the singer appears dropping": Nathan, *Essay*, 67.
168   "faces that are": Lilli Lehmann, *How to Sing*, trans. Richard Aldrich (1902; New York: Macmillan, 1960), 169.
169   "continual sighing": John Gothard, *Thoughts on Singing; with Hints on the Elements of Effect and the Cultivation of Taste* (London: Longman & Co., 1848), iv.
169   "there is no tonic": Ryan, *What Every Singer*, 23.
170   "singing has a refining": quoted in Monahan, *Art of Singing*, 17.
170   "social order and happiness": quoted in Monahan, *Art of Singing*, 17.

170 "natural voice": George Antoine Brouillet, *Voice Manual* (1936; Boston: Crescendo Publishing Co., 1974), 42.
170 "shun low and disreputable": Tosi, *Observations*, 144.
170 "the greater is his price": quoted in Heriot, *Castrati*, 57.
170 "correct management": Louis Arthur Russell (1904), quoted in Monahan, *Art of Singing*, 62.
170 "not at once": quoted in Duey, *Bel Canto*, 79.
170 "as he does": Caruso and Tetrazzini, *Art of Singing*, 58.
172 "Why does it spoil": quoted in Duey, *Bel Canto*, 19.
172 "the mucous membrane": Witherspoon, *Singing: A Treatise*, 45.
172 "Red lines denote": Lehmann, *How to Sing*, 86–87.

• CHAPTER SIX: *The Unspeakable Marriage of Words and Music* •

I have benefited from Susan McClary, *Feminine Endings: Music, Gender, and Sexuality* (Minneapolis: University of Minnesota Press, 1991), and Herbert Lindenberger, *Opera: The Extravagant Art* (Ithaca: Cornell University Press, 1984). For opera's origins, I depend on Robert Donington, *The Rise of Opera* (London: Faber & Faber, 1981); Stanley Sadie, ed., *History of Opera* (London: Macmillan, 1989); Claude V. Palisca, *The Florentine Camerata: Documentary Studies and Translations* (New Haven: Yale University Press, 1989); and Oliver Strunk, ed., *Source Readings in Music History from Classical Antiquity through the Romantic Era* (New York: W. W. Norton, 1950). On relations between words and music, see John Hollander, *The Untuning of the Sky: Ideas of Music in English Poetry, 1500–1700* (Princeton: Princeton University Press, 1961), and James Anderson Winn, *Unsuspected Eloquence: A History of the Relations between Poetry and Music* (New Haven: Yale University Press, 1981).

180 "formally chartered": Palisca, *Florentine Camerata*, 4.
180 "in the habit": Vincenzo Galilei (1581), quoted in Palisca, *Florentine Camerata*, 3.
180 "delightful": Pietro de' Bardi (1634), quoted in Palisca, *Florentine Camerata*, 4.
180 "a harmony surpassing": Jacopo Peri, "Foreword to *Euridice*" (1601), in Strunk, *Source Readings*, 374.
180 "I collect one": Giovanni Bardi, "Discourse Addressed to Giulio Caccini, Called the Roman, on Ancient Music and Good Singing," in Palisca, *Florentine Camerata*, 91.
181 "Vincenzo Galilei, the father," "entirely under my father's," "Caccini and Peri": Pietro de' Bardi, "Letter to G. B. Doni" (1634), in Strunk, *Source Readings*, 363–65.
181 "new allurement": Girolamo Mei, "Letter [to Vincenzo Galilei] of 8 May 1572," in Palisca, *Florentine Camerata*, 73.
181 "excessive delicacies": Ibid.
182 "sung privately": Pietro de' Bardi, "Letter," in Strunk, *Source Readings*, 365.
182 "There are few": Ibid.
182 "the pleasure and astonishment": quoted in Donington, *Rise of Opera*, 108.
182 "has always made my": Peri, "Foreword," in Strunk, *Source Readings*, 375.
183 "tickling": Giulio Caccini, "Foreword to *Le nuove musiche*" (1602), in Strunk, *Source Readings*, 380.
183 "funnel of his ears": Plato, *Republic*, excerpted in Strunk, *Source Readings*, 11–12.
183 "more moved with": St. Augustine, *Confessions*, excerpted in Strunk, *Source Readings*, 74.

184 *"unnaturally* put *asunder"*: Dr. [John] Brown, *A Dissertation on the Rise, Union, and Power, the Progressions, Separations, and Corruptions, of Poetry and Music* (London: L. Davis & C. Reymers, 1763), 25.

184 *"languid Amusement"*: quoted in Winn, *Unsuspected Eloquence*, 252.

184 "text is nobler": Giovanni Bardi, "Discourse," in Palisca, *Florentine Camerata*, 115.

184 "nauseated," "wretched fellow": Ibid., 123.

184 "Emasculating Voice": from an anonymous poem, "ON NICOLINI'S *leaving the stage"* (1714), quoted in Winn, *Unsuspected Eloquence*, 244–45.

184 "monstrous inversion": Count Algarotti, *An Essay on the Opera Written in Italian* (London: L. Davis & C. Reymers, 1767), 58–61.

185 "effeminate and disgusting": Francesco Algarotti, *Saggio sopra l'opera in musica* (1755), excerpted in Strunk, *Source Readings*, 663–64.

185 "turn about and recoil": Ibid., 669.

185 "modern confusion": Benedetto Marcello, *Il teatro alla moda* (1720), excerpted in Strunk, *Source Readings*, 525.

185 *"Songish Part"*: John Dryden, "Preface to *Albion and Albanius,"* in *The Works of John Dryden,* vol. 25, *Plays* (Berkeley and Los Angeles: University of California Press, 1976), 4.

187 "Anything I could tell": letter of Jan. 29, 1924, in *The Correspondence between Richard Strauss and Hugo von Hofmannsthal,* trans. Hanns Hammelmann and Ewald Osers (London: Collins, 1961), 380.

187 "the verses which": W. H. Auden, "Notes on Music and Opera," in *The Dyer's Hand and Other Essays* (New York: Vintage, 1968), 473.

187 "to be rent": letter of Dec. 22, 1912, in *Strauss and von Hofmannsthal,* 151.

188 "friendly intercourse": Algarotti, "Saggio," in Strunk, *Source Readings,* 665.

188 "men of power": quoted in Winn, *Unsuspected Eloquence,* 241–42.

188 "its true office": C. W. von Gluck, "Dedication to *Alceste"* (1769), in Strunk, *Source Readings,* 674.

188 "cut out our finest": E. T. A. Hoffmann, "The Poet and the Composer" (1819–1821), in Strunk, *Source Readings,* 786.

188 "rouse each other's": Richard Wagner, *Wagner on Music and Drama: A Compendium of Richard Wagner's Prose Works,* ed. Albert Goldman and Evert Sprinchorn, trans. H. Ashton Ellis (1964; New York: Da Capo Press, 1981), 232.

188 "thrust forward by *two"*: Ibid., 234.

188 "brotherly Prometheus": Ibid., 159.

189 "painful torments": Ibid., 116.

189 "throat dexterity": Ibid., 95.

189 *"naked, ear-delighting,"* "narcotizing": Ibid., 103–4.

189 "child-bearing," "procreating": Wagner, quoted in Lindenberger, *Opera,* 112.

189 "the glorious marriage": Wagner, *Wagner,* 209.

189 "I lean up": Søren Kierkegaard, *Either/Or,* vol. 1, trans. David F. Swenson and Lillian Marvin Swenson (1843; Princeton: Princeton University Press, 1971), 119.

190 "terrible experiences": Oscar Wilde, "The Critic as Artist," in *The Artist as Critic: Critical Writings of Oscar Wilde,* ed. Richard Ellmann (Chicago: University of Chicago Press, 1982), 343.

190 "musical words said": Oscar Wilde, *The Picture of Dorian Gray* (1891; Harmondsworth: Penguin, 1983), 67.

190 "constantly aspires toward": Pater, *Renaissance,* 106.

190 "Moon-struck": Max Nordau, *Degeneration* (New York: D. Appleton & Co., 1895), 198.

190   "hot, nervously exciting": Ibid., 211.
190   "incapable of profiting": Ibid., 204.
190   "take sides against": Friedrich Nietzsche, *The Birth of Tragedy and The Case of Wagner* (1886/1888; New York: Vintage, 1967), 155.
190   "makes sick whatever": Ibid., 164.
191   "persuade even the intestines": Ibid., 168.
191   "Just look at": Ibid., 172.
191   "immediate copy of": Ibid., 100.
191   "diversion-craving luxuriousness": Ibid., 114–15.
191   "effort to return": Nordau, *Degeneration,* 176.
195   "the inner gayety": Virgil Thomson, "About 'Four Saints,' " liner notes, *Four Saints in Three Acts,* Elektra/Nonesuch CD 9 79035-2.
196   "clarity of enunciation": Ibid.
196   "nowadays poetry and music": Virgil Thomson, *Music with Words: A Composer's View* (New Haven: Yale University Press, 1989), 1.
196   "its elements are mated": Ibid., 13.

• CHAPTER SEVEN: *A Pocket Guide to Queer Moments in Opera* •

198   *"Listening speaks":* Roland Barthes, *The Responsibility of Forms: Critical Essays on Music, Art, and Representation,* trans. Richard Howard (New York: Hill & Wang, 1986), 252.
198   "something had to be sacrificed": Felix Mendelsohn [sic], *The Story of a Hundred Operas* (New York: Grosset & Dunlap, 1913), viii.

Illustrations

Every attempt has been made to locate the proper permissions grantor for each illustration. If an error or omission is found, the publisher would appreciate hearing about it, and will make the appropriate correction in the next edition.

Index